WHEN THE CHEERING STOPS

WHEN THE CHEERING STOPS

Life after the NFL

Gay Culverhouse

ROWMAN & LITTLEFIELD
Lanham • Boulder • New York • London

Published by Rowman & Littlefield
An imprint of The Rowman & Littlefield Publishing Group, Inc.
4501 Forbes Boulevard, Suite 200, Lanham, Maryland 20706
www.rowman.com

6 Tinworth Street, London SE11 5AL, United Kingdom

British Library Cataloguing in Publication Information Available

Library of Congress Cataloging-in-Publication Data

Name: Culverhouse, Gay, author.
Title: When the cheering stops : life after the NFL / Gay Culverhouse.
Description: Lanham : The Rowman & Littlefield, [2021] | Includes bibliographical references and index. | Summary: "In this book, players open up about the difficulties they face once they leave the NFL. Personal interviews reveal how many have struggled with finances, addiction, depression, violence, and finding a second career. While success stories are also shared, the unfortunate truth is that there are far more players left hurt and broken after retirement"—Provided by publisher.
Identifiers: LCCN 2020057019 (print) | LCCN 2020057020 (ebook) | ISBN 9781538145821 (cloth) | ISBN 9781538145838 (ebook)
Subjects: LCSH: Football—Social aspects—United States. | Football players—United States—Social conditions. | National Football League. | Football injuries—United States. | Football—Moral and ethical aspects—United States.
Classification: LCC GV951 .C78 2021 (print) | LCC GV951 (ebook) | DDC 796.330973—dc23
LC record available at https://lccn.loc.gov/2020057019
LC ebook record available at https://lccn.loc.gov/2020057020

CONTENTS

FOREWORD

Jeff Dahl, member of Retired Player Assistance

I write this on behalf of the remaining members of Retired Player Assistance (RPA), a nonprofit group formed by Gay Culverhouse in late 2017 to help former NFL players understand the benefits offered by the NFL and to help those eligible for benefits with their claims. The remaining RPA members include Clark Jordan-Holmes, a lawyer and mediator practicing in Tampa; Paul Scott, who represents former NFL players in benefit claims and appeals; Steven Lewis, a lawyer practicing in New York City; Paul Boone, a lawyer practicing in Jacksonville and Nassau County, Florida; Christopher K. Donis, an Arizona lawyer; Merry Reidenbach, a disability expert; Paul Ed Ward, an IT expert; and me, a lawyer practicing in San Antonio.

I am a lawyer who represents employees who seek benefits under employment benefit plans—an ERISA lawyer, in legal parlance (ERISA is the Employee Retirement Income Security Act of 1974). In that capacity, I have represented former NFL players seeking benefits from the NFL benefit plans. Although many of my clients had difficulty obtaining the benefits they seemed to deserve, after representing a number of former NFL players I realized that they faced even greater obstacles. In other words, I felt they were *really* being screwed. The NFL plan administrators, those who controlled the plan, seemed particularly hostile toward former NFL players seeking benefits. Those who wrote the benefit plan and litigated benefit claims were extremely bright and could be ruthless.

In the summer of 2017, I received a call from Clark Jordan-Holmes, a lawyer in Tampa who was Gay Culverhouse's good friend. While researching case law involving former NFL players seeking benefits under the benefit plans, Clark found my name. He had met Gay many years earlier when she hired him and his law firm to sue the country club where she had become a member—by virtue of her executive position with the Tampa Bay Buccaneers—because they wouldn't allow women to play golf on Saturdays. Gay wasn't necessarily passionate about golf, but she was passionate about fair treatment for women. Gay and Clark succeeded.

Clark invited me to join a group that Gay Culverhouse wanted to form, the Retired Player Assistance, a nonprofit entity to help retired athletes of all persuasions, but especially former pro football players. I had read about Gay and admired her from a distance. I knew that although she had been part of NFL management for a number of years (she was president of the Buccaneers from 1991 to 1994 while her father, Hugh Culverhouse, owned the team), she had advocated for greater protections from head injuries for players at the congressional hearings in 2009, and emphasized that team doctors were often the pawns of management, driven to keep concussed players in the game. Clark spoke with such reverence about Gay. I was anxious to meet her. I jumped at the invitation to fly to Tampa and be part of RPA.

RPA's first meeting was in the fall of 2017. We met where most of our meetings would be held, in a conference room just west of downtown Tampa. Immediately upon meeting Gay and listening to her talk, I understood Clark's admiration for her. Here was someone who had so much inside information—she knew so many former players and knew those in NFL management on a first-name basis—and someone who had a simple agenda: help former NFL players, many of whom were in desperate need, especially "her boys" as she referred to the former Tampa Bay Buccaneers who played when she was with the team. She was smart, courageous, tenacious, and engaging. She knew those in power well and had earned their respect. When she saw a particular injustice, she had no qualms in sending a blistering email to Commissioner Roger Goodell or the NFL's general counsel, Jeff Pash. She was a genuine Socratic gadfly, a thorn in the side of those in power.

On my flight home from our initial meeting, I had already received a couple of emails from Gay concerning former players. Through Gay's passion to help others, I quickly learned that RPA would be a hands-on affair. Within a few weeks I was reviewing players' claim files, and every week Gay and I were talking or texting about players and the difficult issues they were facing. With benefit claims, there is a review process. Denied benefit claims are appealed to a plan fiduciary. In the NFL's case, the NFL Retirement Board is the benefit plan fiduciary. Shortly after our first meeting, Gay spent almost forty hours with one player working on his administrative appeal for disability benefits to the Retirement Board. Her energy was incredible. I knew that I was doing a lot of volunteer work trying to help particular players that she had identified, and thought we could help, but Gay was working ten times harder. Most of her waking hours seemed to be spent on the phone talking with former NFL players and their wives, interspersed with emails to NFL management and their in-house counsel, peppering the latter with questions or chiding them for their treatment of a particular player or players in general.

Gay often shared her emails sent to the men who ran the NFL. When she saw injustice or indifference by those in power—and she saw that often—she wasted no time getting to the point. For example, in 2018, the NFL created a new home page for the NFL Player Benefits website that pictured the face of a player (a White punter) with the phrase "Check out what players had to say about the new NFL Player Benefits Website." She wasted no time getting to the point in a letter to Dennis Curran, an NFL senior vice president; Jeff Pash, general counsel for the NFL; and Roger Goodell, the commissioner:

> This man does not represent the typical NFL retired player. How do you expect to welcome players to the site with a white foreign punter who barely qualifies for benefits?? Where is your sensitivity? Or do you just want to hold onto the money for the League? This site is garnering groans and I told you so's. You are pathetically out of touch. It's truly embarrassing from my point of view that with all your resources you continue to stumble.
>
> Dr. Gay Culverhouse

One of the many claims that we addressed, and another example of her fearlessness, involved a former Buccaneer whom she knew well as a friend who was suffering from early dementia connected with his NFL career. He was being represented by a consortium of lawyers formed for the purpose of helping players file claims in the NFL class action concussion settlement. The player's claim was put in audit, that is, limbo, because of a fraud investigation brought by the NFL against the lawyers' consortium and the medical professionals to whom they referred their players-clients. The former player and his wife pleaded with Gay for help.

I agreed that I would represent the player in the concussion settlement if she could get him released from his fee contract with the lawyers' consortium. She drove to their offices. Gay was met by the lead lawyer in the case who pitched her, telling her that she should work with them.

Gay called me on the way home. "Can you believe it?" she said incredulously. "They wanted me to work with them, told me that I could make a lot of money." She laughed. "Boy, they sure don't know anything about me!" she exclaimed.

After some choice words from her, the lawyer agreed to release the player from the consortium's fee contract, although not without a price, as the consortium insisted in keeping a portion of its contingent fee.

As part of our work for RPA we represented him for free and were able to get him out of limbo and obtain a settlement award under the concussion settlement. Gay did almost all of the legwork, as she always offered to do, setting up the necessary physician appointments and making sure that reports were issued in a timely way and that the claims administrators had the information they needed. She did all this while being constantly available to the player and his wife when they became frustrated with the process.

Gay's maternal instincts were always close to the surface. We were at a conference in Delray Beach, Florida, led by Randy Grimes, a former Buccaneer who organized Pro Athletes in Recovery, an organization designed to help former professional athletes battle drug and alcohol addiction. As we were listening to a speaker, Gay looked at me and shook her head, giggling. "Oh, my Lord, give me your glasses," she whispered. She pulled out a cloth and spray and cleaned my eyeglasses. "How could you even see?"

Although formed late in Gay's life, RPA, along with her family, her dog, and this book, were her abiding passions. Gay's personal phone number was on the RPA website. As Clark told me recently, she felt she needed to be available anytime if one of her boys was in trouble. Gay and I talked, emailed, texted, and reviewed former NFL players' medical records constantly while working for RPA. It was mostly Gay calling me about players who had contacted her or asking me questions or sending me records to review. Her energy, derived from seeing injustice and her incredible concern for other people's lives, was incredible. She couldn't sleep when she knew a former player was in trouble, perhaps a suicide risk. She never discussed her own health issues. I never heard her once complain about her own difficult problems or the infusion treatments that she needed.

During our last phone conversation, less than a week before she passed away in the summer of 2020, I promised that we would keep RPA going in her absence. A difficult task, as she was the heart and soul of RPA. She filled the room. But she told me, "I really needed to hear you say that, that you'all will keep RPA alive." There was no question that we would keep RPA going, to continue her work. I speak for everyone at RPA when I say it was an honor and a privilege to work with Gay, and we hope you get a sense of her passion and devotion in the pages to come.

PREFACE

Gay Culverhouse lived many lives—that of mother, grandmother, sister, daughter of the owner of an NFL team, doctor of special education and psychiatric testing and, in her later years, tireless and selfless advocate for retired NFL players banged up by the game they loved but unable to get the medical attention they needed. In between all this, Gay rode horses, traveled the world (from Asia to Botswana and many places in between), doted on her grandkids, kept in touch with friends, settled all manner of disputes, stared down those who stood in her way, and, sadly, battled a rare form of blood cancer that ultimately took her life, at seventy-three, in July 2020.

When doctors told her one month before her death that the transfusions and chemotherapy were no longer going to work and that she had just a few weeks to live, Gay, with typical aplomb, brushed aside any self-pity and got to work organizing her affairs. There were many people to contact, things to mail, the dog to take care of, and letters to share. But she was particularly focused on two important matters. First, she wanted to make sure that Retired Player Assistance, the nonprofit group she had founded, would continue its work helping players apply for and receive collectively bargained disability payments and other benefits designed to help them deal with their injuries and ease the burden on their families.

Over the years, Gay had assembled a team of lawyers and other specialists from around the country to help her fight the NFL and the boards of these benefits programs, which were often administered by

representatives from the league and the NFL Players Association. As
you'll find out in the pages to come, it was and remains frustrating work.
The law firms and administrators who are the gatekeepers of these
programs can be ruthless in their rejection of applications for benefits.
The lengths they go to in interpreting—or overinterpreting—the rules
governing these plans have astounded player advocates for decades. No
wonder retired players often repeat the mantra "delay, deny, and hope
you die" when referring to these benefits plans.

But Gay, who grew up loving football in Florida and went on to
become the president of the Tampa Bay Buccaneers, was no ordinary
advocate. She knew where the bodies were buried, so to speak, and she
had no trouble firing off emails to Commissioner Roger Goodell and his
assistants whenever she hit a wall. She would remind them of their own
words, that player safety was their highest priority. She almost always
received responses addressed to "Dr. Culverhouse" that were polite
and solicitous.

Her other big concern was the completion of the book that is now in
your hands. Gay had written a book before, in 2011, about the dangers
of football. Entitled *Throwaway Players: The Concussion Crisis from
Pee Wee Football to the NFL*, the slender book came on the heels of her
congressional testimony about concussions and retired players. In the
book, Gay provided a road map to years of stories to sports reporters
who were either willfully blind to the brutality of the sport or only just
waking up to the growing body of research that linked the repeated
head hits in the game to long-term cognitive and neurological problems.

She wanted this book to be both more expansive, covering a host of
issues and a lot of specifics, and a how-to guide for players and their
families. But she also wanted it to serve as a memoir about her role in
fighting for retired players and their families. She talked about the
former players like the friends they were. She knew not only their
foibles, as you'll see, but also where their hearts were. She had a rare
combination of empathy and intuition mixed with stubbornness and a
sense of fairness.

Through the pain and fatigue she endured in the last few months of
her life, Gay pounded out most of the book. She mixed in cases she
worked on with research about the risks of playing football. She per-

suaded friends to contribute sections of chapters that make up the rest of the book.

Knowing her time was running out, Gay started forwarding emails and texts that she hoped would make their way into the book in one form or another. One of them, from the wife of a retired player that Gay had helped over the years, sums up the lasting impact her work had on not just the players but also their families.

> I want to tell you something else . . . heart to heart . . . if it weren't for you I wouldn't understand S and possibly wouldn't be with him to-day. I'm not a sports fan. I'm a music geek. I am possibly the only person around S who has never seen him play football. I don't under-stand the game at all, and I definitely don't understand the whole NFL culture. But when I first met you when you came to Tampa to be with the other players and talk, you helped me see that a lot of what I was seeing in him that seemed like selfish or lazy behavior was in fact the product of playing hard and beating himself up. Because of that I was able to embrace the idea of falling in love with him and perhaps taking care of him for the rest of his life. You gave me a gift.

Gay took solace in these emails and texts, though she never asked for a penny. As frustrating as it was to fight the NFL, it meant that each victory on behalf of a player and his family was that much sweeter. It helped her make amends for loving the game and working in the game. And it brought together the many skills she had sharpened in her varied and colorful life.

Less than three weeks before she died, she sent a brief email to a friend. The subject line was "My Life," and the body of the email continued: ". . . has been a roller coaster. There was rarely peace. People have a difficult time believing all that can happen to one per-son."

INTRODUCTION

This book has been brewing within me for decades. In my eighth decade, it's finally getting out into the sunshine of media attention from the darkness of my mind. I have talked with thousands of players and their families to the point that it is rare I am not awakened with the sadness of their desperate situation.

The path from exultation of being chosen to play in the National Football League (NFL) to the poverty that follows is a quick three-year trip for some players. By the age of twenty-five, they are out of the league and out of work. Usually by then, they have a few other mouths that depend on them for food. Without being able to make mortgage payments, they are soon looking for a cheaper apartment. The fast friends that appeared on signing day are nowhere to be found when the player is in need.

It's such a thrilling time to be a young man in his early twenties with such exceptional talent that the NFL wants you to play on one of its teams. Rarely does a player stop to finish his university degree. The lure of ready money is too enticing. Being crowned a "player" by the NFL is heady stuff. So glamorous in fact that the player will accept any playing conditions just to be on the team. These young men are afraid to rattle the team by asking for changes to their rookie contracts. They keep quiet and barely read the document before signing it. A rookie could protect himself by requesting insurance if injured in training camp; several players each year do not make it through training camp due to injuries. Without insurance, they are lost. No playing in the NFL, no income, and no university degree. Young men need to read the contract because there are conditions in the document that affect their signing bonuses too.

In many ways, this is the beginning of the day the player retires. Most rookies believe they will play ten years in the league. The average is about one-third as long. So on day one in the NFL, players need to prepare for the day when they have to exit financially and emotionally. The best way to prepare is to have a skill besides football that he can use to earn a salary. The best idea would be to complete a degree either online or in the off-season. That is the economic insurance policy that will serve the player well. So is staying in touch with friends from college who work after getting their degrees. They can be good resources for future employment.

Of course, like Icarus, if the player flies too close to the sun, he may crash and burn when he retires. In other words, did he spend too lavishly on his home and entertainment, or did he live within his means? When you believe you will have a solid income for ten years, the tendency is to think you'll save for the future the last few years of your career. All of these factors lead to trouble after players leave the NFL. Rarely is a player prepared for the gut-altering experience of no longer hearing cheers on the football field or the camaraderie of the locker room. The player's world is shaken like a snow globe with no focal point to his life. Since adolescence, players have been told what to eat, when to practice, where to be and when, and what to wear. Without that guidance, players can't function. They are suddenly thrust into a different social environment where they are expected to act politely in ways that can be very different from those in the insular world of sports.

The health concerns mount as the player no longer has access to a trainer to massage stiff muscles. There are no teammates to provide encouragement that things will heal and get better shortly. And there are no free medications available in the open drug locker. Players now have to make an appointment with an outside doctor and explain what drugs they've been taking for the last so many years, assuming they know what they've been taking. Most doctors try to wean the player from his pill regimen. That's not what the player wants; he wants what he had in the locker room with no fuss. As the drugs are withdrawn, players may turn to street drugs or alcohol to assuage the pain of those playing injuries. Things can become tense at home as his wife never knew he was taking so many drugs for pain. They were in the locker room; they had to be all right. As the wife begins to understand the problem, she tries to get him to seek help. The player wants the pain to go away but not enough to go to a doctor. Disagreements lead to fights, and not long after violence breaks out in the home. Women are used to talking out their problems; men are used to action. Football players bust things up for a living, and that's the way they handle problems in the home.

The reason you don't read about these episodes is that the player is retired. He's no longer famous. He no longer makes $750,000 or more per year. He's no longer interviewed on national television after a winning game. His wife no longer models in fashion shows. Her photo is no longer in the social columns of local magazines. Basically, no one cares if there was a domestic dispute. Just one of a hundred that will happen all over town on a weekend night.

When the player Ray Rice from the Baltimore Ravens hit his fiancée, it was news all over the country. The hotel security tape was played on a loop on television and the internet. Even the NFL couldn't squash that tape, although Roger Goodell tried to downplay the incident initially. It's sad to think that we even prioritize domestic violence as to that which is newsworthy depending on whether the player is on a team or retired from the NFL. Men who leave the league are suddenly unrecognizable at the bars or restaurants they used to frequent. That special corner booth in the steak house is no longer reserved for him on Friday nights. He's no longer important enough to showcase.

Nothing prepares young men for this precipitous drop in status.

In the following chapters, I'll explore the hurdles players face in making the transition from the glory of playing in the National Football League to the realities of life on the outside. It's a difficult path to travel for all men in this position. The cheering and the adoration of the fans are as important to the punter as they are to the quarterback on the team. They are town heroes. Some players cope with drugs and alcohol; some have been making plans for years for their postcareer employment. I examine the success stories and the sad stories of the men of the NFL in this book.

I will also peel back the onion to show how, long after these players leave the bright lights of the NFL, the league makes it difficult for them to obtain collectively bargained for and legally protected benefits. You will see how the league spends millions of dollars on lawyers who push for the introduction of incomprehensible rules to thwart all but the most persistent players, who must often hire lawyers to make sense of regulations. Players trying to obtain medical records from their former teams are told they don't exist. Doctors appointed by benefits plans, eager to get more business, reject players' claims. The league goes out of its way to appeal applications, forcing players to spend years trying to get medical benefits promised them by the players association and the owners, all at a cost to their lives and their families who must care for them.

These are real men and true stories. In some cases, identities have been protected at the request of the player. For nearly every "success" story of a player who ultimately received benefits for his injuries, there are many others struggling to make sense of how a $15 billion league that was built on the backs of these players spends so much money trying to prevent them from getting help to repair their bodies that were mangled in the service of the NFL. It's not a happy story, but it's a story that needs to be told.

I

WHY ME?

I know you are wondering what gives me the authority to write this book. In other words, how do I know what I know? Like everything in life, it's about luck and coincidence.

My first year in high school, which in Florida at the time began in the tenth grade, I attended Robert E. Lee in Jacksonville, Florida. Our football team was the most important entity for us students and our parents. Friday Night Lights football games were the events everyone in the surrounding area went to during the season. The star of our team, the Generals, was the quarterback, Harmon Wages. He was everything a star should be: good looking with blond hair and blue eyes, tall and muscular, and deadly throwing the ball.

When Harmon graduated, he considered going to West Point, but his heart was focused ninety miles east in Gainesville, home of the University of Florida. There, he played backup to Steve Spurrier, who went on to win the Heisman Trophy. Wages finally got his chance to start after Spurrier left for the pros, but he broke his ankle in a preseason practice. Because of his lack of playing time, he knew he wouldn't be drafted by an NFL team. Not one to give up, Wages went to Atlanta and tried out on his own for a spot on the Falcons. He made the team as the third quarterback but was switched to running back as the season progressed. In total, he played five seasons with the Falcons and then held various positions in broadcasting.

Like every high school girl at the time, I had a crush on Harmon. This started my interest in football. I decided to attend the University of

Florida so I could continue to follow Harmon's career, and in the meantime, I became interested in the entire Gators team. I had more trivia stored about the team than any knowledge I accumulated in classes. Interestingly, that information made introductions much easier when I could talk about a certain play or remember a player now long gone.

As I continued my graduate education in New York City, I transferred my loyalty to the Giants and their quarterback, Fran Tarkenton. I'd take the subway to Yankee Stadium and enter with twofer student tickets. I'd talk to the fans sitting near me and became a true fan myself. This was my introduction from high school to college to professional football. I never lost my enthusiasm for the game.

At Columbia University's Teachers College, I studied neurocognitive development and ultimately received my doctorate. In the meantime, I had two children and returned to Florida. Life with children was easier without snowsuits and cumbersome strollers. It's much easier if you choose to live down the street from the grandparents of said children too.

Since my coursework was completed but not my dissertation, I enlisted as much help as I could get from my parents. My mother cooked for us occasionally, and my father, not wanting to be left out, volunteered to take the children one Sunday afternoon for a few hours. I was so excited to have the time alone to concentrate and write that I didn't question his plans for entertaining the babies, who were then eight and seventeen months old.

He came over very jolly and confident. He left them in their baby seats and said, "We're off to explore!" About ninety minutes later, he rolled up the driveway and told me they had a great time. I asked what they'd done. He said, "They love riding over the bridges." Now Jacksonville has about seven bridges, and he continually rode over them. The only thing the children could feel was the grating at the top of the bridge, but apparently it made them laugh. Then as the gas was running low, he went to his favorite drive-through restaurant: Burger King. He got them funny hats and each a large chocolate milkshake—his favorite and probably the point of the outing. The eight-month-old who was still nursing had no idea what to do with the shake, so she poured it over her head. She was sitting in chocolate shake!

I had no idea how to begin to clean them up from their outing. Dad jumped in his clean car and said they'd have to do it again someday.

This is the perfect anecdote to explain the man who owned the Tampa Bay Buccaneers. He was so kind and sweet, but he always had a plan that benefited him in some way. The kids thought he was the greatest. Ultimately, that's all that matters.

I was doing my dissertation research, writing and teaching tests and measurements at Jacksonville University at the masters' level. I taught at a couple of private schools that had children with special needs and taught in the public school a classroom for children with language learning disabilities. I can tell you I was a busy mom and had made a successful academic life in Jacksonville.

It was around this time that Dad befriended Pete Rozelle, the NFL commissioner, as well as the owner of the Los Angeles Rams, Carroll Rosenbloom. My dad had met several owners because he was a leading tax and estate attorney. He took them on as clients. Rozelle needed his expertise on antitrust legislation that was a bugaboo for the league. To be honest, my dad had reached the pinnacle of his career as a tax attorney and was looking for his next challenge.

Late one Friday night, Dad called from Los Angeles and asked if I'd be interested in moving to LA if he bought a team. He didn't want to move without his family, and his grandchildren were at the top of his list. We were on board for the move. I'd never heard him so jubilant.

He and Pete Rozelle had met and had a handshake agreement that on Monday Dad would buy the Rams out of the estate of the previous owner who had died. Yet on Monday, we read that Bob Irsay was the new owner of the Los Angeles Rams.

Dad was devastated and immediately filed suit against the league. It seemed that Rosenbloom, who owned the Baltimore Colts, wanted a team in Los Angeles, where he lived. So he helped Irsay finance the purchase of the Rams and then took over the team, giving him the Colts in return.

A settlement was reached with the NFL and Dad was to be awarded the next franchise to enter the league. A few years later, in 1974, two cities were awarded teams: Tampa and Seattle. The league gave the first team, which was Seattle, to Dad. We were shocked. We lived in Florida and assumed the first team would be Tampa. They screwed Dad once again. Dad called and asked if I'd consider moving from Florida to Seattle, and my answer was no. I don't think anyone in our family agreed to move. He was furious at the duplicitous nature of the league.

Three weeks went by, which is the time allotted to place your deposit with the league. The amount was $16 million. The proposed owner for the Tampa franchise couldn't raise the money. Dad had his money secured at the NCNB (soon to be Bank of America), and the team was finally his. Hugh McColl, the head of the bank, had been down this long path with Dad and was his financial man throughout the franchise's history.

The team played its first game in 1976. In the two years between being awarded the team and playing, an amazing amount of decisions needed to be made. Who would the coach be? What would be the name of the team? We needed a logo design, a color scheme, and a theme song. Fortunately, the league was ready to help with every decision. The citizens of Tampa resented the fact that a family from Jacksonville and not Tampa bought the team. There had been no viable owner who was a resident of the city to make a bid for it. This was before current trends where the owner flies in on his private plane for game day and flies out again after the game. In the seventies, it was understood that you would be a resident of the city where your team played. You'd be accessible to the public. After all, you needed them to buy the tickets to your team's games.

My parents immediately purchased a luxury condominium in a new building overlooking Tampa Bay. They knew in a few years they would upgrade to a place more conducive to entertaining. But for the moment, they needed a place in Tampa to call home. Simultaneously, Dad moved his law office to Tampa. He was all in on this new adventure.

My mother's input to the NFL was that the logo shouldn't be a scruffy pirate. Pirates are emblematic of Tampa Bay as Gasparilla is to a holiday that coincides with Mardi Gras. Ships filled with pirates cruise the bay and shoot cannons. Then the pirates dock and capture the city. They parade through town throwing beads celebrating their capture. That night, there are dances sponsored by the local krewes. So clearly the mascot would be a pirate. But my mother insisted it was to be in the mode of Errol Flynn, the most debonair of pirates.

My father wanted orange to be the predominate color as Florida is known for its large orange sun. The NFL design team worked within those parameters and created what the fans jokingly called "Buccaneer

Bruce." He wore a huge swooping hat with a feathered plume, had a knife between his teeth, and one eye closed in a wink. My mother never understood the moniker, but I have to admit that he was the gayest looking pirate you'll ever see on a football helmet. The Buccaneers considered changing uniforms for the coming season. The fans said they wanted to see the Bucs in the original "creamsicle" orange color. I think those fans must not have been alive in the early years of the Bucs.

My father wanted us to have the same orange-colored jackets to wear to the games. In Miami he had a tailor who was paid to dress us in Buccaneer orange cashmere. It was very generous of dad because it was a color that was not popular at the time. Now I see orange dresses and blouses and bags in every window. I often laugh, thinking how easy it would have been if Dad had just acquired the team. I'd have a great wardrobe of orange.

Speaking of wearing clothes to the game, you will never find a more superstitious group than the owners of a football team. If we won a game, which did not happen for almost two complete seasons, you were required to wear the same outfit, including underwear and socks, without laundering them to the next game. If it was an away game and you weren't going, you had to watch the game on your television in said outfit. You can see where this is going. In our fourth year, the Bucs were one game away from going to the Super Bowl. I just had to wash my son's clothes! I made him swear not to tell anyone he was wearing clean clothes.

A couple of years later, in 1981, my father took my young son to a playoff game in Dallas. He was the only family member invited as Dallas was a bit stingy with their visiting owner tickets. The morning of the game my father asked Christopher if he'd like to have breakfast with the team and coaches in the ballroom of the hotel downstairs. My son replied that he'd rather have room service. Dad didn't know how to respond. He so wanted his grandson to appreciate that the Buccaneers were in a playoff game.

You can imagine how the rest of the day proceeded. They rode bus #3 to the game. Bus #1 was the offense; bus #2 was the defense. They were in the "Others" bus. Arriving two to three hours before the game, Dad had to figure out how to amuse his grandson while he met with the Dallas owners and their guests. Dad handed my son his top-of-the-line Nikon and told him to take photos of the players warming up. Christopher didn't know the name of a single Buccaneer. He didn't know the number of a single player. But he liked birds. He focused on the rafters and zoomed in on the birds. He took photo after photo of birds in the ceiling.

When the game began, the cameras panned the crowd looking for unusual shots of the owners. I was watching the game at home in Tampa. All of a sudden, there was Christopher sitting next to Dad with his camera pointed toward the rafters and my father trying to get him to focus on the field. I could only laugh.

When we moved to Tampa, Christopher was in the third grade and his sister was in the second grade. I was very concerned they would be targeted by bullies. My children had no idea at that age what it meant to own an NFL football team. I was super cautious. I made a point of sending them to a small private school and paying for a guard to patrol the school grounds.

In September when I picked up the children from school, eight-year-old Christopher asked me if he and his sister were someone special. I said the common mom thing: "You're always special to your mom." That was not the answer he wanted. "No, Mom. Are we special like in football somehow?" I told him that his grandfather owned a football team, but that was his thing and not ours. Within a few weeks, the other students were pestering my son to tell John McKay, the head coach, who to play in the games. I could see this wasn't going to work out long term and started looking for a boarding school in the woods of Upstate New York. It was for the self-preservation of my son. I wanted him to have his own identity. And why he took pictures of birds in Dallas during the playoff games. He's probably the only person who could not be charmed by my dad being an NFL owner.

As a result, my father would take Christopher with him to exotic locales for the owner's meetings because Christopher wouldn't let Dad just sit in boring meetings. And he introduced Dad to lots of the wives who also accompanied their husbands. Chris was the social butterfly. One year in Hawaii, he arranged sunrise trips to view Diamond Head. He made Dad dress up like a cowboy for a hoedown barbeque and square dance. My mother went to perhaps one owner's meeting before she realized she didn't enjoy it. So Chris became my dad's traveling companion. The upside for Chris was that they got to fly on Dad's Gulfstream plane. Chris obtained his pilot's license at age sixteen, as I did. We shared that experience. Dad had pushed me to fly as he had been in the air force. His grandson was hooked. The fact that they flew everywhere on that plane was a real bonding experience, much more than football.

Our first win in regular season occurred after weeks of being the butt of jokes on *The Johnny Carson Show*. At cocktail parties, my father would play the video he taped of all the jokes at the Bucs' expense. He brought it out in the open because throwing the first shot is a good defense. He acknowledged the defeats but knew they were just on the verge of winning. However, you have to understand that in the seventies, expansion franchises were built from castoffs. The other NFL teams submitted three players for you to choose from their roster. They couldn't be the worst players, nor would they be the best players. But realistically, what team is giving up a potential Pro Bowler? Of course, we got the first pick in the draft and chose Lee Roy Selmon. He, however, was the youngest of three football-playing brothers from Oklahoma and had always been surrounded by his brothers. The Bucs knew they also had to use a draft pick on his brother Dewey in order to get Lee Roy.

By the second to the last game in our second season, a miracle occurred in New Orleans, where the Bucs played the Saints. Everyone was shocked. The Buccaneers won and the Saints were the team to fall to the losingest team in the NFL. The final score was 33–14. When we arrived at One Buc Place after the flight home, thousands of fans greeted us. There was champagne on the bus, and everyone was laughing until the fans crawled on top of the buses and began rocking them back and forth. Our police escort became concerned and called for backup to disperse the crowd. John McKay had some quips about not wanting to die after the win. He wanted to live to play again.

We used the momentum the following week to beat the St. Louis Cardinals, 17–7. I remember my dad and I standing at the top of the stadium watching the fans flood the field. They began tearing down the goal posts. I asked Dad if he wanted me to have the police stop the melee. He said he'd never had so much fun watching the fans. "They deserve this celebration," he said.

In our fourth season we were in the hunt for the Super Bowl. By then the Bucs had gone further than any other expansion team in that short a time. It was something to be proud of, but fans only want wins year after year. Players get injured, they age out, and rookies come in; there's always a changing tide.

I moved permanently to Tampa in 1980. I worked at the University of South Florida College of Medicine in the child psychiatry department as a diagnostician. My work involved traveling around Florida to see students with problems in their classrooms. I then reported to our team what to expect when the students arrived. Simultaneously, I partnered with a friend in Manatee County to run the C & W Cattle Company. On the weekends, the children and I would head south and work the land. We dug fence post holes, castrated calves, sprayed for flies, and worked with the local vets to inoculate the herd. We'd return to Tampa in the evening filthy, dirty, and ready to sleep. Every six months or so, we'd take the calves to auction. The children loved to watch their calves sell for higher prices than those sold by the more established ranchers.

On December 23, 1982, we were in Sarasota having a fun day with the horses. The children had brought a friend with them who was going to spend the night with us in Tampa after we attended a horse show. The children had been riding in the pasture when I decided to hop on a horse briefly. Apparently, that was not on the horse's agenda; he'd already given the children a ride. He was through for the day. He began to buck. Normally, he did three bucks and then settled down. This time, he was pissed. He did three bucks and added a super slingshot. I went flying upward, and when I landed on the hard, sandy ground, I passed out. I suffered a concussion that was so severe one doctor referred to it as a "brain shear." When I came to, I immediately crawled back in the saddle and sent everyone into the house. I rode the horse around the pasture, letting him know he had not bested me that day.

Of course, he got the last laugh. I drove the children to One Buc Place hoping I wasn't too late to catch the team doctor or a trainer. No such luck. However, the receptionist realized something was wrong as I was dragging my left leg. She called the doctor, who said I probably had a hip pointer and to go home, get in the bed, and call in an hour. I drove home and crawled in my daughter's bed because I knew I couldn't climb the stairs to my bedroom. An hour later I tried to walk and vomited instead. The pain was intense. I called the team doctor, and he said I probably broke my back. He was on his way and called an ambulance. He called my parents, and they rushed over to take command of the children. (Notice: Team doctors keep nothing private from the owner.)

The hospital on Friday night of Christmas weekend was very busy. I was housed in a hallway for hours while a room was prepared. The emergency room was flooded with people with gunshot wounds and other victims of violent attacks. By the time I got tested, the doctors found I was leaking spinal fluid in my lower back. There was really nothing more to be done but rest. The next morning, I checked out and prepared for Christmas Eve that evening. I wanted the children to have a normal Christmas.

Three weeks later I flew to New York City to the Hospital for Special Surgery. The orthopedist placed me in traction for three weeks. He then sent me home with a full body brace. For six months, I lived a sedentary life, letting my muscles heal. At that point, the doctor prescribed physical therapy every day for two hours. I did this program for two years and became stronger and healthier. The problem was, initially I could not drive with the brace or sit for any length of time. My back muscles were shredded.

My father approached me and asked if I'd consider working with the team as vice president of community relations. I decided I could manage that job because I could work from home if needed and still have time for physical therapy. I immediately set about pushing the Bucs brand in the community. Dad was involved at the league level on the management council, and we needed a family member to be the face of the franchise in Tampa.

I created the Buccaneer Foundation and placed prominent business owners on the board. We had fundraising events such as donations for field goals and touchdowns at the games. This money went into the foundation. The board members allocated the funds. They became very immersed in the foundation and ultimately donated from their businesses as well. The more a business became involved, the more team spirit they showed by buying skyboxes and more tickets. It was a perfect marriage. The more I stayed out of it, the better it ran.

Meanwhile, I joined several nonprofit boards such as the Moffit Cancer and Research Institute, the Tampa Bay Chamber of Commerce, St. Joseph's Women's Hospital, All Children's Hospital, and Eckerd College. After a few years, I was elected president of the Tampa Bay Chamber of Commerce, the youngest to ever hold that position.

The same year, I was honored with the Executive Woman of the Year Award.

At this time, my father asked why I was not using the country club membership. The Bucs had five memberships, and only the coach and my dad were using the memberships. I had my assistant request an application. She rolled her eyes. I told her it was Dad's request. Well, I opened a tin of worms with that request. Apparently, the club did not allow women to be members unless they were spouse of male members. I thought this was unfair and backward as the president of the largest bank downtown was a woman. The lead attorneys in several law firms were female. Why couldn't women hold corporate memberships?

At the press conference to announce my winning the Executive Woman of the Year, I said that I had hired a powerful female African American attorney to represent me in a discrimination case against the club. The impact was immediate. The media played the story to the hilt. No one had challenged the old boys' network before. My father called to ask what I was doing. "I'm doing what you told me to do. I'm applying for the Buccaneer corporate membership, which is unused currently." His friends were telling him to get me to call off the lawsuit. He was being besieged. Ultimately, the club capitulated and allowed women to hold corporate memberships, but I was personally blackballed.

I rose through the ranks and became the vice president of administration. From that position I oversaw the business side of running the Buccaneers. People assumed I needed to know football. I surprised them by saying it's a business, and the product is football games on Sunday afternoons. The business is exactly the same as manufacturing tee shirts. Marketing, sales, and keeping the back room happy and well staffed is the secret to all businesses. Football is no different. Every Monday we held a staff meeting and put together a plan for the week. During the summer we got the away schedule and put out the list for airline bids. One year, I had a bid that was $20,000 lower from one airline. I was tempted to take it, but my staff was worried because there was talk of that airline folding before the season was completed. I listened to everyone at the meeting and took a few days to think. If I went with the airline and they defaulted, I'd have to charter a flight, which would be costly. But the allure of saving $20,000 was difficult not to consider. I decided to take the gamble. The entire season I read everything I could on the company to get a sense if it was going to quit operations in the middle of the season. My staff stared at me the rest of the meetings that year waiting to tell me "I told you so."

There were many services we had to consider. Early on, we realized the players had no idea how to eat healthy. After work we'd see them at the drive-through fast-food restaurants. The team began to gain weight and fall out of shape. Finally, the strength coach decided there was only one way to keep our men at peak performance: we had to feed them. We could not allow our team to balloon on fast food. A nutritionist was hired to work with the strength coach and trainers to provide a correct diet—but one that the players would eat. When the players arrived, breakfast pizza was served along with vegetable quiches. Lunch was provided, and we kept our fingers crossed that they would learn to choose healthier food options for dinner. The players seemed to enjoy our providing food. However, they really enjoyed the sodas.

One night around 6:30, I was watching the players walk to the parking lot from my office window. I saw them carrying cases of canned soda on their shoulders. I checked our manifest and realized today was the day the soda machines were restocked by the Coke distributer. I looked at our budget and thought we were paying an awful lot for sodas. The machines dispensed free cans. This had to stop. That's a lot of sugar that isn't being accounted for in their diets, and it's very expensive. The next day I called and had the distributer come out and exchange the machines for six-ounce single-serve cups. No more Coke walking out to the door. I never said a thing to the coaches, trainers, or players. They knew they'd been caught.

When I told my father later that week, he was astounded and wanted to know how many years he'd been furnishing sodas for the players' homes and parties.

By 1991, I was the president of the Tampa Bay Buccaneers. Our city had been awarded Super Bowl XXV. The twenty-fifth Super Bowl was a special NFL anniversary, and the league wanted this to be a really special event. Unfortunately, that period in history was rife with conflict because of the looming war in the Mideast, as Desert Shield turned into Desert Storm. Tampa is the home base for Central Command, which is the epicenter of decisions being made for the conflict in the Middle East. To avoid any risk and to provide the ultimate in safety, the large parties that the NFL usually held, such as the commissioner's party, were cancelled. My staff was on call to help the NFL set up for the game but grew to resent the fact that every time they pulled into the stadium, security checked them and the car thoroughly, including mirrors to look at the car's undercarriage. It was a stressful situation.

The city of Tampa and surrounding areas looked forward for years for this huge event that lasted several days. Restaurants ordered extra food, valets, and linens to service the crowds. Caterers ordered more of everything, anticipating parties and dinners. Due to the daily bulletins coming out of the Middle East, most events were cancelled or people just weren't in the mood to celebrate. General Norman Schwarzkopf, the leader of the war in Kuwait, was a beloved neighbor of the Tampa community. We knew he kept us safe from his perch at Centcom. It was a bleak sign when he raised the level of danger to Desert Storm on January 17, 1991. The loss of revenue hit the small businesses particularly hard. What do you do with salads and beef and fish that spoil? There was an uproar among the restaurant owners and caterers. There was no insurance for them to seek recompense.

I was working with the NFL on safety issues, such as having sharp shooters on the light stanchions above the crowds. We worked on how to get fans quickly through the metal detectors and how to get them out of the stadium in case of a bombing. I was having trouble sleeping at night. There was just so much to worry about every day.

The Florida Orchestra was scheduled to play the national anthem accompanying Whitney Houston. However, at practice the day before, the horns and other instruments had trouble with the humidity outside. Clearly, we would have to find the time to pretape their part in the few hours remaining before the game. Whitney didn't think her throat would hold in the January humidity that evening, so she had to lip-sync the night of the game. I assure you no one was happy by the end of the day, so it was a good thing all parties had been cancelled.

The day of the game, I took my children to the NFL brunch where they met an astronaut and an actor. I thought that was great. Highlight of the day. With that, I told Dad I had done all I could do and I was leaving. I didn't want to get caught in the stadium with my children if something bad should happen. I had lived with so much stress before the Super Bowl that I now just wanted to play with my children.

When all was said and done, the New York Giants beat the Buffalo Bills, 20–19. Two teams from the same state was not a big draw for fans except those from New York. As the twenty-fifth Super Bowl anniversary, it was a bit of a bust.

My responsibilities as team president ranged from diets to community involvement and problems that the players experienced. We knew if the player couldn't concentrate on the game when he was at One Buc Place, there were going to be problems on game day. Many players moved to Tampa with their wives or girlfriends. They were often from a college town or perhaps another NFL city and weren't familiar with Tampa. I realized the women were lonely and lost. I hired a former guidance counselor at a Black high school in Tampa. Since the majority of NFL players (now 76 percent) are African American, I wanted someone who would understand their unique issues. We nicknamed her Mama Buc. She met with the women and took them out to lunch and to schools for their children. She recommended churches and dentists. Anything the new-to-Tampa family needed, she was there to help them. She also arranged baby showers for moms-to-be and wedding showers. She helped the women cope with tired and hungry men. Mama Buc was the family member they needed in town but didn't have. She explained what they didn't know about the NFL and tried to help them make the adjustment.

For example, Gary Anderson and his wife had a daughter born with severe handicaps. She organized helpers among the women to see that the family was fed and loved. One night during a preseason home game I got paged in the press box. Gary's baby had died and his wife was at the hospital with the infant. I drove the few miles to the hospital wondering what I could possibly do in this situation. I realized when I arrived that the hospital had requested my presence. The mom had no family there, and the hospital had no one in authority to speak with as the mom was devastated. She kept grooming her little girl's hair. I had an employee get Gary out of the game and drive him to the hospital. When he arrived, the family grieved together but didn't want me to leave them. I got the pastor to come as well as the funeral director. When they arrived, the pastor had brought some congregants who knew the mom. They helped her. The hospital told me it was time for them to separate from their baby. She would only listen to me. I gently and carefully handed the baby to the nurse with the understanding she could say goodbye to her daughter before the night was over. I have to say I was overwhelmed being with the family in that small room with their recently deceased daughter. Gary was a loving dad and husband, and he seemed to know exactly the right thing to say to his wife. Twenty minutes previously he'd been running down a football field. Now he was saying goodbye to his daughter at the hospital. Mama Buc had everything organized by the next day.

In the late eighties my father was diagnosed with prostate cancer. It metastasized in his lung. He had one lobe removed in an effort to halt the spread. Dad had chemotherapy and other treatments, but the cancer kept advancing. We knew it had reached his brain when he had trouble with the stereo knobs. He had to ask my son to tune into the channels he favored. Christopher was the only one he really let help him. He used me like a secretary. I'd get my family settled for the evening and head to the hospital. I kept a legal pad there to take notes. I would stay there until 5 a.m., when the doctors would make their rounds. I'd head home and get my family off to work and school. I'd doze a bit, but Dad would rouse and start dictating things he needed the next day. These requests weren't fresh pajamas, no. It was "call this banker or that owner and tell them the following." His mind was working in overdrive. He asked about the new rookies and how training camp was shaping up. He wanted to know it all. His memory was remarkable.

However, like all good things, life must end. He died August 26, 1994, at age seventy-five. The entire ownership of the league attended the funeral and reception. They had to import black limos from surrounding cities as there weren't enough for all the requests in Tampa. It was truly a long black train of limousines in front of St. Andrews Church. Everyone in the church was the model of decorum except his mistress, who wept loudly at the front of the church. Fortunately, at the time, my mother had no idea about her husband's extras. My brother and I were caught between ushering her out and trying to ignore her.

Negotiations for selling the team had begun during the summer, and during training camp I left to spend time at my father's bedside. I couldn't preside over the Bucs and take care of my dad simultaneously. I never attended another Buc game. My mother kept her skybox and invited friends to join her at the games.

I began teaching at the University of South Florida and doing research there as well. It was wonderful to be back home in academia. It's a world I understood and one in which I was respected. The problem with being the owner's daughter is the preconceived ideas that the public has from movies such as *North Dallas Forty* where the daughter seduces the quarterback. I was no seductress. I was watching my dad's business. It took a while for men to understand and accept my role. I had plenty of men who wanted to get close to me because of football. They realized this was a business not a hobby. I was serious not in the business of flirting in the locker room. Put your fantasies to bed.

In January, as we were getting in our new rhythm, I received a call from the sheriff's department. He blurted out that they had arrested a man who was planning to kidnap me. This is the payback every family in a high-profile sport or entertainment industry fears. The publicity makes you vulnerable. The discussion of money in your family only hurts you. I was on my way to meet Monsignor Higgins, who functioned as our team's priest and had a parish near the stadium. When I appeared at the table, he jumped up and asked what was wrong. I was crying and on the verge of hysteria. He calmed me down and said he'd come back to the house with me to talk to the sheriff and police chief in Tampa. I had a bowl of soup and we left.

The sheriff started by showing me photos of several men. I immediately identified one that I had seen too often to be coincidental. He showed up at a car wash when my daughter and I were washing my car. He asked me if I had change for a dollar. I pointed to the change machine and told him to use it. My teenage daughter searched her wallet to help him. Later when I read his diary, the incident was mentioned. He said I was cautious. The sheriff was thrilled that I could so readily identify the man. They had him in custody. When they pulled him over for a faulty license that didn't match the truck, they found a diary detailing every day that he followed my daughter and me, handcuffs, a stun gun, tape, photos of all the rooms of our house, and a weapon. He was on the hunt for us. He had broken the security code to the house and frequently entered and took photos or souvenirs. My daughter had a floppy-eared pet rabbit in a hutch outside; he broke the rabbit's neck.

The next week or so was a blur. The city of Tampa placed bodyguards with my daughter and me. He had been following her on campus and taken her photo many times. How did he learn where she attended college? He stole the mail from my mailbox. There were vacation photos of my daughter so he could easily identify her. I also wrote the president of the college as I was a board member. I mentioned my daughter attending and being very happy in the college environment. That was all Ralph Gene Johnson, the would-be kidnapper, needed to peg my daughter.

After a week my daughter left school and came home. I did her homework and she took her exams. It was the best of a bad situation. My bubbly daughter was morose. My bodyguards provided the peace I needed to go on with my life. Many friends refused to be in my presence. They said they didn't want to be in the middle of a kidnapping. I quickly found my true friends. In the midst of this chaos, I gave a speech and one of the audience members came up to me and said, "You aren't well. Come by my office this afternoon anytime." His children had attended elementary school with my children and I knew him tangentially.

I saw him and then went to see five doctors, trying to figure out the problem. I ended up at Shands at the University of Florida. I was there on a Thursday and had surgery the following Monday. There was a tumor pressing on my carotid artery. The surgeon told me to get my will in order and visit my priest. The bodyguards never left me. They checked me in under an assumed name, worried about my vulnerable state.

It took quite a while to recover. I had someone take over my teaching responsibilities at the university. I knew I had to relocate. The police were afraid of copycat kidnappers and suggested strongly that I leave the Tampa area after the trial. My friends got in touch with headhunters and soon I was interviewing for jobs in Ohio and D.C. Mentally, this was the best thing to happen as I was quite stressed by all that happened in a very short period of time: my father died, we had a kidnapping threat, and I had life-threatening surgery.

In December I gave my victim's impact statement. The bodyguards were thrilled as the magistrate sentenced Johnson for the maximum counts. I left the courthouse in a patrol car, and we rolled right up to the boarding ramp of the plane to Ohio, where I took a job as a college president. My daughter went back to the dorm, and life was calmer.

I have to admit I thought being a college president would be exciting and busy. After working in the NFL, I was used to high-octane working conditions. I was the first lay person in the seventy-five-year history of the college to be the president. They were used to slow and methodical processes for everything. However, they weren't realistic about life. When I arrived in December, 12 percent of the freshman class was pregnant. The college nurse was driving them to prenatal appointments. The students were afraid to go home at Christmas and wanted to stay on campus so their parents wouldn't know they were pregnant. Furthermore, the staff had the idea of renovating an old building on campus and letting the students and their babies live there the following year. I was apparently the only one who did not think this was a good idea.

I knew I had to leave at the end of the academic year.

The Cooke Center for Learning and Development in Manhattan offered me a job as the executive director. I took it. I worked there and after a few years moved over to Teachers College, Columbia University, where I taught tests and measurements, among other courses. I adored working with the bright students, and many are still my friends today.

The events of 9/11 drove me out of Chelsea, where I lived in a new condo that I had lovingly set up. However, it was covered with asbestos fibers no matter how much I cleaned, months after the attacks in Lower Manhattan. I knew it was time to evacuate. I had been walking my dog on the street that Tuesday morning when the Twin Towers fell. I was engulfed in the jet fuel and falling debris. I thought the world had come to an end. Definitely time to head north to Montgomery County, in Upstate New York, where my cabin sat waiting.

I had been dragging Pepper and Babydoll with me from their original home in Sarasota. Those horses were family in many ways. I began rodeoing with the neighbors and going on long trail rides with the neighbors, no matter their ages. Parents trusted me with their twelve-year-old daughters in the afternoons after school. There were always enough girls for a trail ride through the woods. Since there were hunters year-round, it was always better to have a group of horses rather than one or two. One Saturday I was invited by one of the moms to join their family at a horse show. I saw a horse that was new to me: a Paso Fino. These are gaited horses that are stunning. They look a bit like the knight chess piece with the large curved neck.

I met a few of the riders and trainers and decided I wanted to show those horses. They were smaller than quarter horses and lower to the ground. What could go wrong? Years later, I can tell you I suffered broken ribs several times, broken elbows, and six documented concussions. These horses are on fire. You show them on the verge of their blowing up. After my seventh concussion I visited two neurologists. Both said never to get on a step stool, let alone a horse. I was through with the horse world. I owned twenty-six show horses, four pleasure horses for trail riding, and a Fresian and a jumper. It pained me to close my business, Aquarian Show Horses, Inc. I knew I was pushing the envelope in terms of preserving my cognitive abilities. My balance was shot and I was tending to depression. I could not allow myself to get worse.

I asked Dr. Robert Cantu, a leading neurologist and concussion specialist, what should I do to heal. He said I had to go into a dark room with no stimulation for three weeks. No music, no light, and no reading. Complete sensory deprivation was what he ordered. I asked how to do that. He suggested a three-week cruise where I never got off the ship and had all meals delivered to the room. I followed his directions. By day nine, my headache was gone. I never knew if it was day or night. The ringing in my ears ceased. My balance improved. I didn't have to hold onto the walls to move successfully. My brain began the healing process.

This gave me a deep insight into what football players were experiencing, so I began to write a book shortly before my final concussion. By this time, I was known at the local emergency rooms and the orthopedists' offices. I kept training more horses and risking injury. I was addicted in many ways to the adrenaline rush of riding and competing. So I understood the players' need to be on that football field regardless of the risk to their health. We could say it was for the money, but those of us that compete know we do it for the rush. Nothing beats the minute the gate opens for the horses to enter the ring just like a player taking the field to the crowds' cheering. Nothing can compare.

Nine years later I can still feel the visceral thrill when I watch a horse romping in the field, or one being ridden in competition. I find the pull so strong that I now avoid all horses or talk of horses. It's a true loss for me. My world was set in the barn; the smell of the hay mixed with manure is in my soul. I look at a horse and feel an immediate bond. Likewise, only horse trainers and competitors understand the world I lost. This is why I can easily understand the world the NFL players lose when they retire. It's their soul that they ultimately sacrifice. Football has been their world since childhood. It's their identity. As children, they couldn't wait for Friday night games. They weren't paid. That's not why they played with their heart and soul. Their football team was a set of brothers. They knew the secret: players couldn't live without the game.

Money was not the driving force behind the will to play. Most rookies never even read their contract before signing it. As one player put it to me, "I was so excited to be on an NFL team that I would have played for free. I was now an *NFL player.*" That's the mentality that leads to problems after football. The player doesn't really care what he makes as long as he can play ball. When he is cut, he's devastated, not because of the loss of income but because of the loss of identity and the absence of the rush of playing the game.

I realize this is difficult to comprehend, and most parents don't understand how their son might not read his contract. However, he has been taken over by the addiction to his sport. I know this feeling well. We athletes will do anything to stay on the field of play as long as we can. Someone usually has to make the decision for us to stop. I think I would have competed until I had no cognitive functioning left. I was addicted and still feel the pull to ride.

2

TRANSITION

Few players are as fortunate as Andrew Luck, the Indianapolis Colts quarterback. He was able to choose when it was best for him to leave the league. He stayed at Stanford to finish his degree instead of leaving school a year early to enter the draft in 2011 as many thought he would. He was smart: he had an excellent senior year, his draft stock rose, and he finished his degree in the process. He was drafted first overall in 2012 by the Indianapolis Colts. Luck was "pro ready," immediately leading the team to three consecutive playoff appearances. Although primarily a passer, Luck could scramble when necessary. He immediately turned the 2–14 Colts into contenders in the American Football Conference (AFC) South division.

But by 2016, Luck continued to play through the season with an injured shoulder. In the off season he had surgery and had to take the 2017 season off to rehabilitate his shoulder. He traveled to Europe for special care and then studied with special throwing coaches in California. By 2018, he was ready to return and had one of his greatest years, finishing second in touchdown passes and was voted the Comeback Player of the Year. He was also voted to his fourth Pro Bowl.

However great his accomplishments, he was still aching from the injuries he'd suffered through his years of football. Knowing if he continued to play, he would spend large parts of his life in the training room and rehabilitation center, he made the difficult choice to leave the game that was his focus for many years. He knew there was more to life than pain and rehabilitation. On August 24, 2019, at a hastily convened press conference, Andrew Luck told the world he was retiring:

> I've been stuck in this process. I haven't been able to live the life I want to live. It's taken the joy out of this game. The only way forward for me is to remove myself from football. This is not an easy decision. It's the hardest decision of my life. But it is the right decision for me.

"Luck retires, calls decision 'the hardest of my life'" was the headline on ESPN.[1]

If anyone was prepared to leave the league, it was Andrew. He had the emotional and financial tools to make a successful break. Foremost, he had a strong family who supported him. His father, Oliver, had been the general manager of two World League of American Football teams before becoming president of the league. As a child, Andrew was indoctrinated into the world of football while living in Europe and attending schools in London and Germany. He became an avid soccer fan during this time.

Upon returning to Texas, Andrew was valedictorian of his high school class in 2008 and chose to attend Stanford and play for head coach Jim Harbaugh. While a student, Andrew set many records that still stand today. He stayed to graduate with a degree in architectural design. He never lost focus on the importance of education.

The additional piece to Luck's stability was his marriage in the spring of 2019. He now had the important ingredients to a successful life. With his savings from football safely invested and the skills he obtained through his education and contacts, he was set to start his next career. He didn't need to panic, because he had wisely saved during his football playing days.

It's extremely rare, though, for a player to have the luxury of leaving the game when it suits him. Most players are blindsided when they are told to report to the coach's office and bring their playbook. They cannot believe the call is for them. The average time a player spends in the NFL is fewer than four years. Yet no rookie believes he will be out that soon. The length of the rookie contract is four years and can be extended at the team's discretion for a fifth year for top draft picks. Most men believe that is just the beginning and are confident they will be around to negotiate a well-paying second contract. The value of rookie contracts is spelled out in the collective bargaining agreement, though the most coveted players can also receive signing bonuses. The second and third contracts are where players make far more money.

Unfortunately, some players spend more than they make in their rookie contract because they expect to get a second contract. Merchants do not help these young men. They sell them houses at no money down and put them in cars they cannot afford. These young men have craved these outward signs of success for many years, but they cannot afford them in their rookie years. If these young men are cut after their rookie contracts end, they will have huge debts and no way to pay them off. In a brutal sport where few contracts are fully guaranteed, this happens more than one would think.

Most players will need a job after they leave the league. If they left college before earning a degree, they will have few resources to help them. Most players will not be in the league the minimum of four years needed to receive a pension and other benefits either. The biggest problem players face is the management of their finances in the NFL and afterward. Young men think the NFL will provide for them for many years. This is far from reality. Even though Andrew Luck played for seven years, he still has a college degree that will help him get another job and support his family.

There have been many attempts to educate players and prepare them for life after football, but no one seems to want to hear the truth. Players want to believe they will play for ten years and leave the game as millionaires. The NFL wants players present and future to believe they can make millions by playing in the league and sacrificing their health. The league offers seminars about financial planning and investments but charges up to $5,000 per weekend session. Players, who believe their rookie contracts and future deals will last a lifetime, decide that advice is too expensive. Therefore, the program is underutilized.

In the mideighties the league tried to address this problem by bringing experts to the teams to discuss financial planning over six weeks. The meetings were held on Monday evenings when the players would be on-site to retrieve their game checks. The sessions were one hour in length. During those six weeks, I witnessed only two people attending, and they were the wives of coaches. The NFL abandoned the program as other teams had similar turnouts. You can bring the water to the horse's mouth, but that's as far as it goes.

Most players have thought of themselves as football players for most of their lives. It is their identity. It is rare that a player such as Andrew Luck sees himself as a scholar, family member, and athlete. For the majority of professional players, they are football players—full stop. When that identity is taken from them at the end of their careers, they are lost. Who are they now? Many players exist in a fog of denial awaiting a call from another team that doesn't come. This can go on for years. These men are paralyzed by the fear of the unknown.

This is a recipe for family discord and divorce. Many players meet their wives in high school or college, before they understand the pressures of running a family or a home. Then the stress of football, where a player's job is on the line every day, begins. When the music stops, the stress ramps up further and, many times, marriages suffer. Steven Ortiz, associate professor of sociology at Oregon State, studied the wives of professional athletes. He told the *New York Times* in a story entitled "Taking Vows in a League Hit Hard by Divorce" that wives, too, had to adjust to their husbands being at home. "The fans got the man she wanted all along," he said. "She got someone else."

Keith McCants, a linebacker for the Buccaneers who was an All-American at the University of Alabama, couldn't cope without the structure of football and the easy access to drugs in the locker room. The fourth overall pick of the 1990 draft, he received a $7.4 million contract and played eighty-eight games in his six seasons with three teams. Keith has said that when he left the NFL, he had no access to painkillers so he turned to street drugs to dull the pain of his many injuries. Since leaving the league in 1995, he has been arrested more than a dozen times. Keith has been lost to the world of drugs, courts, and rehabilitation centers. Once a wealthy NFL star, he is now a repeat offender, well known to law enforcement officers in and around Tampa.

Keith never had what Andrew Luck had: a plan to leave the game, an emotional support network, and a financial savings framework. All of a sudden, Keith was out on his own. His main focus was easing his physical pain. He looked for drugs in all the wrong places and kept getting arrested. Twenty-five years later, he has not broken this cycle of arrests, jail, release, and arrest. I might add, several treatment centers have reached out to Keith to help him kick his habit of addiction, but while he has visited several of them, his recovery often does not last long. He still sees himself as a football player. He never found a different role as he aged. This is where many men get stuck and cannot envision themselves as anything other than professional football players. Their focus since childhood has been on sports to the exclusion of other possibilities. If you don't know pilots exist, you can't wish to fly for a living. Many families see their sons as a way out of poverty and will force this dynamic onto them. One way or another, the child's scope is limited to football. Therefore, when it is ripped away, the man is left with no identity or focus. Depression sets in as he struggles to locate his inner and true self. Keith lost his self-awareness to drugs.

In contrast, Nate Wonsley was an undrafted free agent in 1986 when he joined the Buccaneers. He played college ball at Mississippi. Although small at five foot ten, Nate had the heart of a lion on the field. At a preseason home game in Tampa, Nate, a running back, was hit sideways. He laid on the turf and then started to get up. The team doctor kept him on the ground and called for the stretcher and a neck brace. The doctor said to me later, "Gay, I just had a feeling there was more to that hit." Thank goodness he had that sixth sense because scans showed that Nate's neck was broken. Coincidently, this happened after I had broken my back and was using the physical therapy office our team has exclusive access to. Nate and I got to be workout buddies as we both had broken spines. For two years, Nate and I saw each other five days a week as we rehabilitated from our injuries. I watched him process the death of his dream to play football in the NFL after just one season. He had two brothers who were also football players and a supportive family who cheered him on to get better. He and I would have contests running stadium steps toward the end of our two years.

Nate by that time had decided to become a body builder. His high point was placing fourth in the 2012 Europa Show of Champions. He has many trophies for competitions and is featured in bodybuilding magazines. Nate made a new career after a devastating injury. He lost football in one shocking play but was able to readjust and focus on another sport successfully. Many players, though, will suffer an injury and give up.

Head injuries forced Luke Kuechly to make the same difficult decision in January 2020. During his eight years as linebacker playing with the Carolina Panthers, Kuechly had 1,092 tackles, which took a toll on his body and particularly his brain. Luke suffered concussions in 2015, 2016, and probably 2017. In a nationally televised game in 2016, came-

ras caught Kuechly experiencing the aftershocks of an on-field concussion. The cameras focused on his agony and tears while he gasped for
breath.

Although he was celebrated as the Defensive Rookie of the Year in
2012, the Defensive Player of the Year in 2013, a five-time All-Pro, and
notably the 2017 Art Rooney Sportsmanship Award winner, he made
the decision to leave the game he loved. Eight years of concussions and
unremitting aches and pains led him to quit.

> For me, now is the right opportunity to move in a different direction.
> There's only one way to play the game, since I was a little kid: play
> fast and play physical and play strong. That's the part that is the most
> difficult. I still want to play, but I don't think it's the right decision.

Luke should have saved his money during his eight years of play because at age twenty-eight, he has to start a second career. We can only
hope the concussions don't interrupt his postfootball plans. He clearly
had to leave the game for health reasons because he had two years
remaining on his contract that was scheduled to pay him $10 million per
season. No one walks away from that money unless he needs to stop
playing a violent sport.

Some players never make it that far. Tim Meamber graduated from
the University of Washington with a communications degree. He was
subsequently drafted in 1985 by the Minnesota Vikings in the third
round. Life was looking up.

But during his rookie year he was injured and played a total of four
games in the NFL before he was released. His injury ended his football
career. He tried to proceed with a normal life. He married and had a
daughter. He invented a popcorn-like snack but lost the patent in order
to resolve other legal problems.

His life spiraled into a world of drugs and addiction. He had no
guiding coaches or teammates to lean on. He only wanted the next
drug. He was afraid of heroin, but his drug of choice was cocaine. The
$250,000 he received from the NFL concussion settlement was used to
buy drugs.

He lives with his dog in an old van. He has no teeth and is difficult to
understand because he also has Parkinson's disease. He lives in and
around small Washington rural towns and is well known to local residents. He figures since they are used to his presence, they won't arrest

him. He parks at the Pilot rest stop and passes himself off as a truck driver so he can take showers there. Otherwise, he bathes in the local river. Occasionally residents will hold a fundraiser or offer help to Tim. They remember when he was captain of his university team. They talk among themselves about how to help him. Someone is trying to get him dentures, for example. He eats at the food kitchens in town.

Tim Meamber had a college degree. He invented a popular snack food, had a family, and showed potential for much more after his term of football ceased. Unfortunately, he took the opportunity to go down intellectually and financially. His university teammate, Joe Krakoski, summed it up when he told "The Homeless Husky":

> We both went out with knees. I thought I'd play five years in the NFL. Tim probably thought he'd play longer. Then you get dumped on your head. If you don't have a reliable system or catch-all of some kind, anything goes.[2]

Tim Meamber lost his dream of playing in the NFL. He turned to drugs to solve the pain of the loss of his future. In some cases, players' lives change in an instant. That's what happened to Joe Theismann, the Washington Redskins quarterback who suffered a career-ending injury on national television on November 18, 1985. As fans watching the game will never forget, New York Giants linebacker Lawrence Taylor sacked Theismann legally but accidently fell on Joe's leg. The break was midway between his knee and foot. The *Washington Post* called it "The Hit That No One Who Saw It Can Ever Forget." It is probably the most replayed injury in the history of the NFL. The compound break was so severe that it failed to heal correctly and Joe was left with a limp. At age thirty-six, his career as a quarterback was done.

Fortunately, Joe had a gift of gab and an understanding of the game so his move into the broadcast booth was seamless. He worked for a number of networks and shows and even had cameos in several movies. Instead of traveling the self-pitying road to drugs, Joe dug in and created a second career for himself.

Players leave the NFL because they walk away or, more frequently, a team decides it can replace them with a better, less expensive player. Either way, it's a personal trauma as this is the identity the player has established for himself since childhood. Who is he if not a football player? Some men make the transition, yet more do not succeed without football. The player suffers a loss of control and sense of abject failure when he is cut from a team. He wants to sneak out the back door to avoid confronting those players still on the team. He rarely attends local alumni gatherings where he can gather helpful information because his embarrassment is acute in front of his brothers.

Rarely do players have an exit strategy. They believe they will play longer than the average of three to four years. They thought they would be on the team to claim the higher salaries promised after the initial rookie contract. Therefore, it is a shock, and few are financially ready to face a life without their football salary. For those without a degree and no business connections, they are literally lost when it's time to find a new job. Some men just out of the league end up coaching because it is what they know best and because they may have very little other experience.

Some fans who own businesses offer players jobs, but players quickly learn that they are on staff as trophies, not respected employees. They are asked to appear at dinner parties for customers or to impress regional managers at professional lunches. They are only supposed to relive the glory days of their short career. Most players feel like arm candy and leave these positions.

Players need to feel good about their jobs. As professional football players, they were respected because it takes a lot of talent and skill to make it to the NFL. It becomes impossible to duplicate that level of self-confidence at age twenty-six when you are suddenly without a team backing you up. At this point some players might return to their universities to complete their college degrees. They also look to their agents to help them find jobs. But many agents are no longer interested because you don't represent the money you once did. The university might give him an assistant's job with their football team to help him finish his coursework. But it's understood to be temporary and ends when he completes his degree.

However, many players I've known try to complete the coursework but have trouble concentrating. They are now much older than the typical student, and classmates find it difficult to relate to them. And after being out of the classroom for so many years and no longer having an individual tutor, ex-players can find academic work decidedly difficult. The upshot is that many players don't complete their degrees.

For some players, it represents another failure. They might have bought a house with no money down their rookie year, or an expensive car or cars to burnish their image as a professional ballplayer. Those payments continue, yet they have no income. Quickly, things are repossessed and players escape their growing debts by declaring bankruptcy. Unfortunately, these players file for bankruptcy at a higher rate than those men who do not play in the NFL. In a research paper, "Bankruptcy Rates among NFL Players with Short-Lived Income Spikes," economists found that initial bankruptcy filings begin soon after players retire and continue "at a substantial rate" through at least the first twelve years of their retirement.

Critically, bankruptcy rates are not affected by how much a player earned during his NFL career or the number of years he played. "Having played for a long time and been well-paid does not provide much protection against the risk of going bankrupt," according to the writers of a research paper on the topic. The reasons are typically because they didn't save enough because they were too optimistic about how long they'd play, they made poor financial decisions, or they spent too much. "Even in the most conservative scenario, nearly 15 percent of players will have declared bankruptcy by 25 years after retirement," the authors said.[3]

Sadly, rookies face pressure to show off their success. Few players purchase a Prius or a Subaru. They're afraid of looking unsuccessful. They've got to buy the thick, gold chain and the foreign car and the mansion. The public wants them to succeed and applauds the fact that they made it to the Big Time. These enablers are ignorant of the fact that a rookie contract doesn't pay well enough to afford all these payments. He's not paying cash for these new signs of wealth. Fans, friends, cousins, former teammates, entrepreneurs, investment advisors, and hucksters seek out players, pestering them to invest or to buy more of something. The pressure from family members is difficult to ignore. Whether it is outward or subtle, it's understood you've got to buy your mother a new car to show your love and success. You also must get your family an upscale home. That's what good sons do. Rookies don't sit down and explain the realities of their new wealth to their friends and family. It's a lot less money than everyone expects. Players are almost embarrassed by how little they are paid after taxes, their agent's fee, and their living expenses. It may seem like a lot, but players only receive checks for seventeen weeks and must make those last for fifty-two weeks. Taxes need to be paid in April. Players are shocked at the amount that is taken to pay the government taxes, social security, and other fees. Few players have any experience dealing with financial issues before entering the league.

> When you grew up with nothing in very humble beginnings, you tend to want a lot of things when you don't have the money to buy. So there's a lot of wants, and "I wish I had this" and "I wish I had that." So when you're able to purchase some of those items, you know, you wanna go out and buy what you've never had.[4]

After three or four years, they are no longer NFL players, yet they still have payments due on everything they purchased. Agents need to provide reality checks for their rookie clients. College programs could have mandatory financial courses for athletes or provide a guide to finance app for their cell phones. The best stopgap to spending is a frugal wife. Wives see the long view. They worry about what is to come, not what is here now.

> My background's in finance . . . so I've kind of always been a real stickler with him. And it's a blessing. I mean, we pretend like we don't have it and we, basically have a great home and we're very blessed to be where we are but other than that, our home is an investment, so we'll just be tight with our money. . . . So, we've from day one, have planned for the future, and I take control because I hear these horror stories, broke in three years. The minute the career is over like what do they do, and I don't have to worry about that which is great.[5]

Players who relied on financial advisors or their agents for financial advice have experienced mixed results. Although the NFL has a list of certified financial advisors who passed rigorous qualifications, there exists a paranoia among players about letting the NFL know about your financial situation. So players typically find out about financial advisors through their teammates or family.

The players' union also hosts investment and entrepreneurship programs. The most popular of them are the broadcasting "boot camp," a media boot camp, and a coaching boot camp. But however good these courses appear, there are drawbacks. Most players realize these programs are likely best suited for name-brand players such as Tom Brady or Richard Sherman. No-name players don't feel they have a chance to be featured in the broadcast booth or as a coach for a professional team. They are realistic enough to know that playing three or four years in the league doesn't prepare you for a high-profile job. Additionally, these programs are expensive. The NFLPA charges up to $5,000 per course, not including travel expenses, food, and hotel nights.

In the earlier days of football, players had days off and had time to work with local companies, meet business leaders, and learn marketable skills. In the days before free agency, they also didn't make the money players today do, so they had to work in the off-season. And they often stayed many years in one city, allowing them to put down roots.

Today, professional football is a full-time job, even though players are only paid seventeen weeks per year. Players work out all year and are in the training room and rehabilitation center. They attend "voluntary" off-season workouts.

This leaves them less time to work or study elsewhere, so they lean on authority figures they have trusted their entire lives. They are so focused on football from a young age that they aren't aware of what alternatives exist, nor are they as skeptical as they need to be with their money or the investments they are presented with.

When players are offered their first job after they leave the NFL, they are often shocked at how low the salary offer is. They were NFL professionals, so they believe they deserve a large salary because of who they are. They do not understand they are applying for an entry-level position. As one player put it,

> The National Football League does not translate on a resume. . . . It makes you feel so small because, yes, I could maybe generate all this revenue and now I have to fight for work—for maybe a nine-to-five job, which is fine. I might not get the job because a person who's been working for ten years has never done what I've done . . . to the level I've done it, is more qualified than me. . . . That's a bitter pill to swallow because it's not that you're incapable, it's just the fact that . . . you haven't worked on any skill outside of your football. [6]

Not only are work skills important to prepare for life after football, but also social skills are vital to getting and keeping a position. The locker room is a social setting that is not often replicated in corporate business. Football players are relaxed in the locker room and around sports teams, an environment they've called home for the majority of their lives. Social interactions are different in the business world. One needs to understand different social cues. When applying for a position that involves interacting with the public, social intelligence is critical to be successful. If you are applying as a landscaper or UPS driver, social skills are not as important. So retired players need to work with a job counselor to assess their skills and suggest employment opportunities. It would be wonderful if the league offered these services to help players transition into another form of employment. My guess is there would be fewer applications for benefits because the players would have jobs, incomes, and medical insurance.

From my work helping former players obtain benefits, I have found that their number one disability is depression. Players never recover from the shock of being dismissed from the team. Even those with a college degree fall into deep depression. Lower-level jobs cannot make up for the adrenaline rush of playing football. I know of players in their twenties and thirties who stay in the bedroom all day and doze. Three players I know in particular have college degrees and were good students. Losing their football identity was the beginning of the end for them. They are now angry and depressed. No therapy or drugs can make up for their loss of identity.

Scott Goldman, president of the Association of Applied Sports Psychology, recognizes that most athletes transitioning to life after football do not take advantage of sports psychologists. He believes his field can help these men. Goldman's belief is that leaving the all-encompassing life of football is similar to losing a loved one. He works with his clients on the stages of grief similar to those outlined by Elisabeth Kubler-Ross, who wrote about the five stages of grief.

> For some of them, it's as much a shift in identity as dealing with a tragic loss. Most of these athletes get up by 6 a.m. and their day is largely accounted for and scheduled. It can be really intense when they leave.[7]

When tight end Ben Hartsock was released by the New England Patriots in 2013, his sixth team in ten years, he'd been with the club for just four days during preseason.[8] He knew this was the end of his football career and quickly transitioned to becoming an agent. With a wife and two daughters to support, he was afraid he'd lose the mental toughness to work if he didn't immediately take a job. After two years he realized he wanted to be a sportscaster instead, but his mindset was to work.

> Professional athletes, no matter the sport, leave a life of structure and must transition to a life of relative normalcy. More athletes today are already thinking about it, but no matter how well-prepared the transition, it can still cause hiccups, Hartsock said. After twenty years of playing football, Hartsock said it's almost like being institutionalized.
>
> I don't know what other industry or business has a similar experience, he said. The shelf life of an athlete is limited in a way I can't think of any other profession is. Think about going to high school getting great marks, going to college and excelling, and then after five or ten years of being the best surgeon in the world, they take it away from you. That's hard.[9]

Grow Counseling (http://growcounseling.com), professional counselors who help people transition to the next phase in their lives, sees athletes going through a unique set of challenges:

Denial. Not being able to face the reality that the game is over and your life will be different.

Drinking and drug use. Pro athletes may turn to alcohol, prescriptions, and illegal drugs for emotional relief. Often this is an existing problem that becomes bigger during retirement.

Divorce. Statistics are staggering. It is reported that *half* of NFL players divorce within the first year of retirement. Marriage therapy can be a helpful resource for pro athletes and their wives.

Depression. Although the stress may lead to suicidal thoughts and behaviors, only small numbers of pro athletes seek or are provided with mental health therapy during transition.

Isolation. The pro athlete may feel "alone," no longer part of a team. Anger and bitterness, lack of structure, and financial loss may increase the likelihood of isolation.

Many recently retired players and their wives believe the league or union should do more to help players transition out of football. They get cut and then they get angry at the team for not providing a soft landing. All teams have an alumni director, and many have a development director. The problem is the player doesn't want to be seen around the facility as he is no longer a team member. These services are designated for him, but he won't use them. Hence, he never takes advantage of the supports that the union provides for the alumni. Usually, the wives hear about programs through informal wives' groups that exist on the internet and Facebook.

Still, retired players feel they deserve more from the NFL. Their bodies are now broken, and they'll suffer pain the remainder of their days. When they are no longer affiliated with the team, they feel they were underpaid. Some players will suffer from dementia and Parkinson's as a result of having played the game. No matter what benefit they obtain, it will never be enough in their mind for what they are suffering and will continue to suffer.

Football is a tough man's game. There are no cry babies in the locker room. You fight for your position on the practice field and in the stadium. This is an adrenaline rush that propels the gladiator on game day. It's difficult to re-create that feeling of brotherhood linked by a common goal in retirement. Toughness doesn't translate after football to real-world experiences. The player has to tone down his warrior mentality.

Sports psychologists and marriage counselors, like financial planners, could help support players transitioning out of the league. The players, though, need to take advantage of these services.

A LAWYER'S PERSPECTIVE ON ATHLETES, THE CRIMINAL JUSTICE SYSTEM, SUBSTANCE USE, AND MENTAL ILLNESS

This section was written by Mark G. Astor, https://drugandalcoholattorneys.com.

In late 1987, after my parents informed me that they intended to relocate our family from London, England, to Florida, I came to this country and went to visit a long-lost friend who was in college at the University of Michigan, in Ann Arbor, Michigan. In the middle of winter, with snow all around, I fell in love and decided to become a Wolverine and ended up enrolling at the school.

In the fall of 1988, I got to experience my very first college football game as the University of Miami Hurricanes came to the Big House in Ann Arbor. That day 105,000 hearts were broken as the 'Canes won with a last-minute field goal (31–30). Little did I know that one of the players (a redshirt junior linebacker hereinafter referred to as "NW") on the 'Canes roster would become the defendant in a criminal case that I would prosecute in 1998 as a Palm Beach County assistant state attorney. NW was convicted of kidnapping, and as a prison release reoffender (he had two prior enumerated felony convictions) was sentenced to life in prison. NW is still in prison, and despite efforts by his family to seek clemency from the Florida governor, he will remain incarcerated until he takes his last breath.

NW is far from the only athlete that has been in trouble and convicted of a crime. There are fifty NFL players, fifty-one major league baseball players, and thirty NBA players who have also been convicted of crimes ranging from tax evasion to murder.[10] Sentences range from probation to life in prison.[11]

CRIME

While researching this section of the book, the following names came to mind: O. J. Simpson, Mike Tyson, Rae Carruth, and Pete Rose. They are among the best-known, or most infamous, cases of athletes getting mixed up in crimes.

O. J. Simpson

I was a young Palm Beach County assistant state attorney in 1994 when O. J. Simpson was arrested for the murders of Ron Goldman and Nicole Brown Simpson. I recall watching the opening statement of the so-called Trial of the Century with many of my colleagues in the County Court library of the Palm Beach County State Attorney's Office. While O.J. was acquitted of the murders, but later found liable in the wrongful death suit that followed, he just could not stay out of the public light. On October 3, 2008, O.J. was convicted of kidnapping and armed robbery stemming from an incident in a Las Vegas hotel.[12] O.J. was paroled from prison on October 1, 2017, after having served almost nine years.

Rae Carruth

Rae Carruth was drafted by the Carolina Panthers in 1997, but in 2001 he was convicted of conspiracy to commit murder of his girlfriend Cherica Adams.[13] Rae was released from prison on October 22, 2018, and since that time appears to be leading a quiet life in Charlotte, North Carolina.[14]

"Iron" Mike Tyson

Mike Tyson is regarded as one of the all-time greatest professional boxers. I recall seeing him knocked out by James "Buster" Douglas while I was in my third year at the University of Michigan (February 11, 1990). A year later, on February 10, 1992, Iron Mike was convicted of the rape of beauty pageant contestant Desiree Washington and served three years in prison.[15]

Pete Rose

Pete Rose, a.k.a. "Charlie Hustle," was a switch-hitting baseball player who holds the records for most hits, games played, at bats, singles, and outs.[16] In August 1989, Rose was thrown out of baseball after betting on games while both a player and a manager. On April 20, 1990, Rose was convicted of filing false income tax returns.

Why Do Athletes Get in Trouble?

How often have we heard about a professional athlete who comes from nowhere and make millions of dollars only for it to be squandered, ending their career? Athletes who lost all their money due to "temptation" have a number of common traits, namely, bankruptcy, domestic violence, and substance abuse.[17] There appear to be two reasons athletes get in trouble: their background and temptation.

Background: Trauma

The very first podcast I did, Darryl and Tracy Strawberry were my guests.[18] Darryl and Tracy were such incredible guests, and both are true inspirations. On one of my later podcasts, I interviewed Super

Bowl winner Vance Johnson.[19] Both Vance and Darryl talked about their own personal battles with trauma and how they used substances to douse their pain. Both Darryl and Vance talked about their infidelity and their pain and how they used substances to calm the voices in their head. And both Darryl and Vance have found peace, and a calling, as both work and serve others to help them in their battle against addiction.

Last year I had the opportunity to interview former NBA player Jayson Williams on my podcast.[20] What Jayson revealed was a childhood that was marred with sexual abuse, trauma, and the use and abuse of alcohol. This behavior spilled over into multiple run-ins with the law. In 2010, Jayson was convicted of manslaughter following an incident in 2002 wherein he shot and killed his limo driver.[21] In 2009, Jayson was tasered by the police after entering a Manhattan hotel intoxicated. That same year he allegedly punched a man in the face at a bar in Raleigh, North Carolina, and in 2010, he was arrested for driving while intoxicated, which resulted in an additional year in prison.[22] Jayson now owns and operates his own program, Rebound, and he has helped hundreds of men, many like him who have suffered from sexual abuse and trauma.[23] Check out Jayson's Facebook page for all the fun activities he gets up to that help him and his clients maintain sobriety.[24]

Temptation

According to the ESPN documentary *Broke*,[25] 78 percent of NFL players are out of money within two years of retiring from the game.[26] When you consider that many professional athletes, especially football players, who have an average playing life of 3.3 years,[27] have a small window of opportunity to earn money, you can begin to understand how the window of opportunity to squander that money is large.

Few athletes learn to manage their money and the temptation of houses, fast cars, and jewelry is too much for many to resist. A prime example is Vince Young of the University of Texas. I don't have such fond memories of Vince, who torched my Wolverines in the 2005 Rose Bowl (a game that the Wolverines should have won). Then in 2006, on fourth down and five yards, on the USC nine-yard line, with just nineteen seconds left to play, he ran for a game-winning touchdown to beat the Trojans.

Young appeared to have it all, physical size and strength, lightning speed and illusiveness, and despite an awkward throwing motion, he was accurate enough to play in the NFL. Young was drafted in 2006 by the Tennessee Titans, despite reportedly doing poorly on the Wonderlic test that is given to prospective draft picks.[28] At first blush, Young appeared to be a good fit for the NFL. However, from 2007, things went downhill, including violations of team rules, injuries, and poor play. (He was benched in favor of Kerry Collins during the 2008 season.)[29] By 2014, after failing to catch on with several other teams, Young was out of the league, finally being cut by the Cleveland Browns.[30]

The contract that Young signed with the Titans in 2007 included $25 million in guaranteed money, but by 2014 he was broke.[31] Here is the list of some of the crazy things Young spent his money on: $600 shoes for all of his friends; $6,000 at TGI Fridays; all the seats on a Southwest flight so he could avoid sitting next to anyone; $5,000 per week at the Cheesecake Factory; an investment in the Vince Young steak house that went south; and, reportedly, Rolex watches for his entire offensive line.[32]

Young is not the only athlete to have been financially decimated by temptation. Here are some other athletes who lost all their money (some of whom could not keep either their checkbook or their manhood in their pants): Dan Issel (unknown), Rick Mahorn ($6 million), Robert Swift ($11 million), Randy Brown ($15 million), Delonte West ($16 million), Glen Rice ($33 million), Jason Caffey ($35 million), Eric Williams ($39.8 million), Charles Barkley ($40 million), Larry Johnson ($40 million), Dennis Rodman ($50 million), Kenny Anderson ($60 million), Darius Miles ($61 million), Christian Laettner ($61 million), Joe Smith ($61 million), Cliff Robinson ($62 million), Eddy Curry ($70 million), Derrick Coleman ($91 million), Shawn Kemp ($92 million), Latrell Sprewell ($100 million), Vin Baker ($100 million), Antoine Walker ($110 million), Scottie Pippen ($120 million), Gilbert Arenas ($160 million), Allen Iverson ($200 million), Deuce McAllister ($70 million), Terrell Owens ($80 million), JaMarcus Russell ($61 million), Andre Rison (unknown), Mark Brunell ($50 million), Warren Sapp ($82 million), Luther Ellis ($11 million), Tiki Barber (unknown), Raghib Ismail (unknown), and Bernie Kosar (unknown).[33]

Substance Use

When it comes to this topic, there are various modalities in which substance use can be defined: (1) performance enhancement; (2) recreational use; (3) to deal with stressors, including mental illness; and (4) pain relief.[34]

Performance Enhancement

The idea that some professional athletes "cheat" to get a performance advantage is not new and is not limited to athletes who play sports for a living or to any specific age.[35] Performance enhancing drugs are not illegal substances, or those that can be prescribed by a doctor, and they include those that can be purchased over the counter.[36]

In the 1950s, trainers in the Soviet Union gave their athletes supplements with testosterone to increase their strength and power.[37] More recently, it has come to light that many East German athletes were using performance-enhancing drugs (PEDs).[38] This had a profound effect on some of the female members of the East German teams.[39] Perhaps the most famous of all the PED cheating athletes is Ben Johnson, who won the 1988 hundred-meter gold medal at the Seoul Olympics, only to be stripped of his medal twenty-four hours later when traces of a banned steroid were detected in his post-race urine sample.[40]

Recreational Drug Use

The most famous recreational drug user of modern times is heavyweight world champion boxer Tyson Fury.[41] Fury claimed that he used cocaine as a way to help him cope with depression.[42] Another athlete from my own past, who was a recreational drug user, was World Cup–winning soccer player Diego Maradona, perhaps the best known athlete from Argentina.[43] In both cases, and similar ones like this, it seems the disease of addiction took hold until treatment was sought and a plan for long-term sobriety implemented.

Mental Illness

A 2014 article published by the NCAA indicates that as many as 30 percent of the 195,000 college athletes questioned about their mental health state reported an issue.[44] Only about 7 percent of those athletes who noted an issue were being medicated, and 34 percent were having problems with their sleep.[45] Here is a list of some famous athletes who have had issues with depression:

Michael Phelps. Fell into a deep depression after the Olympics and used drugs and contemplated suicide.

Amanda Bears. Self-harmed and suffered from anorexia, bulimia, and drug abuse.

Ricky Williams. After becoming a millionaire at twenty-three years of age, he felt isolated and suffered from depression and social anxiety disorder.

Jerry West. Suffered abuse from his father as a young boy that left him not wanting to live. Suffered from depression and during a low point would not speak for days.

Serena Williams. Suffered from depression after she won Wimbledon and from postpartum depression after she gave birth in 2017.

Rhona Rousey. After she lost two straight fights in the UFC, she suffered from depression, contemplated suicide, and isolated herself.[46]

Pain Relief

It's hard for us to appreciate the physical punishment that professional athletes put themselves through on a daily basis. Sports that take a toll on athletes include football, basketball, baseball, ice hockey, and tennis. But really, given the years of work that athletes must spend honing their craft, it's impossible to avoid injuries. Some athletes who have retired due to injury include Luke Kuechly (football), Andrew Luck (football), Doug Baldwin (football), Brandon Roy (basketball), Sandy Koufax (baseball), Patrick Willis (football), Bobby Orr (ice hockey), Bjorn Borg (tennis), Calvin Johnson (football), Jim Brown (football), Bo Jackson (football and baseball), Yao Ming (basketball), Ken Dryden (ice hockey), Barry Sanders (football), Dave Nilson (baseball), Earl Campbell (football), Isaiah Thomas (basketball), and Tiki Barber (football).

One of the most famous cases of pain relief medication and abuse involved my good friend Randy Grimes, who was a starting center for the Tampa Bay Buccaneers. You can listen to my interview of Randy here: https://drugandalcoholattorneys.com/drug-and-alcohol-attorney-interview-with-randy-grimes.

While Randy was worshipped as a hero on the field for his toughness, off the field he was in big trouble. If you ever get the opportunity to meet Randy, and I would encourage you to do so because he is a wonderful human being, you will see the scars on and around his knees from the multiple surgeries. While Randy's playing career ended in 1992, his addiction to pain pills was just getting started. Randy was consuming anywhere from thirty to forty-five pain pills a day,[47] an addiction that would last twenty years.[48] Randy's addiction almost cost him his life and his family. "In football I always had a playbook and a team to get me through the day. . . . Without structure I didn't know what to do. . . . I lost myself as my addiction took over," he said.[49]

After finding the courage to ask for help after a teammate suffered an overdose, Randy found sobriety. "I literally crawled into treatment. . . . And the tools I found there saved my life. I prayed that God would open the gates of heaven and let me in. . . . Instead he opened the gates of hell and let me out."[50]

ATHLETES AND DOMESTIC VIOLENCE

While there seems to be a constant barrage of athletes who get in trouble for arrests, use of performance-enhancing drugs, and controlled substances, no topic seems to have garnered more attention than athletes who get arrested for domestic violence.

The topic of athletes and domestic violence came to a head during the mid-1990s when O. J. Simpson was arrested for allegedly killing Ron Goldman and Nicole Brown Simpson. As a former prosecutor and member of the Florida Bar since 1994, while I have my own personal belief about the innocence, or lack thereof of O.J., the jury determined that the state had not proven guilt beyond a reasonable doubt, so O.J. remains presumed innocent.

It was around that time in Palm Beach County, where I was a young assistant state attorney under former state attorney Barry Krischer, that domestic violence cases and the way they were prosecuted changed. In the past, we had allowed victims to agree to drop charges, which they frequently did. Additionally, a defendant who agreed to take a domestic violence course could do so and then have the case dropped. All that stopped after O.J. All defendants who wanted their charge dropped had to plead guilty and take the course. Cases were not dropped even if the victim wanted them dropped. And anyone arrested for domestic violence would not be entitled to bond out of jail (and potentially return to kill their victim); they were required to spend the night in jail and see a judge the following morning (after they'd had time to cool off).

In recent memory, two of the worst offenders in the NFL have been Ray Rice and Kellen Winslow Jr.

Ray Rice

Who could ever forget the video of Ray Rice knocking out his fiancée.[51] In February 2014, Rice, a running back with the Baltimore Ravens, got into an elevator with his fiancée when an argument ensued, and Rice proceeded to strike her and knock her unconscious. He was then seen dragging his unconscious fiancée out of the elevator, appearing not to care that she was still partially in the elevator. This incident was the beginning of the end of Ray Rice in the NFL, which changed the way it handles domestic violence matters. Rice never returned to the NFL

Kellen Winslow Jr.

Kellen Winslow Jr. played in the NFL from 2004 to 2013.[52] In 2018 he was arrested for rape and kidnapping.[53] In 2019 he was arrested for two counts of lewd conduct.[54] In June 2019 he was convicted of the aforementioned, and due to the Corona virus, his sentencing has been delayed.[55] That being said, his attorneys have claimed that he suffers from frontal lobe damage and that should be taken into account when he is eventually sentenced.[56]

When the Punishment Does Not Fit the Crime

While several of the athletes who have been outlined here have suffered severe consequences, such as prison, many have not. The simple fact is that we place our professional athletes on a pedestal and treat them as such. If we break it down by league, we will see how few professional athletes suffer the appropriate consequence.

For instance, from 2010 to 2014 in Major League Baseball, there were four players accused of sexual misconduct and five of domestic violence.[57] Of those players only two were formally charged and only one was convicted. None of these athletes were punished by their respective teams.[58]

In the NBA there were two sexual assault allegations and fourteen domestic violence allegations against players from 2011 to 2014. Only three had formal charges brought against them and none were convicted of a crime.[59] Only one player was punished by his team.[60]

In the NFL twenty-seven players were accused of domestic violence, but only seven were actually charged.[61] Of those seven athletes, four pleaded guilty to a lesser charge and three went to trial, and none resulted in convictions.[62] Of the twenty-seven allegations, only five were punished by the league, and one was punished by his team.[63]

Why Is There a Lack of Punishment?

As a former domestic violence prosecutor, while there may be a "no drop" policy, the simple fact is that if a victim does not want to cooperate (and there are many reasons for that), the state is unlikely to further inflict emotional distress on her (in most cases it is a female victim, but not always).[64] There are three factors that appear to influence the lack of punishment: (1) lack of victim participation, (2) team complicity with law enforcement, and (3) lack of league action.

Lack of Victim Participation

When I was young prosecutor and routinely prosecuting domestic violence offenders, it was extremely frustrating when a victim declined to prosecute the case. These factors include, but are not limited to, the following: the victim is financially dependent on the attacker; the victim fears retaliation if she cooperates with the prosecution; the victim fears she may be made to appear as if she made up the allegations; by the time the case goes to trial, the situation has been diffused (the attacker has apologized and promised never to do it again); the relationship is over; the victim does not want to relive the situation; and the victim and attacker have children so the victim does not want to potentially be responsible for breaking up the family.

Team Complicity with Law Enforcement

When trying to prosecute a professional athlete, one aspect that is frequently overlooked is the relationship among team security, a player's personal security, and law enforcement.[65] A prime example of that was Ben Roethlisberger, who was accused by a woman of rape. Not only was it reported that one of the officers warned Roethlisberger and security personnel of the complaint, but also he tried to dissuade the victim from even pursuing a case.[66] On other occasions, law enforcement officers, many of whom work the games as additional security, and who are fans in their own right, get caught up in the wild idea of seeing their hero getting in trouble.[67]

Lack of League Action

Prior to the Ray Rice video,[68] it seems that professional sports leagues took very little action against their athletes, especially the star athletes, when it came to addressing their bad behavior. When it comes to PEDs, it wasn't until the Balco scandal in the 2000s came to light that Major League Baseball became serious about punishing athletes who cheated.[69] There seems to be credible evidence that ever since the Ray Rice video emerged, the professional leagues are being more assertive when it comes to punishing players who are arrested, especially for domestic violence.[70]

The bottom line is that athletes are just like the rest of us: they make silly decisions, they suffer from substance use and mental health disorders, and occasionally they commit the unthinkable crime, murder. Others find all that money they receive fuels their outrageous behavior and can ultimately lead to bankruptcy. We place our athletes on a pedestal, and sometimes it's not deserved.

3

HEALTH IN THE LOCKER ROOM

Every NFL team doctor quickly realizes the Hippocratic Oath that they take does not cover the ethical problems they face daily in the team's locker room. Is the doctor loyal to the player and his health needs or to the team that employs him and the coaches who need to win at all costs? This dilemma is faced in every NFL locker room, and while an owner, coach, or doctor may have to grapple with the moral dimensions, it is the players who must deal with the long-term physical consequences of the choices made by his bosses. Let's look at this closer.

Players need to play or they won't get paid. There is always a man behind you wanting to be a starter, a member of the practice squad hoping to move up, or a rookie trying to knock off a veteran. This forces players to stay on the field and play through pain, often masking that pain with drugs and showing as little vulnerability as possible. The owners years ago recognized that in a sport as brutal as football, with a 100 percent injury rate, it makes little financial sense to offer guaranteed contracts. So most contracts in the NFL are not guaranteed but are instead filled with incentives—roster bonuses, bonuses for games played, bonuses for being an All-Pro, and so on. However, you can't earn an incentive if you aren't on the field. You have to start so many games, or gain so many yards, or catch so many passes; it's endless. You must play. So when you're hurting—and all players hurt during the season—you often go to the team doctor and ask for the needle filled with a painkiller. Toradol, which amounts to a high dose of Advil, is routinely dispensed by clubs before games so players won't feel as much pain after getting hit and thus can stay in the game longer.

The first game I attended with my children, they noticed the trainers building a human wall around Wally Chambers, a defensive end with the Buccaneers in 1977 and 1978. Of course, their interest was piqued. They saw a doctor stick something into Wally's knees. This was unusual to them. However, unfortunately it was not unusual for the Buccaneers. Every game, players were shot up with pain killers on the sideline so they could continue to play. Our doctor was so invested in keeping the players on the field that he once yelled "time out" from the sidelines, stopping the game and costing the team a valuable time out. He was stressed and too involved, even though he was not the coach and not allowed to call for halts in the game.

It was clear to all that he was the doctor for the team. And I mean for the team, not for the individual players. The players were treated so they could do their part to help the team. If a player got "his bell rung" in a bruising tackle, the doctor held up two fingers and asked the player, "How many?" It was always two and every player knew to say "two." There was no rest after a player got a concussion or double vision. Players would vomit on the sideline or in the huddle and be ready for the next play.

Prior to 2009, the NFL didn't take concussions seriously. That's around the time Alan Schwarz, writing for the *New York Times*, did a series on the concussion crisis and the league's denial of the facts. This culminated in a hearing conducted by Congressman John Conyers Jr., a Michigan Democrat and chairman of the House Judiciary Committee. Conyers and his committee wanted to understand the impact of head injuries sustained by NFL players "and what can be done to limit them and compensate the players and their families."

Conyers called the hearing after the *New York Times* published a story about a study commissioned by the NFL that indicated that retired football players, especially those in their thirties and forties, appeared to have been diagnosed with Alzheimer's disease or related cognitive disorders more often than the general population.

During the scathing testimony, countless experts disputed the NFL's claims that there was no harm from hits to the head. This led to a tidal wave of articles and television reports on concussions. By 2013, *League of Denial*, a book by Steve Fainaru and Mark Fainaru-Wada of

ESPN, was published, and the evidence was so overwhelming that the league had to finally admit there was a connection between hits to the head, concussions, and players' cognitive and neurological health later in life.

The avalanche of stories about concussions and brain disease left the league with a full-blown crisis to confront. For the league, which is the standard-bearer for the football universe, the attention being shown to the violence of the game and head injuries were fundamental threats to football itself. The more parents read stories about the brain-damaged ex-players, the less likely it was they would enroll their sons into Pop Warner and other youth football leagues. Suddenly, parents, school districts, youth leagues, and everyone involved in sports were having to consider the potential legal liability from head injuries. Would parents of injured children sue the coach? The league? The athletic director? As a result, the cost of liability insurance soared so high that some youth leagues folded.

Many of the leagues that continue require that coaches learn how to spot concussions and how to steer those players off the field. Now, coaches are being told that old euphemisms like having your "bell rung" or "getting dinged" actually meant the athlete has suffered a mild traumatic brain injury. Coaches are now learning that the brain is a gelatinous mass inside a bony skull, the base of which has sharp ridges that can cause damage if the brain rattles around. The interconnected brain cells, or neurons, get injured when a player has a concussion, and he needs time to recover afterward.

Most importantly, players who suffer one concussion have a higher risk of getting another, and children and teens, who are more likely to suffer a concussion than adults, take longer to recover.

Worrying for the NFL, two-thirds of the roughly three hundred thousand mild traumatic brain injuries that happen each year in sports occur in football, according to doctors at the University of Cincinnati. Sports like wrestling, soccer, basketball, and baseball for boys, and softball, field hockey, and volleyball for girls, also produce many concussions.

The vast majority of young athletes stop playing competitively once they leave high schools. The athletes—and particularly football players—who make it all the way to the pros, though, put their bodies through far more abuse and brain trauma. And their problems can manifest themselves even before their professional careers are over.

While they're in the NFL, though, players are still fairly complacent about their long-term health. They have yet to experience severe health breakdowns. They are interested in meeting their performance measures in their contracts. Pills were handed out after games, with no prescription, advice, or discussion of the long-term consequences. Doctors and trainers just said, "take these when you get home," and so they did. They would fall asleep and wake up feeling better.

However, the new generation of players, having read about retired players with dementia, and having seen the movie *Concussion*, starring Will Smith, about Bennet Omalu, the first doctor to identify chronic traumatic encephalopathy in NFL players, are less trusting of team doctors. In 2019, two players took their health into their own hands and questioned the medical care they were receiving from their team's experts.

Trent Williams of the Washington Redskins and Kelechi Osemele of the New York Jets asked the ultimate question: "Is the team doctor and staff looking out for me, or are they just trying to keep me on the field?" For six years, Trent Williams had been asking his team's doctor about the growth on his head. The reply was always the same: "It's a cyst. Leave it alone." In January 2019, Williams finally obtained a biopsy of the cyst. The seven-time Pro Bowler learned at the Pro Bowl that the cyst was anything but benign—it was not a cyst but the cancer he had been afraid it might be. Although the owner Dan Snyder flew Williams to another doctor for a second opinion on his private plane, Williams said he could not trust the team management and team president Bruce Allen in particular. He had witnessed too many medical problems with quarterbacks Colt McCoy and Alex Smith, and running back Derrius Guice, to not be suspicious.

Williams spoke up in his defense, and when the season was over, the Redskins traded the seven-time Pro Bowler to the San Francisco 49ers. After the trade, Williams gave a half-hearted nod to Snyder. "I'm thankful this is over," Williams told NFL Network. "Thanks to Dan and the organization for all they've done for me. Still a lot of love for the fans and that locker room."[1]

Kelechi Osemele became a New York Jet in the spring of 2019. He had been with the Oakland Raiders organization, and before that, he was drafted by the Baltimore Ravens. On August 5, during training camp, he suffered a shoulder injury but continued to practice with his team. On September 22, he reinjured his shoulder. With anti-inflammatories and Toradol injections, the team doctor and trainers believed he could play through the season. When the Toradol ceased to mask his pain, the Jets doctors told him that he'd need surgery, but with cortisone shots and a shoulder brace, they thought he could continue playing. Osemele was not new to the league. He knew, at age thirty, he needed to protect his body for the long term. He felt playing in pain masked by increasingly potent painkillers was not the best option for him. When he refused to practice, the team fined him a week's pay ($580,000) for each week he did not practice. Osemele filed a grievance against the team. He consulted several doctors and had the shoulder surgery he so badly needed to clear the pain. He felt disrespected by the Jets and their staff for not recommending the surgery during the season.

Over the many years I was associated with professional football, I met a number of doctors who treated team members. I knew it was difficult for some to come to grips with their loyalties. However, there were many who tried to do what was in the best interests of the player. Some players, however, pushed the doctors to make choices that were not in the best interests of the player. The doctor would make certain to explain the downside of taking a drug or following a certain treatment, and the long-term consequences. This is particularly fraught in the case of players who suffered repeated hits to the head, whether or not they were diagnosed as concussions. That's because these hits can have a cumulative effect: the more hits to the head, the higher the risk of developing cognitive problems like dementia later in life. To put it another way: hits to the head can have a dose response. But playing football is the only way many athletes know how to make a living, so they ride it out as long as possible. It's difficult to persuade young men earning six- and seven-figure salaries, with family and friends to support, that there are other realistic options. I know doctors who tried to help these men. However, the players are often addicted to the noise of the crowd and that adoration from fans that is difficult to give up, particularly at a young age.

As problematic as injuries are when players are in the locker room, the health problems mount even more once they retire. Hobbled by injuries, many players stop doing the intense exercise needed to offset the calories they consume. So these retired men have a tendency to gain weight after they leave the NFL They are conditioned to eating large numbers of calories, however well monitored and prepared, and the habit is hard to break. The player never feels "full" unless he eats as if there are two-a-day practices. He feels deprived. Eating is a way of life for players. Upon leaving the training table buffets, they are lost as to where and what to eat. Many return to their hometowns, some of which are in the South and West, where fried food and other unhealthy options are standard meals.

When their weight begins to creep up, players will deny it is fat. They will fool themselves into thinking it is muscle weight. But in reality, weight is weight. When computing obesity, the numbers that are important are your height and weight. No extra points for muscles. They contribute to your obesity ratio the same as fat. The heart doesn't know the difference and your feet, ankles, knees, and hips recognize they are supporting the weight.

This is when other health problems emerge, including diabetes at the top of the list. Players have problems with hypertension and sleep apnea more frequently than the general public. Football players are usually larger and more muscular than the average American. But when they no longer have to work out under the eyes of the trainers and strength coaches, many players are reluctant to go to a gym and put in several hours of intense work needed to shed their extra weight. They feel they deserve a rest. Some are too depressed to get off the sofa and start a new routine. And the problems compound if they do not cut the amount of food they consume.

Then there is arthritis, which is ubiquitous in players who retire from a collision sport like football. Players often need joint replacements. The surgery can be tricky though if they have hypertension and breathing difficulties. Rehabilitation is particularly difficult because of the weight being put on the new joints. Using crutches presents problems for the player's hands and wrists that must help support his heavy body's weight. The player might then resist going out. The lack of mobility slows down the rehabilitation process even further.

Take David Lewis, a linebacker who was drafted in the second round by the Buccaneers in 1977, their second season. David had played for Coach John McKay at the University of Southern California and wanted to stay in California. Coach McKay, who was by then lead-ing the Buccaneers, called David's mother, and David was in Tampa by the end of the week. Now you have to remember that no one wanted to go to the Bucs because, in their first season, they lost every game. Most players want a shot at the Super Bowl, not a spot on a team that resides in the cellar of the league.

At six foot four and 236 pounds, with a smile as wide as his entire face, David was hard not to befriend. He was comical and kind. His quips were memorable. Everyone grew to love this new linebacker. David played five years with the Bucs and made it to the Pro Bowl in 1980. In his two final years, he got his wish to return to Southern California where he played with the San Diego Chargers and Los An-geles Rams, before returning to Tampa to live.

David and his wife remained friends of mine. I became his represen-tative and helped him apply for benefits through the 88 Plan, which provides up to $140,000 a year to players with dementia, Alzheimer's disease, Parkinson's disease, or amyotrophic lateral sclerosis (ALS, or Lou Gehrig's disease). When his attorney moved too slowly and David got upset, I intervened and worked directly with the attorney and his staff to push the process along more quickly. I helped translate the process for David, who didn't understand the legal terms being used. At the same time, his attorneys didn't know how to respond to his frustra-tions except to repeat the same legalese to him.

David received a diagnosis of Alzheimer's disease, which allowed him to apply for a onetime payout from the concussion settlement, and he was readily approved for the 88 Plan. His Alzheimer's disease has created other health problems. During his time away from the NFL, David reached three hundred pounds. But after he left the league, he ate as he always did. Even though David now has type 2 diabetes and is on dialysis, he still insists that his wife bring him lunch from Taco Bell each day. Bonnie gets really frustrated, as David will never lose weight eating Taco Bell every day. "It's hard for me," she said. "I want to make him happy. I know he doesn't eat right."

Not long ago, I spoke to Bonnie, and she was thrilled that David was down to 293. She's going back to work and arranged for someone to take care of David and drive him to his appointments to get dialysis. She is like a new mom leaving her baby at daycare for the first time. They know that although they received money from the concussion settlement, it won't last two lifetimes.

Her other concern with going back to work is David has congestive heart failure from hypertension. He'd like to have his knee replaced, but the heart problems preclude the surgery. David hates not being able to exercise the way he used to. He's not happy being connected to a CPAP machine every night because of his sleep apnea. Bonnie has to sleep on the sofa because the machine keeps her awake during the night. David was upset about that as well. Many health issues could be resolved if David was willing to seriously lose weight. But reversing the cycle is hard.

When I had dinner with them in Tampa in 2020, I was shocked to see David in a wheelchair. He simply cannot put weight on his knee any longer with the confidence that he won't collapse. His balance is compromised as well. The wheelchair is now a necessity. Bonnie made the reservation months in advance at Bern's Steak House, where they celebrate special occasions like anniversaries and birthdays. To watch David order almost took my breath away. The waiter was very cool, but even he raised his eyebrows. David's meal, which he ate in its entirety, started with French onion soup and escargot, followed by a salad, a twenty-ounce rib-eye steak with two lobster tails, and one fully loaded baked potato as well as creamed potatoes. He finished his meal with a huge double scoop of macadamia nut ice cream covered in hot fudge sauce. My only response was to smile. What else could one do? David has Alzheimer's. He understands he should eat less, but that thought doesn't last when he nears food.

There's the part of me that understands why Bonnie capitulates to David. Our dinner was postponed for months because David was in the hospital with sepsis, a very serious infection of his heart. We were afraid he wasn't coming home from the hospital. David's health is precarious. How can you deny him his Taco Bell?

Postscript: David passed away after we met. The Buccaneers lauded him on Twitter, and the *Tampa Bay Times* wrote that for more than thirty years, he coached at Tampa Catholic High School and had a positive effect on hundreds of young men.

David is only one example of what I see on a regular basis among retired players. With rare exceptions, they gain weight after they leave the NFL. With no mandatory weigh-ins with the trainer or monetary incentives to stay at a certain weight, players let their health routines lapse. They may play golf, but riding in a cart for eighteen holes and visiting the bar afterward doesn't make for true calorie-reducing exercise. The rounds of golf also continue the pain associated with deteriorating joints and vertebrae. After a while, the player must consider whether that bit of exercise was worth the pain he is going to suffer as a result.

Many of my friends from the NFL have taken up swimming. I know three players who have recently had swimming pools built in their yards with the money they received from the concussion settlement. The water buoyancy supports their weight, which allows them to move their aching joints almost pain free. There are rails and steps to assist with ingress and egress. My guys can exercise in the privacy of their own yard with no gawkers. It's embarrassing to see fans stare, not believing this man was the Pro Bowler they watched on the field. When players age, they age quickly, particularly linemen who took a banging on each play. However, every player suffers in retirement. No one's body is engineered to take the stress that football metes out.

Getting a full view of the scope of the health problems that retired players face is not easy. There have been studies over the years that have looked at player mortality; their incidence of hypertension, diabetes, and other medical conditions; and, more recently, their cognitive and neurological conditions. But retired players scatter to the wind when they leave the NFL, and finding enough of them to study can be difficult. Having made their names as finely tuned athletes, many of them do not to want to share information about the conditions that will, ultimately, show how they have deteriorated.

Then there is the issue of funding and objectivity. University professors have done some research. So has the federal government from time to time. But the organization with the biggest incentive to learn about the health of retired players is the NFL, and the league has ulterior motives. First, the league does not want to advertise that the game of football is destructive. Second, it funds retiree benefit programs, and the more damaged players are, the more they are likely to have to pay.

Then there are flaws with the studies themselves. In a league where about 70 percent of the players are African American, some research includes a high percentage of White retired players, which skews the results. While this may be a function of who the researchers were able to contact, it distorts the total picture of retiree health because some conditions, like hypertension, are more prevalent among African Americans.

One of the largest studies began in 2013 at the peak of the concussion crisis. Thousands of players were at the time adding their names to what became a massive class action lawsuit against the league. The retired players accused the league of knowing about the long-term dangers of concussions and not telling the players. The league wanted to avoid the possibility that discovery would unearth a smoking gun from the NFL files, or the possibility that former players would testify about their injuries in court. So the NFL settled the case with the players' lawyers for $765 million, a figure that was later uncapped so there were no longer any upper limits on the amount of payouts.

In the midst of this turmoil, the NFL Players Association teamed up with researchers at Harvard University on a ten-year, $100 million research project designed to treat and prevent health problems, including brain trauma, skeletal injuries, and the use of painkillers. The study aimed to include about a thousand former players, or about 5 percent of all retirees.

Among their biggest findings thus far is a study published in 2019 in the *American Journal of Sports Medicine* that found a correlation between the number of years a player was in the NFL and the position he played with greater risk of cognitive and mental health problems. Running backs, linebackers, and defensive linemen had the greatest risk for cognitive problems, according to the study.

Based on a survey of nearly 3,500 former players, the study showed that players who experienced concussions had higher risk for serious cognitive problems, depression, and anxiety that lasted as long as twenty years after the injury.

The problem with the study, which the authors acknowledge, is that their analysis relied on the memories of the players rather than on any objective diagnosis of their concussions or other injuries at the time. They also pointed out that their findings "do not mean that everyone with concussion will necessarily experience cognitive or mental health problems."

Still, according to their analysis, the authors said that players who reported "the most concussion symptoms had 22-fold risk of reporting serious long-term cognitive problems and six times the risk of having symptoms of depression and anxiety, compared with those who re-ported the fewest symptoms."

What this and other studies end up finding is both self-evident and unlikely to change: players leave the NFL injured, and they suffer more when they retire, and the longer they played, the more problems they end up having.

4

RACIAL DISPARITY

The NFL's record on race relations has been checkered at best during its century-long existence. At first blush, this would seem odd. After all, roughly 70 percent of the current players are African American. Some of the league's biggest stars, from quarterbacks like Patrick Mahomes of the Kansas City Chiefs and Russell Wilson of the Seattle Seahawks to defensive standouts including Richard Sherman of the San Francisco 49ers and defensive end Jadeveon Clowney, are African American. The swagger, style, and fashion of the league are all influenced by African Americans.

In June 2020, when Commissioner Roger Goodell apologized for not listening earlier to the concerns of African Americans on issues of social injustice, he made a shocking (for him) but remarkably self-evident statement: "Without Black players there would be no National Football League."[1]

But that was far from the case decades ago. Fritz Pollard, an all-American running back from Brown University, was one of two African American players in 1920 in the American Professional Football Association, the predecessor to the NFL. He helped the Akron Pros become the league's first champion and became the fledgling league's first African American coach a year later. But a half decade later, African American players were pushed out and the league's owners entered into a so-called gentleman's agreement to keep out Black players between 1934 and 1946.

That year, the NFL, which lagged far behind college football, finally broke its own color barrier when the Los Angeles Rams signed Kenny Washington and Woody Strode. But as former *New York Times* columnist William Rhoden has noted, the league was not, nor does it continue to be, motivated by altruism. In 1946, the Rams moved from Cleveland to Los Angeles. The local chapter of the NAACP as well as Black-owned newspapers in the City of Angels pressured the Los Angeles Coliseum, the future home of the team, to require that the Rams be integrated in order to be allowed to play in the stadium.

"Even as black players at every position have become the foundation of this multibillion dollar enterprise, their relationship with the NFL, from the league's perspective, has largely been a marriage of convenience, with progress only being brought about by pressure," Rhoden wrote.

In 1946, another league, the All-America Football Conference, opened for business, threatening the NFL's already shaky business model. The AAFC started signing Black players that the NFL was ignoring. So the NFL grudgingly started drafting and signing Black players as well. The AAFC was out of business a few years later, but the door had been cracked open.

Still, the NFL's embrace was lukewarm. Coaches and general managers filled many key positions, most notably quarterback, with White players. Blacks were used primarily as running backs and defenders. Once again, it took an upstart league to change the dynamic. The newly formed American Football League (AFL) in 1960 needed talent wherever it could find it. The flashier, more entrepreneurial league had Black players at many of the key positions, including middle linebacker and quarterback. The Oakland Raiders drafted Eldridge Dickey in 1968, a quarterback in college who was used as a wide receiver as a pro, and the Denver Broncos tabbed Marlin Briscoe, who became the first Black quarterback to start a pro game.

To keep up, NFL teams copied the AFL. In 1967, the Pittsburgh Steelers hired Bill Nunn Jr., a sportswriter who closely followed football programs at historically Black colleges and universities. In no time, he helped the Steelers—one the league's worst teams—identify talented Black players, including Mel Blount, L. C. Greenwood, Ernie Holmes, Donnie Shell, and John Stallworth, who formed a nucleus of a Steeler dynasty that included four Super Bowl titles in the 1970s.

The percent of Black players in the NFL has steadily grown, but the percentage of Black team executives and top coaches remains embarrassingly low. There are no Black team owners, and Jason Wright became the first Black team president only in July 2020. There weren't many more Black coaches and general managers, the two biggest roles in a team's football operations. The NFL, aware of the disparity, has tried to cajole teams into hiring more people of color, with limited results. At the end of the 2019 season, there were just four head coaches of color and just one Black general manager. In 2020, the league once again strengthened its so-called Rooney Rule, named after Dan Rooney, the former Steelers owner. The rule obligates teams with openings for head coach, general manager, and other key positions to interview candidates of color.

The disparity between the overwhelmingly Black players and the overwhelmingly White managers has a number of consequences for retired players. The most notable of these are related to their health. African American men are more prone to the comorbidities of obesity compared to African American women, White men, or White women. They have a much higher incidence of hypertension and obesity, according to Dr. Henry Buchwald, professor of surgery at the University of Minnesota. These problems are particularly acute among offensive and defensive linemen, who need to bulk up to do their jobs effectively. When they leave the league, they are more prone to developing diabetes, hypertension, and cardiac problems.

According to a study published in August 2020 by researchers from Harvard Medical School and the Harvard T.H. Chan School of Public Heath, Black retired NFL players are "significantly more likely than white players to experience diminished quality of life due to impaired physical function, pain, cognitive troubles, depression, and anxiety."

The research, published in the *Annals of Epidemiology*, was based on a survey of 3,794 former NFL players between the ages of twenty-four and eighty-nine as part of the Football Players Health Study at Harvard University, an initiative funded by the NFL Players Association. The survey was based on self-reported data by the retired players, 1,423, or 37.5 percent, of whom were Black. Another 2,215 respondents, or 58.4 percent, said they were White, while the remainder identified as Hawaiian or other races. Given that currently about two-thirds of the players in the NFL are Black, it is possible that this research understates the health problems of retired Black players.

A survey of retired players showed that Black NFL players were 50 percent more likely than White NFL players to have pain that interferes with their daily activities, depression, and anxiety. Black players were also 36 percent more likely to have "cognitive symptoms—including memory deficits and attention problems—that impacted their quality of life."

According to Marc Weisskopf, one of the authors, the gaps between Black and White players "echo well-documented health disparities in the general population."

The gap in health outcomes for Black and White players was the same even when accounting for how many seasons the players were in the NFL, the positions they played, the surgeries and concussions they had, and a host of other factors. Age also had no influence on the gap. The researchers said that "discrimination prior to, during, or following a player's time in the NFL could account for the disparities."

Based on a census of NFL players compiled by Michael Gertz at ProFootballLogic, it appears that the Harvard study undercounted the percentage of Black players among the retiree community. At the same time, if the percentage of Black players is as large as Gertz estimates, then the gaps in health outcomes will likely be as pronounced as well.

According to Gertz, in 2016, the largest group of players in the NFL—about 1,200, or roughly 60 percent of the league—were between the ages of twenty-three and twenty-seven. Gertz also classified the number of players by position and race. The NFL overall is about 68 percent Black, though that number could be higher because some players' race was unknown or unidentified. The racial breakdown also varies greatly by position.

For instance, Blacks made up the vast majority of cornerbacks and safeties, defensive linemen, linebackers, running backs, and wide receivers. When you cross-reference those positions by head injuries, you see that Black players absorbed many of the recorded concussions. According to Nancy Armour of *USA Today*, cornerbacks suffered the most concussions—22 percent—in 2015 and 2016, followed by wide receivers and linebackers.[2] In other words, almost half of all the concussions were to players in those three positions, which are overwhelmingly filled by Blacks.

According to *Mental Health Daily*, a team of neuroscientists agrees that brain development likely persists until at least the midtwenties, possibly until the thirties, and that the last portion of the brain to become fully developed is the prefrontal lobe. This area is said to be responsible for attention, complex planning, decision making, impulse control, logical thinking, organized thinking, personality development, risk management, and short-term memory. The prefrontal lobe, as the name suggests, is at the front of the brain. In a sport where many players "lead with their head" when running with the ball or trying to tackle a runner, it is possible that the prefrontal lobe is more at risk of traumatic brain injury.

According to the Boston University CTE Center, chronic traumatic encephalopathy (CTE) is a degenerative brain disease found in athletes, military veterans, and others with a history of repetitive brain trauma. Most of what we have learned about CTE has come from the research of director of the VA-BU-CLF Brain Bank Dr. Ann McKee, who has revolutionized our understanding of CTE. In CTE, a protein called tau forms clumps that slowly spread throughout the brain, killing brain cells. CTE has been seen in people as young as seventeen, but symptoms do not generally begin appearing until years after the onset of head impacts. In support of this information, McKee and her team at Boston University suggest that symptoms of CTE include "memory loss, confusion, impaired judgment, impulse control problems, aggression, depression, suicidality, parkinsonism, and eventually progressive dementia."[3]

The NFL funded a study that investigated additional potential harmful behaviors that may be responsible for altered brain function. The study, titled "NFL Funded Study Identifies Football Positions Most at Risk of Brain Injury—Not All Concussions Are Created Equal" (Yasmin Tayag, October 31, 2017, *Inverse*), found that alcohol abuse, chronic stress, drug use, poor diet, relationship troubles, sleep problems, and social isolation also had an impact.

All of this comes back to inequities among NFL players and, ultimately, retired players.

5

NFL BENEFITS

We've discussed the rough road players take when they leave the NFL, the depression, the lack of employment, the mounting health problems, and in many cases, the mounting financial problems. Over the years, the National Football League Players Association (NFLPA), which acts in the players' best interests as their union, has won retired player benefits in negotiations with the NFL owners.

To some players, it's money they fought for and deserve. For others, it's never enough or equal to what they believe is their contribution to the game. But the reality is that the union is most directly obligated to its dues-paying members, who are the current players. Whatever money they fight for to help retired players is done because the current generation of players thinks it's a priority, either morally or because they recognize that they, too, will leave the league and need some assistance.

In the past decade or so, more players have become aware of the health problems that retired players are facing, as well as the landmark concussion settlement that was largely a result of the bad publicity of players with cognitive and neurological problems. As a result, the players have placed a greater emphasis on retiree benefits when they are at the negotiating table with owners.

The negotiations are led by the union staff and its executive committee, which is made up of veteran players and retired players. They report to the union representatives that each team elects. The representatives attend union meetings, keep their teams informed on the latest developments, and vote on issues that are important to their teammates. The NFLPA president is elected by this committee of union representatives. That president then represents the players' interests to the rest of the NFL, including the commissioner and owners.

The most important negotiations involve the collective bargaining agreement, or CBA, which in recent years has been ten years long. This contract covers a wide range of issues, including retired player pensions, health care, the number of games per season, minimum salaries and the salary cap, required practice sessions, and penalties for players caught using performance-enhancing drugs or illicit drugs. The agreement is so voluminous that negotiations begin a year or more before the previous agreement expires. Every cycle, players have heated debates about what issues to prioritize. Not surprisingly, money in the form of minimum salaries and a share of the league's total revenue are at the top of the list. But retiree benefits are increasingly part of the mix.

Player pensions are part of the CBA and have become a bigger priority, thanks to intense lobbying by prominent former players. All vested players—those who played or were on a roster for at least three seasons—are entitled to a pension. The value of the monthly pension is based on the number of years played. But not all retired players are treated alike. In fact, there are two broad classes of retired players: those who retired before 1993 and those who retired after that year, even though many players' careers spanned that year. From 1988 to 1993, the league and union were unable to reach a new labor deal. But when they finally agreed on a new contract, players who retired after 1993 were given bigger pensions, annuities, 401(k) accounts, and other benefits.

Players who retired before 1993 were left with less lucrative pensions and few of the other perks. In the latest round of negotiations, which culminated in a new ten-year contract that was signed in March 2020, advocates for the players who retired prior to 1993 argued yet again that they deserved a bigger slice of the pie. Those players had to have played for four years in order to be vested. Additionally, their salaries were far lower before 1993, when players had less leverage because there was a more limited version of free agency, if any, depending on when they played. These retired players feel they have been cheated compared to their brothers who, through the luck of the calendar, retired after 1993.

For most current players, 1993 is a long time ago. In fact, many of them were not even alive then. They might know the names of Joe Montana or Walter Payton or even Joe Namath, but the labor conditions under which they played are alien to them. Many players today aren't ready to fight to fund the pensions of the pre-1993 retiree players. Owners have a track record of never giving anything away for free. If players want bigger pensions, then the owners will demand something in return. Or the union can pay for the pensions out of their share of league revenue. The players get a finite amount of money each year, and any money they give to retired players comes out of their share. To a twenty-five-year-old who has mouths to feed and an unending belief that his money will last a lifetime, helping increase the size of the pensions for older players is not a popular concept.

But Lisa Riggins, the wife of former New York Jets and Washington Redskins running back John Riggins, helped change that narrative. She formed a nonprofit called Fairness for Athletes in Retirement, or FAIR, whose goal was to increase the size of pensions for pre-1993 retired players so they are more in line with those players retiring from the NFL today. The average pension for retired NFL players now is approximately $46,000 ($760 per month for each season played). Additionally, they may receive health reimbursement accounts, 401(k) plans, annuities, and free health and dental insurance for five years.

John Riggins, who played fourteen seasons and retired in 1985, before full free agency was introduced, and never made more than $1 million in a season, receives $3,300 per month before taxes in his pension. In the collective bargaining agreement signed in 2011, a "Legacy Benefit" was added to increase the size of the pension of older retirees to bring them more in line with current pensions. The increase amounted to an additional $108–124 per month, or a few thousand dollars a year for a veteran player who finished his career before Bill Clinton moved into the White House. Outraged by this discrepancy, John's wife took on the challenge to bring parity to the player pensions.

A lawyer living in the Washington, D.C., area, Lisa naturally went to the halls of Congress and spoke to representatives and senators. She tried to expose the inequity of the situation. They were impressed that she was an attorney and the wife of a Redskins legend, but lawmakers hear many stories of unfairness. Nothing happened. Lisa then hired a former *New York Times* sports reporter and a public relations firm.

They crafted articles pleading the players' case and began releasing videos that featured former NFL stars discussing their financial problems that stemmed from their puny pensions.

This onslaught of publicity prompted Hall of Fame inductees to demand lifetime health insurance and additional monies. Eric Dickerson, the former Rams superstar, spearheaded this effort. He toured the country promoting the concept that Hall of Fame inductees deserved more than the average retired NFL player because they created so much more wealth for the league. They also wanted appearance fees, or they would not appear in their gold jackets that all Hall of Famers receive at NFL-sponsored events. This was not a popular stance, and little has been done since.

Calculations show that to achieve pension parity for all retired NFL players, teams would each have to pay $6.6 million per team for six years. Owners are unlikely to pay out of their own pockets, so these contributions would have to come from the money they would otherwise pay to the current players who risk their bodies and health each season. The teams split the revenue with the NFL, and the collective bargaining agreement outlines how that money is spent. If the current players want to vote to fully fund pensions for pre-1993 retired players, it would cost them about $1.2 billion. Team owners are unlikely to persuade their players to effectively take a pay cut to help older players. Bob Stein, an attorney in Minnesota and a former NFL player, put it this way: "I don't think the owners or players are bad guys. But here's the problem: Every dollar they allocate to retired players is a dollar that doesn't go to them."[1]

Ultimately, Riggins's efforts prevailed. In the new collective bargaining agreement signed in March 2020, players who retired before 1993 received a bump in their pensions. They will not be equal to players who retired after 1993, but it moves them closer to parity. And for the first time, roughly seven hundred players who played at least three seasons and retired before 1993 will secure pensions worth $1,650 a month. When they left the league, those players needed four seasons of service to qualify for a pension. Now, these players are in line with the requirements for those who retired after 1993.

Pensions, though, are only one part of the benefits puzzle. The league and union administer an extensive set of disability benefits that retired players can obtain. The benefits can be substantial, but the rules can be complex and the administrators of the program have a track record of rejecting claims and fighting players they believe are getting benefits they don't deserve.

To start with, the following benefits are available for vested players who were on an NFL team for at least three seasons:

Total and permanent disability. If you are actively playing and become totally disabled, this benefit is worth up to $22,084, or $11,250 if you are no longer playing and become disabled within fifteen years from the end of your last season. This benefit is payable for life or until the player has recovered. It is understood that the player receiving this benefit is unable to be employed in any capacity. It's important to add that the retired player will be checked at intervals of about five to seven years by medical personnel affiliated with the benefits plan office to ensure the player continues to need this benefit.

Line of duty disability. Players who qualify receive a minimum of $4,000 per month for up to ninety months.

Neurocognitive disability. For fifteen years or until the player reaches fifty-five years, a monthly payment of $3,000 to $5,000 per month.

There are a number of benefits that are negotiated every ten years in the collective bargaining agreement. Players need to monitor the rules for eligibility to these benefits because the league and union are adding and subtracting benefits that could help or hurt a player or his family. It's difficult to learn about these changes if you are not following closely, but there are player alumni chapters in many cities, including NFL team cities or those close by, like Orlando and Fort Meyers, which are near Jacksonville, Tampa, and Miami, which each have NFL teams. Each alumni group has a president who keeps up with the latest NFL news and benefit data. The meetings are usually held quarterly and include NFL-sponsored meals and speakers from the local community to discuss health issues such as diabetes or the Trust, an organization that helps players transition out of the league. There are also courses on learning to be a coach, a scout, a referee, or access to a financial planner to help you set up a business. There are many other services available, particularly for recently retired players, including memberships to gyms and access to counselors.

If a retired player decides he's had enough team bonding and wants to go it alone, it can be difficult to keep abreast of the changes in benefits and other services, such as health screenings held around the country under the auspices of the Tulane Medical School. The health screenings are paid for by the NFL for the benefit of the retirees. The NFLPA website usually keeps all benefits-related news up to date. However, many retirees forget to check for updates. They can miss important notices or new benefits additions that may assist them in their daily living or financial planning.

The other group that is a wealth of information for former players is the NFL Alumni Association, which is partially funded by the NFL. The NFLAA is open to anyone who played football, or a spouse, or anyone who worked in any capacity for an NFL team or is a fan. Whereas the NFLPA is free to join but limited to former NFL players, the NFLAA charges a yearly membership fee. Their main purpose is to raise funds for their children's charity, usually through local golf tournaments.

APPLYING FOR BENEFITS

Applying for NFL benefits is a two-step process: a committee review and then approval by the board. The rules and requirements that govern these bodies are spelled out in the CBA and are currently monitored by Groom Law Group, which represents the league's interests. The rules that are in place must be followed closely, especially the timelines and appointments for medical evaluations set up by the benefits plan. These rules can flummox former players who have physical limitations on where and how long they can travel, since many players are forced to visit doctors who are not located near their homes.

Let's look at the case of Daryl Ashmore. He played eleven years in the NFL as an offensive lineman. In 2015, he applied for disability benefits by submitting his file of medical tests. A plan coordinator on October 9, 2015, sent him his schedule for further testing to confirm his medical records. One week later, on October 16, he was supposed to be evaluated in Texas, and four days later, he was scheduled to be seen by an orthopedist in South Florida. Then, on October 22 (forty-eight hours later), he was to be evaluated by a neuropsychologist in Tampa. Due to

Ashmore's size (six foot seven and three hundred pounds) and orthopedic disabilities, his attorney asked that the medical examinations be moved to within one hour's driving distance of Ashmore's home. His doctor in Florida fully endorsed this suggestion.

Instead of agreeing to this recommendation, the plan coordinator scheduled all three examinations in Atlanta, Georgia, for a few weeks later. The attorney asked for accommodations for his client who cannot fly because of his size and ailments. The plan provided no accommodations and the appointments were cancelled. When the plan reviewed his application for benefits, Ashmore was denied because he had failed to attend the medical examinations. He appealed the decision and was again denied. The plan maintained that Ashmore's request for accommodations was unreasonable and that he did not even try to attend the appointments. Ashmore's attorney argued that it was impossible for him to attend the examinations and the appointments had been cancelled in advance of the two-day notice period. The plan office maintained the player never officially notified the office that he would not be attending the scheduled examinations.

Ashmore went to court to dispute the plan's rejection, and on June 15, 2018, U.S. district judge Kenneth Marra in the Southern District of Florida found in his favor. "The Plan cannot reasonably expect a player to attend an examination that is subject to an unresolved request for accommodations. Because the Plan's decision to reject Ashmore's claim for benefits due to his failure to attend assessments that both parties understood would not occur defied all reason and common sense."[2] Marra granted Ashmore the benefits he was twice denied by the plan.

Jesse Solomon, who had a nine-year NFL career as a linebacker, faced another procedural roadblock that the plan can throw up as a way to reject a claim. The issue in his case involved the date that Solomon became disabled. According to plan documents, in order to qualify for the highest-paying benefit, the player must have declared that he was disabled within the first fifteen years after leaving the league.

Solomon retired from the NFL in 1995. In 2009, he applied for benefits due to his orthopedic problems. He was denied. A year later he applied for benefits for players with cognitive disabilities that resulted from the many hits he had absorbed in football. It was estimated that he sustained at least sixty-nine thousand hits during games and practice. His doctors and the NFL doctors concurred that Solomon had severe symptoms consistent with chronic traumatic encephalopathy, or CTE, a degenerative brain disease associated with repeated hits to the head. However, Solomon only received the lower level of benefits because his claim was filed after the fifteen-year deadline had past. Solomon argued that the information regarding his cognitive decline was in his medical file within the fifteen-year time frame.

Solomon was persistent. In 2017, the U.S. District Court in Maryland ruled that the disability plan administrators ignored the medical opinion of their own neutral physician who stated in 2011 that Solomon had suffered repeated brain injuries while playing for the NFL. The court found in Solomon's favor that he was due a higher level of benefits. Judge Marvin Garbis found that Solomon was hit so hard "too many times to count" in "helmet-to-helmet collisions" that he "experienced triple vision" and "lost sense of who he was." An MRI of Solomon's brain showed deterioration, and he had to retire from his job as a teacher and has been unable to work since then.[3]

Not unexpectedly, the NFL plan office appealed the decision. That legal gambit failed as well. The U.S. Court of Appeals for the Fourth Circuit rejected the plan's argument. "The Board failed to follow a reasoned process or explain the basis of its denial. The NFL Board failure was in neither addressing nor even acknowledging the plaintiff's application, including that of the Plan's own expert."[4]

The questioning of the plan's lawyer by the judges showed their skepticism and incredulity:

JUDGE DENNIS SHEDD: Why is the Plan fighting him so incredibly hard? . . . And when he makes the claim through your own doctor that he's got a problem? . . . Why in the world would you—I guess current players don't want money to come out for past players. Or something?

MICHAEL JUNK (attorney for the Plan): I don't think that's the motivating factor.

JUDGE SHEDD: Then why in the world would any player playing professional football . . . look at this and go, This is one heck of a great deal for players. We play as hard as we can, give everything we got, get banged up . . . I saw something in the record about 69,000 tackles, that's incredible. We do all we can, and then we apply and when doctors say, You're not orthopedically disabled, go away.

JUDGE ALLYSON DUNCAN: Forever.

JUDGE SHEDD: I'm not counsel, you are, but somebody ought to scratch their head and say, Does this really look good? We don't have much of a legal argument, but we're willing to fight it to the death to deny somebody. . . . Does that make sense to you? Do you think that looks good to lawyers, what's going on in this courtroom today? It's not necessarily part of the determination, I'm just asking a real world question.[5]

The judges' questions have been pondered by many retired players and their advocates who have had to fight the benefits plan tooth and nail to win benefits that the union fought for in the collective bargaining agreement. Why would the NFL pay to defend a case in which they were so clearly in the wrong? The player had the damage, according to several doctors, including the ones paid for by the NFL. They agreed that Solomon had a brain injury of the highest order. One doctor went so far as to say he thought Solomon had CTE, which can only be diagnosed after death. Even so, Solomon exhibited all the signs and symptoms consistent with CTE. So why did the NFL force him to take the case to federal court? And was the NFL aware, or did it even care, how these strong-arm tactics were viewed by the NFL community?

My guess is that the NFL bet that Solomon could not afford to keep fighting this case. Within five years, a large number of professional NFL men declare bankruptcy. The attorneys probably figured that Solomon had spent all his money fighting their denial and wouldn't have any money left to fight the appeal in the Fourth Circuit. Jesse had smartly hired one of the best disability law firms in the country, well known for its support of retired players against the NFL. Not only did Jesse Solomon prevail in court, but his legal fees were paid by the NFL.

But for every victory that a player like Solomon wins, there are many other cases of players who fight losing battles against the benefits plan. Dwight Harrison did not hire a competent attorney, and his application for benefits had a decidedly different outcome. When going up against the NFL's attorneys, it is vital that you hire the most experienced attorneys in ERISA law. The lawyers need to be fully versed in the complicated world of NFL benefits as well. There are many benefits with differing criteria for awarding benefits. Harrison hired an attorney that he assumed could represent him. Unfortunately, the lawyer had no experience litigating ERISA cases against the NFL. He was over-matched, unlike the firm Jesse Solomon employed.

Harrison was awarded benefits for depression and anxiety disorder in 1993. The plan office found he had been disabled since 1984 and paid his back benefits as well. A year later, he filed a lawsuit pro se (on his own), claiming his disabilities were caused by his employment in the NFL and therefore he was entitled to a higher monthly pension.

The plan office countered by claiming that the benefits Harrison already received should be returned because, they claimed, Harrison exaggerated his condition and never met the league's definitions for being disabled. Harrison asked the court to appoint him an attorney, but they refused because the case had been filed pro se. The court struck his request to counter claim. Therefore, in 1996, the plan said that Harrison owed $352,252.06. This included his disability payments, attorneys' fees, and litigation costs. In January 1997, at the plan's first meeting of the year, the plan decided to offset the present value of Harrison's entire pension and apply it to the 1996 judgment.

Five years later, without counsel, Harrison filed another suit to re-gain his pension. His wife appeared in court instead of Dwight, saying he was unable to participate. The judge ruled in the favor of the plan, stating, "The Plan decided to offset his (Harrison's) future retirement benefits and cannot be challenged as unlawful, unreasonable, or in bad faith."

Due to an alleged clerical error, payments resumed from 2003 to 2007. The payments stopped when the error was discovered. Harrison continued on his own to file lawsuits to have his pension returned but was unsuccessful.

The league and the players' union renegotiated the CBA in 2011 and established a legacy benefit for those players who were vested before 1993. This paid these players up to $124 a month more for every year they were in the league. Harrison applied for this legacy benefit, and the NFL Retirement Board notified him by letter on May 24, 2012, that his benefit had a current value of $134,199.77. It was then taken by the trustees of the disability plan to help settle his debt. That left a balance of $162,851.43. The board described it this way in their letter to him:

You are "akin to a person who received a lump sum payment of his entire benefit under the plan" and "wasn't therefore eligible to make further claims under the plan." With these words, Dwight Harrison was cut off from the benefits afforded vested NFL retired players. He could not request money to reimburse him for surgeries, the 88 Plan long-term assisted living benefit, or the many other perks of having played in the NFL.

In 2007, Harrison was informed that he would no longer receive his pension benefit of $1,440 per month. This was his only source of income. He subsequently learned that his disorder, according to the NFL, occurred in college and not during his professional career. The league went so far as to discount his depression and say it was a recent problem, not one of long-standing.

Harrison lost his bid for benefits because he missed a couple of scheduled doctor's examinations, not surprising for a man whom six doctors independently diagnosed as having postconcussion syndrome, memory loss, and severe depression. Doug Ell, a lawyer for Groom Law Group, speaking for the league-appointed trustees of the board, determined this to be "both fraud and frivolous litigation by Mr. Harrison." Ell wrote that "Harrison lost benefits because he did not take a medical exam. Mr. Harrison was explicitly and repeatedly warned of it, and a federal judge even ordered him to attend, and he refused to do so."[6]

The Social Security Administration declared that Harrison's disabilities, including memory loss and early onset of dementia, were the result of his head injuries. A seasoned attorney could have argued successfully for Harrison's benefits. Cy Smith, the lawyer for Solomon, also worked to obtain benefits for the family of former Pittsburgh Steeler Mike Webster.

Jeff Dahl, a well-respected ERISA attorney from Texas, took over Harrison's case to battle for the benefits that were taken away. By this time, Dwight was living in a FEMA-type trailer with no running water. His situation was dire, particularly considering he played ten years in the NFL and had many injuries. I asked Jeff for a summary, and this is what he wrote:

> Well, we lost in the trial court and then took it to the Fifth Circuit Court of Appeals in New Orleans, lost there in an unpublished opinion, and then I petitioned the Supreme Court to hear the case (in regards to the taking of the pension), but they didn't take it on. As for

Dwight, he's hanging in there, I think, but he's had a couple of strokes. Thankfully he did receive a little money from the concussion settlement.

Some retired players hit snags because of procedural changes, such as when the rules governing the plan were changed in the new collective bargaining agreement approved in 2011. Previously, to be eligible for the Total and Permanent Disability (T&P) benefit, a neuropsychologist could examine the player and make the determination of his condition. When the new CBA was approved, that mandate was changed so that three doctors had to evaluate the player to make the same determination: a psychiatrist, a neuropsychologist, and an orthopedist or a neurologist. After a player is determined to be totally and permanently disabled, he can expect to be retested every five to seven years to assure the board that the player is still disabled and deserving of his monthly payout of $11,500.

Recently, I had three players contact me whose T&P benefits were being reviewed. They were astounded that they now had to attend at least three scheduled medical examinations. I filed an appeal to retain the full benefits of one player. A board-appointed neurologist and neuropsychologist determined he was well enough to work. However, his orthopedic injuries qualified him for T&P. We dodged a bullet and he was allowed to keep his monthly benefit. In five to seven years, his status will be reviewed again. Most orthopedic problems do not resolve quickly, so unless there is another change in the rules, we can assume he will be able to keep his benefit. However, like other players with this benefit, he must send the benefit plan his IRS filings each year to prove that he is not making more than the allowable amount of money.

The second player, Mr. P, played defensive end for the University of Central Florida. He received his diploma in three and a half years and was drafted in the seventh round by the Cincinnati Bengals. He played with them for two years and then played for the Jacksonville Jaguars for two more years. He was also on the roster with the Minnesota Vikings as well as teams in Europe and Canada. After completing his football career, he returned to the University of Central Florida and obtained his master's degree in sports leadership while assisting the football coaches at the university.

Mr. P spent the next three years looking for a job while continuing to work out, hoping to be picked up by a professional team. Those hopes waned as his pain increased and his memory deteriorated. He could not balance his checkbook or remember what groceries were needed at the store. He was quickly slipping into depression and unable to find a job. After a series of visits for health evaluations, Mr. P realized he needed to apply for NFL benefits.

Here is how I outlined his case in my letter to the Plan Retirement Board dated July 10, 2019.

> In considering Mr. P's appeal, your prior decision, and the evidence considered when the decision was made, is important. At your meeting on August 18, 2010, you decided to award Mr. P Inactive T&P benefits. . . . As your prior decision reflects, in February 2010 you referred Mr. P to Medical Advisory Physicians for a "final and binding determination of whether you are medically totally and permanently disabled within the meaning of the Plan."

Mr. P was referred to an orthopedist who agreed that he suffered from arthritis and pain related to his damaged arms and legs and cervical spine. "I believe all these injuries are football related. I believe Mr. P could work at a sedentary occupation as long as breaks were allowed every forty-five minutes to an hour for pain."[7]

The neurologist that evaluated Mr. P on April 26, 2010, summarized his findings for the board as follows:

> Postconcussive syndrome. Recommendations: His history and neurologic examination is compatible with traumatic brain injury secondary to multiple concussions. After reviewing the records of [four doctors], I believe that Mr. P has suffered a traumatic brain injury with residual neurocognitive deficit and would be unable at this time to take on any gainful employment unless cognitive therapy is initiated to see if any improvement occurs and if he is employable at any level.

The examining neurologist, Dr. Herskowitz, clearly made note of the fact that Mr. P suffered these brain traumas as a result of playing for the NFL. The Retirement Board responded that they were placing him in the inactive category for the following reasons:

The Retirement Board noted that you have a complicated set of orthopedic and neurologic impairments, some of which arise out of League football activities and others, which may not arise [sic] out of League football activities. The Retirement Board could not conclude that your total and permanent disability has the required connection to League football activities so as to allow an award of Active Football or Football Degenerative T&P benefits.

Mr. P appealed the classification of his benefits. He was denied at the May 12, 2011, meeting based on an evaluation by a psychologist.

As I noted previously, the board periodically reviews the player's status to make sure he still fits the T&P category to which he is assigned. These reviews usually occur at five- to seven-year intervals. In January 2017, Mr. P was reevaluated by the plan neurologist. Dr. McCasland determined Mr. P was not totally and permanently disabled because of a neurological condition. He recommended more neurocognitive testing. Mr. P remained in his inactive T&P category. Fourteen months later, in April 2018, another review was made by the committee and again they decided to keep him in the same category.

Seven months later, in November 2018, the plan office sent Mr. P to see a plan neuropsychologist. Stephen Macciocchi, PhD, reported that he was unable to make a determination because the test scores were "invalid." This is code for "the client was malingering" or "he was not trying during the testing procedure." (Personally, I believe this is an artifact of the testing protocols, which are not appropriate for clients with head trauma.)

Dr. McCasland posited from his testing that Mr. P was not showing enough effort during the testing and that his scores were "unexpectedly low." The same basic results from Dr. Macciocchi led the committee to deny Mr. P his inactive T&P benefits. When Mr. P received his January 2019 check, it was noted that it would be his last payment for his disability benefits. He has no other source of income. He's unable to work. He believed the NFL took care of its own. He never thought the NFL would abandon him after he'd given them his body and brain.

Prior to these recent tests, Mr. P's cognitive and emotional problems were clear to every doctor he visited. As far back as 2009, Dr. Mary Hibbard of the Rusk Institute of Rehabilitation Medicine found "impairments in the domains of reaction time, gross motor speed, sustained visual attention, verbal processing speed, learning, memory and executive skills." Her final assessment: "Impaired cognition due to multiple concussions."

In 2011, Dr. Eric Larson at the Rehabilitation Institute of Chicago diagnosed Mr. P as having "symptoms consistent with Adjustment Disorder with Anxiety and Depressed Mood . . . his distress appears to be complicated by Pain Disorder Associated with Both Psychological Factors and a General Medical Condition."

I appealed this decision for Mr. P. On October 10, 2019, he attended a neuropsychological evaluation by Rodney Vanderploeg, PhD, at the behest of the Plan Retirement Board. The assessment in brief:

> He currently demonstrated the ability to learn and retain information and had delayed recall memory scores with the average range on multiple measures. In addition, he was able to demonstrate intact cognitive functioning on one or more measures within every cognitive domain. However, psychological testing is consistent with a Major Depressive Disorder with vegetative symptoms such as psychomotor slowing, low level energy, excessive fatigue, and difficulty sustaining a mental focus, all of which will adversely impact his cognitive performance on a day-to-day basis. As a result, I recommend a psychiatric evaluation.

The following day, October 11, 2019, Mr. P was seen by Dr. Stephen Sergay, a neurologist. After examining Mr. P, he wrote that he was unable to render a decision as to total-and-permanent disability on a neurologic basis.

At the November meeting of the Retirement Board, it was decided that Mr. P receive a psychiatric evaluation to determine whether his benefits could be restored.

On January 16, 2020, Mr. P was examined by the plan neutral psychiatrist, Mathew Norman. His report follows:

> Diagnosis: Adjustment Disorder with mixed anxiety and depressed mood.
>
> Mr. P. reported some symptoms of anxiety and depression and anxiety. Despite his reported symptoms, he had no objective signs of overt anxiety and few objective signs of impairing depression on examination in this office. His examination is consistent with an Adjustment Disorder. He has some depressive symptoms and reported anxiety symptoms.

Even Mr. P's self-reported symptom severity does not rise to the level of placing restrictions or limitations on Mr. P.'s work status. That is, there was insufficient evidence noted in the medical records reviewed and in his in-person examination to support him being out of work from a psychiatric standpoint. In addition, Mr. P. does not present evidence of depression or anxiety lasting more than twelve months.

In my opinion, Mr. P. does not meet criteria for Major Depressive Disorder, Generalized Anxiety Disorder, or Panic Disorder. He does meet criteria for Adjustment Disorder with mixed anxiety and depressed mood.

It should be noted that Mr. P.'s clinical presentation was clearly not consistent with someone suffering with an impairing Psychiatric condition. Specifically, he was able to maintain his attention, concentration, and focus during examination. He related to me very well. His reported depressed mood and anxiety did not interfere in his interaction with me. Therefore, Mr. P. is not restricted or limited as to work capacity.

Mr. P has not been employed in a meaningful way since he left the league. Despite holding an advanced university degree, he could not find a job he could handle. With depression, anxiety, and physical pain, he simply could not hold a job to support him and his family. Fortunately, the NFL awarded him T&P benefits. For almost seven years, the league supported Mr. P and his children. But because the league and union agreed to change the ground rules in the collective bargaining agreement, he no longer qualifies for any disability benefits. There is no money coming in for Mr. P.

He has applied for a payment through the NFL concussion settlement. He's in the middle of testing for that diagnosis. However, with the examination results he has attained recently, I don't hold any hope for a big award. The other option for him is to be deemed disabled by the Social Security Administration. His attorney is applying for this government benefit, but it is not easy to attain. He applied previously and the Social Security disability board declared that just because he was unable to do one job did not mean he could not be employed in another job.

These are the situations that keep me awake at night. I know these men so well that I literally internalize their pain and frustrations. I keep running scenarios in my mind thinking of ways to get the NFL to see what is happening to their warriors after they leave the league. These men need help, yet they are often blocked by the Retirement Board from attaining the benefits they deserve by an antiquated system of medical examinations tailored for the general public, not for men who have had their brains and bodies battered repeatedly. It is only quite recently that the NFL even acknowledged that concussions are not some transitory "ding to the head" but can be linked to degenerative brain disease.

And so retired players have to continue to confront a league (and union, which co-administers these programs) that throws up roadblocks. Take Mr. C, who was drafted in the first round in 1993 by the Tampa Bay Buccaneers. He played a total of seven seasons at defensive end for three NFL teams. After retiring he tried to work as a trainer and a football coach, but his body was in too much pain. Going for something more sedate, he tried selling cars and landscaping, but both proved to be too taxing physically. Even though he had a college degree in criminal justice, he couldn't get a sedentary job. He had always been the financial resource for his wife and four children. He became depressed. He'd suffered many concussions through the years and knew all the trauma was catching up with him. At that point, he applied for NFL benefits.

On behalf of the benefits committee, on February 4, 2012, Dr. Rodney Vanderploeg performed a neuropsychological evaluation on Mr. C. The following is his summary:

> Mr. C has invalid performance validity scores and therefore it is not possible to determine if Mr. C's poor performance in the areas of new learning and memory, as well as aspects of executive functioning (cognitive flexibility and mental control) and visuospatial abilities were an accurate reflection of his actual ability. However, he consistently performed poorly on all memory measures, had difficulty on measures of mental control and performed very poorly on a drawing task during which he demonstrated a disorganized approach with poor planning. Mr. C also presented as clinically depressed. He was diagnosed as having a Major Depressive Disorder, Chronic and Severe, with Psychotic Features (paranoia and disorganized thinking).

Based on this, his clinical presentation at this time, he was deemed to be disabled and was awarded benefits.

Unfortunately, Mr. C did not receive any cognitive or behavioral therapy to help remedy his depression or adjust to his constant pain. He spent his days in his room watching TV or sleeping. He and his wife continued to argue, and his children didn't know their dad at his best, if at all. He almost started a fire in the kitchen, so he is banned from cooking. He screwed up the checkbook, so his wife took that over. He is afraid to drive because he's had some minor accidents running over construction signs and pylons. He has few if any friends due to his depression.

Imagine the drop from college all-American and NFL defensive end to hiding in your room with migraine headaches and full body joint pain. Any of us would suffer from depression. Add to this that he has not been employed since he left the league. His ego has taken a beating.

Mr. C was reevaluated to make certain he still qualified for T&P benefits. On November 15, 2019, he once more saw Dr. Vanderploeg. The final report stated:

> Results from a comprehensive neuropsychological evaluation were invalid and cannot be used to make a determination about any neurocognitive impairment or cognitive disability. Psychological test results also were invalid due to overreporting of psychological problems. However, based on his history, Mr. C appears to have a significant depressive disorder. A psychiatric evaluation is indicated to determine if psychiatric issues are resulting in a functional disability.

Although the evaluation in 2019 had the same results as the previous one in 2012, the same doctor could not render the opinion that Mr. C was permanently disabled. The rules at the plan office had changed. So Dr. Vanderploeg, still believing Mr. C suffered from depression, recommended he be seen by a psychiatrist. Interestingly, he had seen one in Ohio a week before he saw Dr. Vanderploeg. However, the reports were still being written and not yet a part of Mr. C's file. Dr. Brett Plyler on November 8, 2019, diagnosed Mr. C with

- Major depressive disorder
- Multiple orthopedic injuries
- Chronic pain
- Headaches
- Cognitive problems

After reviewing Mr. C and reviewing his application, I do not feel that he meets the criteria for total and permanent disability for psychiatric reasons. Currently, Mr. C does suffer from major depressive symptoms but they do not impair his ability to work. His primary issues seems [*sic*] to be his physical pain and limitations, and these greatly affect his mood, cognition, and anxiety. His symptoms of depression are—depressed mood, insomnia, hopelessness, cognitive problems, anger, anxiety, tearfulness, lack of motivation and fatigue. Mr. C reported nightmares or "night terrors" that frequently disrupt his sleep but the symptoms do not appear to meet criteria for Night Terrors per DSM 5. He also has some social anxiety and unreasonable fears about the safety of his family. Mr. C is not in active treatment. His chronic pain also plays a role in his mood, anxiety, and sleep problems.

As for employment, Mr. C would not have any restrictions from a psychiatric perspective. I would recommend employment in the criminal justice system as this was Mr. C's degree of study and he has a previous history of helping youth and teens.

Realistically, who is going to hire a man with major depression who has never worked since he left the NFL twenty years ago? In order to be employed in the field of criminal justice, the first prerequisite is that you have no mental problems. Working with youth when he can barely tolerate his own children is short sighted and impractical. The anxiety and social pressures of being a guard or police officer would be intolerable for Mr. C. Additionally he cannot be on his feet for long periods due to his joint pain. This fact was confirmed by the orthopedist who evaluated him. His report stated that Mr. C could work if the job was sedentary and that he could take breaks to deal with his ongoing pain.

Whereas in 2012, one neuropsychologist declared Mr. C was incapable of working and eligible for T&P, in 2019 three doctors ruled that he could work. The NFL Retirement Board changed the rules in the 2011 collective bargaining agreement. Mr. C was initially awarded benefits under the original ruling. During the interim, the goal posts moved and he was no longer eligible. I assure you no one gets better as they age physically.

You might reasonably ask, "Is this the end?" He does have one more option. Mr. C, with the assistance of an attorney, applied for Social Security disability benefits. It's a long process and a long shot, but if he qualifies for Social Security disability, the NFL Retirement Board will have to reevaluate their rulings that he is not disabled. The rulings for T&P usually go in favor of the player at this point.

Interestingly, in 2019 four doctors were essentially removed by the plan as neutral physicians. Speaking to two of those doctors, it was found that they were not fired per se, but their appointments were canceled by the plan board and no more appointments were scheduled. They believed this occurred because they were too lenient in their diagnoses of impaired NFL retired players seeking benefits. As one orthopedist said, "I diagnosed what I found; I did not care about pleasing the NFL in order to get more referrals." I looked at a large group of players seen by these four doctors and could tell immediately why the NFL Retirement Board would want these doctors replaced. They empathized with the player's chronic pain and wrote reports that reflected their sound medical opinions and training, not the answers that would preclude the players from obtaining benefits.

THE 88 PLAN

This benefit was the result of the collective bargaining agreement in 2007 and was revised through 2016. It was named after John Mackey, the first man to receive the benefit, who wore the number 88 on his jersey during his distinguished career with the Baltimore Colts. Basically, this benefit reimburses players for medical treatment, assistive equipment, or doctors' appointments to help with a diagnosed neurocognitive impairment such as ALS, Parkinson's disease, or dementia. Players can receive up to $100,000 a year. The greater benefit that this plan offers is assisted living in the facility of your choice when you are no longer self-sufficient. This is a straight payment from the Cigna insurance company to the facility, not a reimbursement of dollars spent. Assisted living facilities provide occupational and physical therapy, along with speech therapy. Most have a gym and a communal dining area. You have a private room and are allowed visitors. However, residents are carefully monitored so no one gets lost. It's a secure environment, but one with much freedom to move and socialize.

As I completed my testimony before Congress in the fall of 2009, the final question directed to me was, What did I plan to do next? My

response was that I was going to find Jerry Eckwood, a former Buccaneer who I had heard was not faring well. I intended to get him help.

"A lot of this doesn't make sense," Eckwood said, looking at the
forms, as conveyed by Alan Schwarz of the *New York Times*. "I don't
think I could have done this all by myself. I would have probably just
forgotten about it."[8]

When I returned home, I put out feelers to former players, asking if
they had heard from Jerry. He was from Arkansas, but the word was
that he was near his daughter in Tennessee. Piece by piece, we put the
puzzle together and located Jerry at a supervised home. His daughter
had found it, and he paid for it with his social security payments. Not
knowing how Jerry would react to a woman, I partnered with a male
friend of long-standing who traveled to Tennessee with me and helped
with the transportation details and doctor visits. We had an appointment with Dr. Allen Sills from Vanderbilt University to evaluate Jerry
for the 88 Plan. (Dr. Sills currently works as chief medical officer for
the NFL, appointed by Commissioner Goodell.)

After several tests, Jerry qualified for the 88 Plan. Now you might
think this is the fairy tale ending we desired. Yes. I was thrilled, and
those who loved Jerry were thrilled. But Jerry didn't understand what
was happening. The first assisted living facility was not to his liking
because he wasn't allowed to walk to the stores down the street alone.
That didn't stop him, but the facility panicked each time they found him
missing. He was developing paranoia, which is common in people with
dementia. He accused the housekeeper of stealing his phone. When she
found it and gave it to him, he threw it at her. Jerry was asked to leave.

After reassessing our situation, we found another assisted living facility that would emphasize working out in the gym and physical therapy.
This was more like the locker room or football training that he understood. He flourished. He was happy and felt at home with the physical
routine.

Jerry Eckwood never would have known about the 88 Plan if we had
not interceded. I literally found him, had him tested, and placed him in
assisted living. Players who qualify for this plan must have dementia,
Alzheimer's disease, or Parkinson's disease. They are rarely able to apply for this benefit without someone to help them. It's too complicated,
particularly when your brain isn't working to capacity. You need a representative who knows about the benefit and how to access an applica-

tion. You need insurance to pay for the tests, or about $1,500 in your checking account.

The 88 Plan is a reimbursement system for all services other than assisted living. If you are able to remain at home but need help with transportation to medical appointments or with daily living skills, you may hire a qualified person. They in turn will give you a receipt, which you pay. Then once a week or so, you send the receipts to the administrator of the benefit, and you will receive a check to cover what you spent.

The Player Care Foundation hosts a variety of programs and health benefits for players, including a lifeline for depression, spine treatment, and prostate testing at various venues around the country. While these programs are generous, the problem is that most players don't know they exist.

When a player is cut from a team, he is upset and angry. The last thing he's thinking about is health screening or assisted living. He basically wants to get away from the locker room and find another job. That remains the focus for about two years on average. Players are not ready to accept that their playing days are over. Some of them keep at it in the gym in hopes they will get a call from a team in need. By the time the player realizes his football career is really finished, he's lost contact with his former teammates and is out of the loop on NFL news about benefits and alumni programs.

The first thing I do is recommend that players connect with either a union representative or the NFL Alumni Association. These groups have meetings in the NFL cities and many other cities that are populated by former players. This is where speakers come to keep players up to date on benefits and programs to assist them. It's also a good social group that will help make the transition to retirement or another career easier. This is a group of men who have walked in the player's shoes and survived life without football. More important, this is where you learn about the benefits you have earned during your playing days. Yes, if you are web savvy, you can find this material at www.nflpa.com, but most players have too many questions to suffer through the website, patiently looking for the answer to their specific question.

For those players who are confused and lost in some way, I created Retired Player Assistance, Inc. Our goal is to obtain benefits for former professional athletes. Most retired players don't have any idea what benefits they may be entitled to receive. We take their information and determine if they are vested. Then we help them apply for those benefits. Some players have applied previously and been denied. We'll then craft appeals for them or suggest Social Security disability or the 88 Plan. We always answer the phone ourselves. We are volunteers, but if you need specific legal help, such as an ERISA attorney well versed in employment law, we'll recommend someone we have vetted.

Our group meets twice a year to address new issues that confront retired players. Most recently we have been focusing on financial education. We believe players who receive concussion settlement money need to understand that legal fees and Medicare liens will be subtracted before they receive their money. This is a little-understood issue. We created a video to address this process and educate the players and their families as to why some money is held out.

Additionally, we travel to alumni meetings to explain NFL benefits and answer the players' questions. We are volunteers and will travel wherever we are asked to speak. We want the players to be aware of the benefits they fought for in the collective bargaining agreement. Most are surprised to learn these benefits exist.

We maintain a website where players can register and speak with us to answer their questions: www.retiredplayerassistance.org. We have several attorneys, as well as disability experts and psychologists, and a computer wizard on staff. Working together, we can answer most questions.

6

CONCUSSIONS AND
THE NFL SETTLEMENT

For years, players and coaches called them dings, bell ringers, or anything other than concussions. They were routinely treated with smelling salts during the game and a bit of rest after the game. If a player was really hit hard, doctors would ask them a few questions—such as, What's the score?—and perhaps have them sit out a play or two. For years, coaches held full contact practices three and four times a week during the season. Randy Grimes, a longtime center on the Buccaneers, said that practices were so brutal he and his teammates were worn out by game day, which, thankfully, involved less hitting.

Even players who were warned about getting too many concussions didn't listen. In a league with a 100 percent injury rate and nonguaranteed contracts, players saw them as the cost of remaining employed. But by the late 1980s and early 1990s, players started to speak up about how the concussions were affecting their memory and cognition. New York Jets receiver Wayne Chrebet played eleven seasons in the NFL and retired early because of repeated concussions. Chrebet, signed as an undrafted free agent, said his gritty style of play allowed him to last that long in the league.

"It's my own fault," he told reporters. "I could have gone out of bounds more. I could've ducked under tackles. They told me, 'Be careful. One more concussion and you're done.' I played the same way. Whose fault is that?"[1]

Chrebet only knew the half of it. The NFL knew about the long-term consequences of concussions and that they were a problem for the players and the league. Otherwise, they wouldn't have established the Mild Traumatic Brain Injury Committee in 1994 to study the issue. The commissioner at the time, Paul Tagliabue, put Dr. Elliot Pellman, a rheumatologist with no formal training in neurology or brain science, in charge. Pellman did know a thing or two about concussions though: he was the Jets team doctor while Chrebet played on the team. It was later disclosed that Pellman had repeatedly sent players back onto the field despite signs of concussions. For good measure, Pellman was Tagliabue's personal physician.

Independent researchers accused Pellman and others on the brain injury committee of promoting "junk science" and downplaying the long-term effects of concussions. These efforts to obscure the dangers of concussions and repeated head hits turned into the NFL's biggest existential crisis—a problem so large it ballooned into a $1 billion legal settlement. The roots of that very expensive agreement started around 2011.

That's when I started to see a pattern develop from the many players and wives with whom I spoke. Head injuries and concussions were the main topic of conversation. They were worried that they were losing their mental acuity. Word had traveled among retired players and family members that I had testified about concussions in 2009 in congressional hearings in Washington, D.C. I was vocal and clear in my presentation, going so far as to shame the NFL for their lack of care for head injuries on the field. Tiki Barber, who played ten years for the New York Giants, was more subtle. After all, he still was earning a living from football. Sitting near the front of the room, he held two helmets designed by a company called Vicis. They were very large and looked as though they were meant for the Conehead family. They were shaped similarly to a football standing on its point.

Barber was helping the start-up in Seattle market their new helmets that several players had endorsed and claimed were a safer option. The helmets led to many conversations. He was clearly stating without words what most players knew: hits to the head are dangerous. Better-designed helmets are needed. Even though the NFL continued to follow their line that head injuries weren't a problem, the players knew differently. Several players recognized the need for an alternative helmet and were investing in companies doing research into more absorbent, protective headgear. Vicis's new technology included a helmet shell that had more give so that the impact from a hit was distributed over a broad surface, mitigating the impact to the player's head. Ultimately, this helmet was accepted by the NFL and universities and used by many teams. In fact, the NFL was so smitten with the technology that it awarded the company more than $1 million in grants.

However, the prohibitive cost of the helmet, retailing at $1,500, made it too expensive for most amateur players. Unable to raise enough money to cover its costs, the company declared itself bankrupt at the end of 2019. Once you saw Barber with an alternative helmet at the congressional hearing, you knew that players were getting wise to the truth about concussions no matter how hard the NFL tried to keep the public in the dark. Even though the league continued to deny the evidence that was building, linking concussions to cognitive disabilities later in life, researchers were becoming more adamant about the potential damages and the players were starting to mobilize.

The NFL tried to push back. Pellman's committee published several articles in the medical journal *Neurosurgery* that essentially refuted common sense. One point made by the committee was the belief that NFL players' brains had advanced to the state that they were less affected by injuries to the head than the public at large. What was also difficult to understand was the committee's statement that returning to play after a concussion in no way increases the chances for a second injury. In 2005, the committee published another article in *Neurosurgery* that boldly stated that "chronic brain injury has never been reported in American football players."[2]

That same year, Dr. Bennet Omalu outlined the findings of his autopsy of Mike Webster's brain in an article for *Neurosurgery*. He thought he had discovered a new brain disease and named it *chronic traumatic encephalopathy*, or CTE. Later, Omalu recanted and said he did not discover CTE. A year later, in 2006, the NFL's Mild Traumatic Brain Injury (MTBI) Committee requested that the article be retracted. The article made the connection between concussions and brain disease later in life. That was not the connection the league wanted made public because it could not only leave them legally liable but also scare youngsters and their parents away from football.

The doctors, including Omalu, who examined Webster's brain believed he suffered severe frontal lobe damage, which affected his ability to think and make decisions. After retiring, he bounced between jobs. Then, as his mind deteriorated and he became wracked with pain from the years of abuse his body had suffered, he basically lived in his truck. He was demented and depressed. Friends and teammates offered him money and assistance, but Webster was beyond help. He died of a heart attack at age fifty in 2002. Although the league refused to admit the connection between concussions and brain deterioration, the Retirement Board awarded substantial disability benefits to Webster's family.

Embarrassingly, during the congressional hearing in 2009, a video clip from *60 Minutes* was shown of an interview with Ira Casson, the chairman of the NFL's MTBI Committee. Casson vehemently denied any cause and effect of head injuries and long-term brain injury. The hearing went dead silent. I don't think anyone believed a man, especially a doctor, could tell such a lie with such a straight face. His critics called him "Dr. No." Of course, he was being paid well not to let the truth out about concussions damaging players. His committee was supposed to give a professional cover to the ludicrous medical messages that the league wished the public to believe.

Dr. Omalu published another article on the autopsy of Terry Long, another NFL player whose brain resembled that of Mike Webster's. Long, too, exhibited many of the same symptoms of paranoia and memory loss. He, too, died a premature and tragic death. The statements coming from Casson's committee became more difficult to believe, with all signs pointing to a connection between head injuries in football and severe brain disease in later life.

The NFL began to react by changing rules vetted through the Competition Committee to make the game safer but still entertaining. No fan wanted to pay money to see what amounted to flag football at a professional level, so the league tinkered around the edges of the game. New, "safer" tackling techniques were instituted to reduce head injuries, although they were unpopular with the longtime players. Spotters were to be in several positions on the field and in the boxes above the field to check for concussions. Concussion protocols instituted by the league were supplemented by monetary fines for those who tried to skirt the league's rules.

I began to speak to attorneys from 2010 to 2012 about what I would need to do to have a class action lawsuit brought against the NFL on behalf of the former players with head injuries. I knew there was a legal issue in some way that should benefit the former players. It was common sense that if you did not warn your employees of the dangers of their job and they suffered career-ending injuries or were left with cognitive problems such as dementia, there must be some form of recourse. I'm not a legal scholar, so I called Harvard Law School and spoke to the lead scholar in sports law there. He said that what I proposed made sense to him, though he'd never thought about it. He recommended several attorneys who practice in the courts. I went to their offices. We had many long discussions. One firm represented retired players who were trying to win NFL benefits. It was an expensive firm that usually had good results for their clients. Although the firm was interested, this was too massive a project for them to undertake. Another viable firm was in Baltimore. The lawyers and I spoke for a total of three days, usually with the entire cadre of the firm. On our last day, the lead attorney told me he'd commit to the project if I paid $2 million upfront. I left without saying a word. I was too shocked. The following day I called the firm and requested to speak with the lead attorney. He was "in conference," I was told. I asked to speak with his son. He, too, was "in conference." I asked the receptionist if there were any firm attorneys available. They "were in conference." I said, "Please take a message: I'm not using your firm now or in the future for any reason whatsoever."

All of a sudden, someone was available to speak with me. I told him that he was missing out on the biggest lawsuit of his career and he'd be really sorry and embarrassed that he passed up the opportunity. He was speechless.

Dozens of cases sprang up around the country, some in state court, some in federal court. Players were filing complaints in California, Florida, Texas, Mississippi, Pennsylvania, and many other places where former players lived. The NFL would face an avalanche of legal bills if it tried to fight the cases in their jurisdictions one at a time, so they asked to consolidate the cases in one federal court. At the same time, the plaintiffs' lawyers who had many players signed up as clients formed an executive committee to take on the NFL. (While this is standard in these types of cases, there was a lot of politicking to decide which lawyers would be on the executive committee and which ultimately had control, among many other things, of how legal fees would be divided.)

The federal courts approved the NFL's request, and all the cases were swept into something called multidistrict litigation (MDL). The National Football League Players' Concussion Injury Litigation (MDL 2323) was filed on January 31, 2012, in the U.S. District Court for the Eastern District of Pennsylvania. Judge Anita Brody, a senior judge appointed by President Bill Clinton, took over the case. Sol Weiss and his co-lead counsel, Christopher Seeger, were chosen as the lead lawyers for the plaintiffs. While Seeger and Weiss were new to sports litigation, they had made a name for themselves by winning a $5 billion settlement from Merck & Co. for its mishandling of the drug Vioxx.

Unsurprisingly, the league filed a motion to dismiss the lawsuits brought by the 4,500 or so retired players who accused the league of fraud and negligence, for knowing about the dangers of concussions and head hits but failing to warn them.

The legal teams for the league and plaintiffs faced off in April 2013 in Judge Brody's courtroom in Philadelphia. The league's lawyers argued that the case should be dismissed because the players agreed to a collective bargaining agreement, which specifies that all issues against the league should be heard by an arbitrator, not a judge. In the packed and steamy courtroom with an overflowing gallery, the plaintiff's lawyers argued that their case should be heard in court because the accusation of fraud would supersede any labor agreement.

After the forty-five-minute hearing, the debate spilled onto the plaza outside the courthouse. Paul Clement, a lawyer for the NFL, was asked to respond to the plaintiffs' charge that the NFL had glorified violence and profited from it. "The collective bargaining agreements address player safety," he said. "Nothing in this collective bargaining agreement speaks to the marketing of violence."

The plaintiffs' lawyers took a different route. They brought out former players to talk about their injuries. One of the players was Kevin Turner, a former fullback who, at forty-three, was grappling with amyotrophic lateral sclerosis, or ALS. Turner, who lent his name to the case, said he was certain his brain injury was caused by hits to the head he received while playing in the NFL. "The NFL was acting like we were idiots, that there was no correlation," he said, his speech slurred and halting.

Lisa McHale, whose husband, Tom McHale, was found to have chronic traumatic encephalopathy after he died in May 2008, said the NFL did not care about the suffering of players like her husband. "I don't want to believe that they could have been so callous," she said.

The case was a tricky one. The league's argument that the collective bargaining agreement (CBA) preempted any attempt by the players to try their case in a court did not cover players who were in the NFL between 1988 and 1993, when the league operated without a labor agreement. So even if the judge agreed that the players had to argue their case in front of an arbitrator, those players from the late 1980s and early 1990s might still be able to proceed in court because they were not beholden to a labor deal.

If the judge ruled in favor of the league, both sides could win and lose at the same time. But Judge Brody did what many judges do: she sought a way for the parties to settle before the case proceeded to a trial, which can take years and millions of dollars and delay any relief for the players. So on July 8, 2013, Judge Brody appointed a mediator and ordered both sides to try to reach a settlement.

Less than two months later, the league and plaintiffs' lawyers agreed to a settlement amid much media fanfare. The league agreed to contribute $765 million, with $675 million set aside for medical help for more than eighteen thousand former players. Critically for the league, it admitted no fault and no relationship between playing football and suffering long-term consequences of concussions. The league also demanded—and won—what it really sought: blanket immunity from future lawsuits. All retired players—not just the 4,500 who filed claims—would be covered in the settlement, which meant that these players would give up their right to sue the league for similar claims in the future. Only players who opted out of the agreement—about two hundred ultimately—would be able to continue to fight in court. Nearly all of those cases have been resolved, either with the players opting back in to the settlement or by reaching a separate deal with the league.

Actuarial estimates, though, suggested that far more players were going to get sick and the $675 million the NFL was putting in would not cover all of the settlements. So Judge Brody got the league to agree to "uncap" the agreement, which meant the NFL was on the hook for an unlimited amount of damages over the sixty-five-year duration of the settlement. In recognizing that the league had underestimated the severity of the injuries, Brody handed the players a major victory.

In July 2014, the concussion settlement agreement was announced. Free phone lines were set up and answered by trained staff to assist the players in applying for the settlement. A handful of players opted out of the deal, but the vast majority—about 99 percent—opted in.

But almost from the moment the players could apply for settlements, the process was plagued by delays, unnecessary audits, and rejections that led to frustration. Many players were also surprised to find out that money from their settlements would be taken off the top to pay their lawyers and Medicare liens for treatments they had already received for their injuries. That could shave tens of thousands, maybe even hundreds of thousands of dollars off of settlements.

There were other, deep-seeded problems. After years of fighting with the NFL over other benefits, the players did not trust the league to pay them money from the settlement. The process was too difficult for most players to understand because it was couched in the language of the court.

Another problem was that the plaintiffs' lawyers came out of the woodwork because they saw the NFL deal as an opportunity for riches. While this is not unique to class action lawsuits, it was particularly insidious in the NFL case because many players, some of whom had severe financial problems, were too easily swayed by fast-talking lawyers promising seven-figure payouts, but also taking 20, 30, and even 40 percent from the settlements as payment for their work. Many players also had cognitive problems and were unable to understand the implications of the documents they were signing, or to recognize how much time and effort was needed to win an award.

But the smell of money was in the air, so some lawyers started flocking to retired player alumni meetings to sell their services. Nowhere was this more flagrant than Tampa, Florida. There, some lawyers hired former players as "runners" who got a fee for every new player they brought. The members had no idea that their chapter president was being paid by the attorney. They thought he was recommending a vetted attorney.

One of the biggest offenders was from the newly formed firm in Tampa called the Neurocognitive Football Lawyers, LLC (NCFL), which was made up of seven small law firms. They specifically targeted football players seeking concussion settlements. Lawyers from the firm spoke to the alumni groups at their regularly scheduled monthly meetings. The players were told to take so-called Baseline Assessment Program (BAP) tests with neurologists and neuropsychologists approved by the settlement administrator because, if those doctors determined a player was eligible for an award, there would be no need for the results to be reviewed by a court-appointed neurologist. Time would be saved and money would be paid, except when you are trying to game the system.

The NCFL figured it could streamline the process by bringing in their own doctors. But the settlement administrators got suspicious and began auditing the players' claims. Why would lawyers risk their reputations? They didn't in the case of NCFL. The names of the attorneys were hidden behind their newly created entity. They approached the retired players with a get-rich-quick scheme. However, they took the step of forming a new law firm just to process these claims. They employed doctors and paid them for qualifying diagnoses. The more cognitively impaired the doctor found the client, the more he was given as a bonus. This is how NCFL guaranteed players they would receive a settlement award. In one case, a father and son neurology practice in Tampa saw eighty-four NCFL clients. A sample of these claims was sent for medical review, and on February 5, 2018, they received the following notice: "The ratings were inconsistent with and did not reflect with the history information in the doctor's own notes, history information in the neuropsychology notes, and/or the information in the third-party affidavits submitted on the claims."

Chastened, the firm has since disappeared on social media. No advertisements anywhere. I can only imagine they have closed their concussion law firm and gone back to their regular practices with no one being the wiser. But what has happened to the clients?

Not all lawyers have used dubious tactics. In fact, more than a thousand players have, as of early 2020, received a settlement. But many former players struggling with brain injuries remain frustrated. The following story is an example of one player's winding road to obtaining his concussion settlement award.

In 1980, I was in the Buccaneers' "war room" when the player, SB, was drafted out of the University of Florida, which happened to be my alma mater. He had a history of playing hard at linebacker as a Gator.

His senior year he was benched because the coach and trainers were worried about his brain after all the concussions he'd suffered. Still, Coach McKay considered him a very good player and targeted him as a third-round pick. I was in the room when the coach called SB's father and asked if he could draft his son. The dad said that all his son had ever wanted was to play for the Gators and in the NFL, and he wouldn't stand in his way.

Once SB joined the team, our equipment manager designed a helmet with pneumatic bladders that were filled with a bicycle pump once the helmet was on SB's head to ensure a perfect fit. SB played eight seasons in the NFL with the Buccaneers. By the time SB retired, he'd played in 114 games, starting 71 of them.

But like many players back then, SB had his "bell rung" too many times to count throughout his playing days. Double vision and smelling salts were standard by the time he retired. Over the years, his cognitive abilities declined. By May 22, 2018, his condition had so deteriorated that he was the focus of a *Real Sports* episode on HBO. The lead-in was "Former Gators and Bucs linebacker SB, also once a popular sports radio host in Tampa, is battling Alzheimer's disease and has been rejected from the NFL's concussion settlement, according to tonight's episode of HBO's *Real Sports with Bryant Gumbel*.

SB's attorney was from NCFL in Tampa. Frustrated that SB's claim was not being processed fast enough, his lawyer got HBO interested in his story. He thought a full-court press in public might change his luck with the concussion settlement decision makers. Instead, his client was embarrassed on national television. When asked his age, SB said he was ten years younger than he actually was at the time. Everyone who knew him picked up on it as a sign he was in bad shape. Who of us when faced with a wall of lights and cameras has not made a mistake on a simple question? However, SB was mortified. He had not wanted to go public with his problems but had been pushed into it by his desperate attorney.

Reputable law firms keep their client lists small in order to properly process their settlements. Then there are the firms that gather four hundred or more clients and hire workers at $10 per hour to complete the forms and document the doctor reports. SB's attorney fell into this group. The lawyers believe the more clients, the better. Not only did they believe it raised the odds of making their money back in fees, but also having a long client list gave them more leverage with the judge and with the plaintiffs executive committee. However, these lawyers had no time to properly advise their clients. The settlement directions are easy to follow, but someone has to follow through and do the work.

After several years, SB had not received an award letter. Neither had any players he knew who were also represented by this firm. SB and his wife contacted me for help. As I looked into NCFL, I was shocked to see that not one client had progressed through the settlement guidelines and received compensation. Clearly his attorney had tried everything, including putting his client on national television to bully the claims administrator into approving SB's claim. What was the problem holding up this monetary payment? I knew SB had been diagnosed with dementia and other neurological problems. He had suffered a stroke while broadcasting a radio show and was having difficulty with his eyes and memory. He was no longer driving because he would get lost traveling the three blocks to his mother's home. Surely if any former player deserved compensation from the concussion settlement, it was SB.

I began my research by contacting the claims administrator's staff to ask why SB had waited so long and heard nothing about his application for a settlement. After a bit of digging, I discovered that all the claims submitted by NCFL were being audited. There are several legal reasons claims go to audit. The bottom line was that I had to extract SB's application from the 186 others held in audit. I needed a new lawyer to handle his case because the settlement guidelines insist that only an attorney can represent a player or he can represent himself. Fortunately, I had a professional friend in Jeff Dahl, who had represented several players in ERISA suits against the league. I explained to Jeff my personal relationship with SB and his wife and asked that he do us a favor and represent him in the concussion settlement going forward. I promised to do as much work on it as allowed and not take up time being frivolous. With that agreement in place, I told SB's family my plan and that I saw it as the fastest way to solve the problem. After all, he could remain in audit for the remainder of the settlement as there was no mandatory timeline for reviewing claims in audit.

I made an appointment with their attorney. I had the foresight to reserve a conference room at my attorney's office and ask a professional mediator (also a longtime friend) to accompany me that day. I explained to the lawyer the situation: SB was seriously cognitively compromised and was frustrated at having to wait for his settlement. He was ready to move on with a new attorney. It was my role that day to come to terms that were amenable to all parties as SB had signed a contract giving 25 percent of the award plus expenses to the law firm. I mentioned that his fee was too high because the judge had since capped legal fees for attorneys at 17 percent, with an additional 5 percent going into a fund for future legal expenses. His lawyer said he knew that and would correct it, of course.

The strangest thing happened next. He put his wallet on the table and asked that I work for him and his firm. I ignored him and said I was there to come to an agreement on his termination as SB's attorney. He threw out an absurd percentage. I said I was authorized to offer 12 percent. After an hour of charades, during which I left the room to speak with SB's wife, we completed a deal for 12 percent plus expenses. The smartest things I did that day were making sure we were on neutral territory and having a witness to the proceedings who was an officer of the court.

In all, NCFL registered 188 retired players. All their NCFL claims were based on diagnoses made before January 7, 2017, which is the effective date of the settlement agreement. The law firm hired six neurologists to evaluate its clients. Although their clients lived in twenty-six states, with one exception, 143 former players either lived in Tampa or were flown to Tampa to be tested by one of the five doctors that NCFL preferred. In order to speed up the process, one doctor set up evaluations in an office in the law firm, a clear breech of the regulations of the settlement, which require all evaluations to be done in a doctor's office.

Because these NCFL claims were based on doctors' reports before the pre-effective date, they had to be reviewed by a court-appointed neurologist. Eleven of these claims were not medically eligible. Two were thrown out because the doctor was not qualified to make the diagnoses. The remaining claims (131) were audited. I knew SB had been evaluated independently and had a neurologist that was well respected. However, he was tainted by his association with NCFL. He was in audit even though he had a bona fide head injury. His case may not be reviewed for years. That was my impetus to switch attorneys.

After we extracted his application, we reapplied. We had him see a physician chosen by the settlement administrator. After being tested by a neurologist and neuropsychologist, his claim was accepted and he was awarded his settlement.

The smoothest award from start to finish was for David Lewis, a former Tampa Bay Buccaneer and a good friend. He may not say it was smooth, but I made it go smoothly for him. The problem was that he and his attorney and the paralegal couldn't understand each other. David had a well-respected attorney from up North. David lives in the South. The northern speech patterns are rapid fire, and the attorney spoke in legalese, as did the paralegal. We reached a compromise. David would tell me his concerns (usually daily), and I would then call the paralegal. She'd speak to the attorney sometime during the day and return my call. I'd then explain to David the answer. On occasion, I'd explain to the attorney why we had to employ this method. I mentioned, if he looked at the file, he'd remember that David had Alzheimer's disease. That was a simpler explanation than saying "you talk too fast." Seeing the doctors and getting the diagnoses was easy. David is a real people-pleasing giant. He and his wife traveled to South Florida to see the neurologist. She worked with his local doctor for a few weeks. The paperwork was completed and submitted. Checks never arrive as quickly as you want, just as Christmas takes its time in getting here to celebrate. In David's case, it was about four months from doctor exam to receiving his concussion award. That's what I call fast and smooth.

Player J had the opposite experience. He was tested in the spring of 2014 by a neuropsychologist and a neurologist. Neither doctor found cognitive problems that would justify a cash award. On June 8, 2015, the claims administrator was notified that Player J was now represented by Gibbs and Parnell, a member of the NCFL.

In the Monetary Award claim from NCFL for Player J submitted to us on July 25, 2017, the Diagnosing Physician Form signed by Doctor 1 asserted Level 2 Neurocognitive Impairment. We received a tip about Player J that there had been previous examinations finding no Qualifying Diagnosis while he was with another law firm, which is how we then found the medical records from the 2014 examinations. We then put Player J in audit.

Player J is very active writing posts on Facebook, almost daily. On January 28, 2018, he gave a 17-minute long radio interview, during which he had no apparent trouble speaking. He has posted on Facebook on January 29, 2018, that he is publishing a book regarding his personal life. He had mentioned that book in his radio interview. On March 3, 2018, he posted on Facebook that he was relaunching his foundation.

We sent a Notice of Audit of Claim to NCFL for Player J on December 5, 2017, asking for the names of all health providers he had seen in the last five years. NCFL responded to that notice on January 4, 2017, listing fourteen medical providers. But the doctors who had evaluated Player J in 2014 and found No Qualifying Diagnosis were not on that list.

All of this could have been avoided and time saved if NCFL had used the Baseline Assessment Program (BAP) that was provided at no cost to the players. These doctors were approved by the concussion settlement administrator. If they reported a certain diagnosis for a retired player, it was assumed to be correct and the process could rapidly proceed.

The number of troubled cases continues. On April 23, 2020, a former player reached out to me. He lives in Atlanta and was referred to me by Gridiron Greats, a program started by Coach Mike Ditka to help former players in medical and financial need. This player is forty-five years old and is vested in the NFL's benefits and pension program. His problem was that he didn't think his attorney was doing a good job for him. "When I call his office, he acts like he doesn't know who I am," he told me. I asked the attorney's name. This attorney had a reputation for taking more cases than he could handle. He didn't live in Georgia; he was in the far north. His operation took all cases and then farmed them out to smaller firms and took part of the fees they generated from the clients he sent them. The client never knew the attorney they hired wasn't doing the work.

I told the player that, of course, the attorney didn't know who he was. They never met, and the attorney wasn't doing the work on the case. He was shocked. He told me that the attorney was highly recommended and had more than two hundred clients. "And you think he should know you out of two hundred men?" I said. As we talked over several days, he asked how he could get out of his contract. The problem, as I told him, was that he had this attorney also applying for Social Security disability in hopes of getting NFL disability benefits more easily. He was stuck. "Why didn't someone explain this to me?" he asked.

My response, "You didn't ask."

I went one step forward and asked if he'd been tested for the concussion settlement. "Oh, yes. I'm waiting for my money. I got a 2.0." Over several days, I spent hours talking with this man; never would I have guessed he qualified for a 2.0 neurological impairment. At forty-five, he spoke perfect English and was the author of a book on football. I ventured one step forward. "Who is your attorney?"

"He's in Tampa," he responded, and then he named one of the NCFL attorneys that has had so many of their cases audited. I knew then this player was not going to get the money he was waiting for. I gave him the name of a claims administrator and told him to email and ask for the status of his claim. I said to expect to hear that it was in audit. I didn't go into all the problems with the firm as I had burst enough bubbles for him recently.

At this point, the player had no money and had moved in with family members. He's been waiting on attorneys to make his money appear. He said he needed three surgeries and was in pain. The COVID-19 virus was rampant, many parts of the country were on lockdown, and unemployment was soaring. I had no further advice for this former player as there are no jobs for which he could apply and most government offices, including Social Security, were closed. The NFL had canceled all doctor appointments for benefits assessments.

This player lives in Atlanta but for whatever reason had chosen attorneys in two different states. I cannot advise this. However, I suspect that he was taken in by runners shilling for the attorneys. It's the only explanation I can figure.

I have received calls from a few players who've realized what has happened. I've found them reputable attorneys. The problem is that we have to pull the player's original applications for claims and start from the beginning. That's not difficult because there are only certain doctors we can use at this point in the settlement process. The court prohibited players from going to BAP doctors starting in June 2019. Those appointments were free to the players. The newer Monetary Award Fund (MAF) doctors are chosen by the plan administrators, like the BAP doctors. However, the player must pay or have their insurance pay in order to be assessed. Usually, the player's attorney will make these appointments. However, these exams, according to new rules from the court, must be scheduled close to your home if at all possible, usually within 150 miles. The settlement website has a geographical list of all the MAF physicians. This distance restriction was implemented to prevent players from traveling to distant locations to see "friendly" doctors.

The other problem I've run into is that not all MAF physicians take all forms of insurance. It seems to be very specialized, and occasionally MRIs are requested. This also limits a player's access.

But players do not have much choice if they want to see if they qualify for a settlement. So some of them pay for a specialized exam. There are no cheap ways around it. In the beginning, attorneys might front the money for the exams and pay the player's travel expenses if they were seeing a BAP physician. But as years have passed and the awards have been slow to arrive, many attorneys could no longer afford to front the travel money. In the beginning of the settlement, everyone was sure that money would be flowing. The attorneys never thought their players wouldn't be approved for awards for their dementia or cognitive impairments. So they got greedy and signed up hundreds of players. Then the attorneys had to pay from their pockets for travel and local transportation, meals, and hotels for a player and his wife. These men did not travel on their own. They could get lost, or more likely, it could turn into a two-day vacation with their wife. The bills started stacking up as two hundred or more clients had to travel and be transported and housed. And in the end, the men weren't getting the diagnoses that the attorneys expected.

There were so many reports of fraud that the claims administrator appointed a special investigator to help clear the backlog of pending claims. In the "Memorandum of Law in Support of the National Football League and NFL Properties LLC's Motion for the Appointment of a Special Investigator," the claims administrator noted that 46 percent of the total claims submitted raised red flags and signs of fraud. For example:

> One of the neuropsychologists who evaluated players represented by Law Firm-A expressed concern that a lawyer from Law Firm-A would call and ask what answer to a question would make a difference to the outcome. The Claims Administrator also obtained evidence that Law Firm-A told players that Law Firm-A could secure

qualifying diagnoses and that it was willing to pay doctors directly out of their pocket for these diagnoses.

In addition, the Claims Administrator developed evidence that Law Firm-A directed at least one Settlement Class Member to show up for his diagnosing appointment hungover and on Valium, in order to make it appear that he had cognitive impairment.

A particularly egregious case involved a Dr. H. In December 2017, the special master, who works for Judge Brody, found reports that were startling. Dr. H claimed to have evaluated at least three and as many as eight players on twenty-five consecutive days, including eight players on New Year's Eve. Dr. H claimed to have spent 139 hours in one twenty-four-hour period evaluating and writing reports and another 134 hours in a different twenty-four-hour period. In December 2016, she diagnosed Player C with level 2 neurocognitive impairment (moderate dementia). He reported that he was unemployed and had memory issues and an inability to complete tasks. He was thirty-two. However, he was highly visible as a registered wealth manager for a large investment firm.

In another case, a Florida-based pediatric neurologist diagnosed 75 percent of the thirty-six players she saw with Alzheimer's disease, even though they were mainly in their thirties and forties. She also reported that twenty-one of these men had identical vital signs.

The worst attorney by far that my players saw was from Tallahassee. When the concussion settlement went into effect, the lawyer hired a few employees to help in defrauding these men and their families. He rented office space and hired a "runner" who had played football locally and knew the Florida State University graduates who were now retired men seeking the concussion settlements. He received cash for every player he brought into the firm as a client. The players trusted him as if they'd known him for years.

This lawyer hired a doctor to do the evaluations of his clients in his office. Dr. W was a longtime client of the lawyer's. He had been charged with groping a female patient in 2014. By 2016, he had lost his license to practice. However, he continued testing former players for the lawyer's firm.

Not content to take a commission on the settlement awards, the lawyer hired a friend who was recently out of prison for tax and bankruptcy fraud. He was banned by the Securities and Exchange Commission (SEC) from working in the financial industry. Without registering as an agent, they formed a new hedge fund.

Using his confident, booming voice and relying heavily on his Christian upbringing, the lawyer coerced many of his clients into moving their NFL 401(k) investments to his fund. He promised above-average market returns. He had the players walk down the hall and meet with his friend, who would seal the deal. The players were also allowed to borrow money from the hedge fund at exorbitant rates. The players didn't understand their liabilities. They were snowed by the fast-talking duo. They were sold on the fact they might double their money. The loans the players took in no way disturbed the principal of their investment as their loans would be repaid when the settlement money arrived. Or so they thought.

Soon this lawyer had more than two hundred clients and had opened several offices and hired additional employees. Many of the players were existing on the loans they had taken out with him. They weren't worried about paying them back as they were constantly told their concussion award settlement would cover the loans plus accrued interest. Men and their families were now relying on this monthly payout to survive.

Disaster struck in 2017 when the friend was arrested on aggravated child assault charges. The local paper ran the story, and soon all the investors began to panic. The monthly payments stopped, no one answered the office phones, and no one returned emails. The affected players called the claims administrator, and an investigation was begun. At this point the players discovered their claims had not even been submitted. The losses were unbelievable. Not only did the players lose their entire football savings, but also they weren't even being processed for the concussion settlements. Men threatened suicide; they lost their homes and other entities that required monthly payments. The money they had invested was the same money that was being paid to them as a high-interest loan.

The lawyer continues to practice law in Tallahassee.

Despite all this, many other players have been getting paid. As of February 24, 2020, 20,553 former players registered for the settlement. The administrator had received 2,989 claims, with 1,092, or about one-third of them, having received awards worth a whopping $750,044,475.40. Judge Brody was right: the original offer by the NFL to spend $675 million on claims was not enough and would have been exhausted just five years into the sixty-five-year settlement. Five years into the settlement, 11,960 former players had attended medical exams, and another 12,569 were pending.

Originally, the majority of those involved were pleased with the rules governing the distribution of the concussion funds. The NFL had agreed to uncap the amount of money for distribution at the judge's command. The retired players were given plenty of notice and allowed to visit doctors in many different venues. There was $20 million allotted to publicize the settlement. The administrators wanted to reach every retired player who was qualified to receive money under the settlement. Public relations firms were hired, and attorneys advertised heavily to attract clients who might benefit from the money now available.

In their eagerness to inform retired players and to gather clients, the lawyers did not mention that the players had to pass tests showing they had cognitive impairment. Players initially believed everyone who applied would be compensated. This was a failing that set the tone for the players to once again feel neglected by the NFL. They felt they were led to water and not allowed to drink from the well of wealth.

7

CHRONIC TRAUMATIC ENCEPHALOPATHY

On Christmas Day 2015, Bennet Omalu, a Nigerian American pathologist, officially became a household name. Of course, he looked nothing like the actor Will Smith who played him in the movie *Concussion*. Smith, tall and wiry, is not a short, round man like Omalu. The movie, which opened to rave reviews, was on everyone's lips that holiday season and beyond. The timing of the movie's release was interesting because the NFL playoffs were about to start, when attention on the football world is at its highest.

Scenes were added for dramatic effect, and conversations were combined to move the storyline forward, but the essence was intact. The crux of the movie was about Omalu trying to get the NFL to accept that head injuries were causing long-term brain disease in football players. His pleas starting in 2005 fell on deaf ears. Not only would the NFL not accept Omalu's research, but also they tried their best to suppress his information gleaned from autopsies of Mike Webster and Terry Long, two former Pittsburgh Steeler offensive linemen who died prematurely and, according to their autopsies, had an aggressively degenerative brain disease called chronic traumatic encephalopathy, or CTE. Omalu was certain he had discovered a unique pattern of destruction in the brains of these two men. The league, which had formed a committee of scientists as a front to push its point that there was no relationship between concussions and cognitive decline, tried to have his research removed from medical journals and suppressed. The league tried to substitute research from its own committees, much of which was later discredited as "junk science."

The league's efforts to cover up or distract from the growing associations between CTE and repeated head hits did not go unnoticed. In October 2009, I spoke in front of the House Judiciary Committee, which held hearings on the issue. Commissioner Roger Goodell was there. So was DeMaurice Smith, the head of the players union, as well as former players. Linda Sanchez, a congresswoman from California, was among the lawmakers who repeatedly challenged the league's denial that there was any link between football and brain disease. "The NFL sort of has this blanket denial or minimizing of the fact that there may be this link," she said to Goodell at the hearing. "And it sort of reminds me of the tobacco companies pre-'90s when they kept saying, 'Oh, there's no link between smoking and damage to your health.'"

Fast-forward six years, when the movie *Concussion* was released. Moviegoers were amazed at the lengths the NFL went to hide the truth, even years after public congressional hearings on the topic and the flood of articles in the *New York Times*, ESPN, and other news outlets. It was as if the public was hearing the information for the first time. But that's the powerful dynamic of movies. Alec Baldwin, who played Dr. Julian Bailes, a former Steelers team doctor who was sympathetic to Omalu, and Will Smith, who portrayed Omalu, sold the movie and the sordid history to NFL fans. People now understood what the issues were and why they should be concerned. It may have been a dramatic re-creation, but it made the topic accessible to the public.

Suddenly, more parents were asking questions about the risks of playing football, especially in young boys. Should my son play Pop Warner? When should he be allowed to tackle in football? What's the best helmet? What if my son gets a concussion? Eyes were opened to these and other questions about the safety of the game, and youth football in particular, as well as other contact sports like hockey and lacrosse.

Research, which had been confined to a handful of laboratories, began in earnest at many medical centers and universities as well as the VA hospitals. An explosion of interest occurred in head injuries and concussions, whether from sports contact or the military, where soldiers have suffered brain trauma from exploded bombs. The world was focused at one time on concussions. But in a stunning congressional hearing in 2016, the vice president for safety at the NFL was forced to acknowledge publicly for the first time that there was a link between head injuries and brain disease later in life.

However, even with millions of dollars being spent on research by the top doctors in the world, it's still impossible to diagnose CTE in a living person or to accurately describe the symptoms or incidence in the population. There is still no cure and no way to mitigate the symptoms except to treat it the way a patient with dementia or Alzheimer's disease is helped. Although CTE mimics amyotrophic lateral sclerosis (ALS) and Alzheimer's, it is not the same as those diseases. There is great controversy in the research community as to what it is and what it is not. Many agree, though, that someone with a brain injury may think irrationally, be paranoid or schizophrenic in certain settings, or have trouble with balance, walking or ambulating, or speaking. Or that they might have tremors, cognitive impairment, or trouble with their motor skills. This is certainly not the entire list of symptoms as each person responds differently depending on which section of their brain suffered the most trauma.

As an example, would you pick up a turtle egg on the beach and throw it around and then replace it in the nest? No? Why not? You are afraid of disrupting the growing cycle of the turtle. Its yolk is fragile. It's protected by the white of the egg and a hard shell. Turtles are endangered. They are precious. Likewise, the brain is covered by a hard shell (the skull) and floats in a gelatinous fluid. You wouldn't pick up a brain and toss it around.

And yet that's what we do when we play contact sports. These sports make us think we are invincible. No amount of padding or head protection can halt the movement of the brain in a skull because it is floating in liquid. It's not attached to the skull. When you stop abruptly by hitting the ground or hitting another player, the brain continues shaking while the rest of your body comes to a halt. The brain crashes into the inner surface of the skull. It's bruised. The brain then ricochets in the opposite direction like a cue ball on a pool table. It hits the opposite side of the skull and collects a second bruise. This continues until the motion comes to a stop slowly. Newton discussed this in his laws of physics. This is basically how concussions occur.

The brain is stunned from this event, so it needs to rest. Rarely do athletes suffering a concussion think they need to lie down and let their brain heal. Their first instinct is to head back into the game. Once a player has suffered a concussion, he or she is much more likely to suffer a second one within forty-eight hours. This concussion is more damaging. It's not 1 + 1 = 2; it's 1 + 1 = 3 (or more). Team trainers and doctors rarely describe the effects of concussions in terms that the players can understand. I do believe if the NFL players understood what happens on a physical level inside their skull, there would be fewer men racing back into the game after a strong hit to the head. The favorite phrase "I got my bell rung" to describe a football concussion doesn't do justice to the true damage. It makes light of the event. It makes the player look like a weakling to his teammates if he goes to the treatment tent to be examined. Although there are NFL spotters looking for possible concussed players on the field, most concussions go undetected unless a player self-reports, and players rarely feel it's in their best interest to take themselves out of a game. Some teammates are also reluctant to call attention to their concussed brethren because they might be seen as turncoats.

Although brain damage is immediate, the cumulative effects build over years until manifesting themselves as outward symptoms that are difficult to ignore, and difficult to reverse. The tremors and a shuffling gait combined with memory loss are usually the first signs to alert friends and family that something is not right with former players. Visits to the family doctor usually result in a recommendation that the player consult a neurologist. This might lead to a diagnosis, but the family needs insurance because the tests are numerous and expensive. Most neurologists are not quick to mention chronic traumatic encephalopathy even though it is usually the player's first fear. There are a number of conditions that mimic symptoms associated with CTE, and those must be ruled out before a more precise identification of CTE can be made. Once the player is diagnosed with symptoms consistent with CTE, the goal is to keep his brain intact as long as possible and to keep the player safe in his environment. Those players who are vested— usually with at least three seasons of service—can apply to the NFL's 88 Plan. After testing by NFL-designated doctors to ensure the player suffers from dementia, Alzheimer's, or ALS (or like symptoms), the player's family can choose to put the player in an assisted living facility. The league pays the fees directly to the facility. It is not a reimbursement program. However, should you wish to have in-home help instead, there is a reimbursement program through the 88 Plan that will pay for transportation, home health care, cooking, cleaning, and so on.

Not all players qualify for assisted living, nor do they want to live in a facility that doesn't allow freedom of movement. When Mike Webster suffered his fatal heart attack, he was living in his truck. He was incoherent and paranoid. He tried living with his adult son but couldn't take the stress. He was in constant pain and couldn't focus. There was nothing anyone could do to help ease his pain and confusion. Homelessness was his only recourse. He died at fifty, a sad irony for a player whose nickname was "Iron Mike" for his endurance and strength.

Apple Valley (California) still remembers their local legend, Chris Brymer, who was an offensive lineman on the local high school's team. He was huge and powerful. He anchored the team and protected the quarterback. He was the town's hero and the most popular football player to graduate from Apple Valley High School. USC recruited Chris as an offensive lineman, and he played his college years there. He was one of the strongest men on the team, and except for being academically ineligible one year and redshirting his freshman year, he was an important contributing member of the team.

After leaving California in 1999, Chris played for a German team in NFL Europe during their summer league. He returned at the end of the summer and was invited to summer camp with the Dallas Cowboys but never earned a spot on the roster. Before his career was over, he put in one year with the Los Angeles team of the XFL. In each location, Chris tried to impress his coaches with his strength and size. It wasn't enough, so he moved on with his postcareer plans.

Chris married his high school sweetheart, and shortly after they had a son. He started a mortgage loan company using the first letter of his name, his wife's name, and his son's name: CMG (Chris, Melissa, Grant). The business was a success. He purchased several homes and was riding high in the business world. Then his years of concussions began to affect his behavior. He became angry at his wife, he lost his patience, and he became destructive. His business failed as his paranoia grew. He accused Melissa of infidelity. Finally, she had enough and took their two-year-old son and moved out of the family home. She didn't want her son harmed or exposed to his dad's out-of-control behavior.

When Melissa left, Chris resorted to living on the streets and visiting the local soup kitchen. Occasionally, Chris would set up a tent across the street from his parents' home and live there for a bit. He never wanted to enter the home and never ate the food they offered him. Instead, he fished for food in the dumpster behind the tattoo shop in his neighborhood. Remembering that Chris Brymer was once a very successful businessman in a highly competitive business, it was difficult to reconcile his current state. Melissa knew it was the result of CTE. She had read everything she could on the topic and believed her former husband had all the classic signs. He was no longer well groomed but rather resembled a mountain man who didn't bathe or wash his clothes. He was attacked as he slept on the sidewalk. He arose and beat the attacker severely. It made the evening news and then people recognized it was former pro football player Chris Brymer. All signs point to Melissa being correct about Chris's diagnosis. However, nothing can be diagnosed definitively premortem. His friends from high school and business want to help Chris, but he rejects all offers and says he doesn't need anything.

THE STORY OF KENNY GRAHAM, BY MARK DOWNING

Where do I begin? I first met Kenny at the post office in downtown Bakersville, California, where we both have a P.O. box. I saw him intermittently for a couple of years but never really talked to him. He was always very cordial to me and acknowledged me with a "Hey, how are you doing?" every time I passed by him.

One day I noticed he had an awful lot of mail that he was going through, so I stopped and said, "Why do you have so much mail?" He replied without missing a beat, "I'm playing the sweepstakes. I'm trying to get some capital to build on my land which my father left me."

I said, "You have some land?"

"Yeah, I have three lots," he said.

"Do you have a house on those lots?"

"No," he said, "I live under the fig tree."

"Do you have any income?"

"Yes. I get $2,000 a month just for breathing."

"Why don't you rent an apartment?"

"Why should I rent an apartment when I can live free and clear on my land?"

"Because it's 100 degrees outside! Do you have running water? Do you have electricity?"

Kenny replied, "No."

I inquired further. "How are you doing this?"

"I'm roughing it."

"What did you do for a living?"

"I played pro ball. Look me up on the Google machine," he said.

And that's how our relationship started.

Well, sure enough, I found him on the internet, and I was quite impressed that he had been an All-Pro strong safety for the San Diego Chargers in the 1960s. It must have been meant for Kenny and me to cross paths that day because I have a web design business, I'm very active on Twitter and other social media platforms, and I am very comfortable advocating when I feel that somebody isn't being treated properly.

It was obvious Kenny was suffering from concussions because of his years playing in the sixties. I mean, if I had $2,000 a month coming in without any bills to pay, the first thing I would do is rent an apartment. Kenny likened living under the fig tree on his vacant lots to wearing twenty pounds of pads during spring training. Kenny didn't mind at all. Kenny related everything in his life to football. Football was his life! When I started talking football with him, he would light up like a sailor talking about his first time out on the high seas.

I'm a big sports fan, NBA basketball more than anything else, but as a kid my dad watched football every Sunday, so I knew the players from Kenny's era. This made for an interesting conversation, and I noticed it was very therapeutic for Kenny when we talked about his playing days.

When I hung around Kenny, it felt as if I was hanging around LeBron James at seventy-five years of age. His hands were big, and the tips were broken from tackling big running backs. Kenny was very intelligent about all the aspects of football, so it was fascinating having lunch with this living legend and talking football. The more I got to know Kenny and develop a friendship with him, the angrier I got at the NFL commissioner Roger Goodell and the NFL Players Association for ignoring my pleas for them to help Kenny, who was obviously suffering with short-term memory loss and the inability to process commonsense things such as renting an apartment. When I asked him, he said, "Why would I rent an apartment when I can live free and clear on my land? That is crazy!"

Because Kenny couldn't process things properly, it was very difficult to deal with him because I didn't understand the effects of concussions or CTE. After doing some research, I discovered when someone is suffering with symptoms associated with CTE and they cannot process something, it makes then very angry and agitated.

To make a long story short, Kenny's good friend, Howdy Miller, saw one of the articles on Kenny and began assisting me. Lois Henry, a newspaper reporter, and many other good Samaritans also got on Kenny's bandwagon.

After a series of very controversial tweets directed at the NFL, someone from the Players Care Foundation, which is affiliated with the NFL, contacted us. They offered to help Kenny with his medical issues and rented Kenny an extended-stay hotel room that very day. They were the only ones that seemed to care about Kenny and were instrumental in getting Kenny out from under the fig tree where he lived for almost two years.

The NFL, the NFL Players Association, and the Chargers did not so much as lift a finger or show any interest in Kenny's situation.

After taking Kenny to a series of appointments with brain specialists, the NFL Player Care Foundation helped him get approved for medical benefits and assisted living (through the 88 Plan) at the beautiful Brookdale retirement center in Bakersfield where Kenny is today.

After the NFL concussion settlement was finalized, I tried to help Kenny get a $300,000 settlement, but the settlement administrators made it very difficult and did not accept the diagnoses from the brain doctors we had already taken him to in Los Angeles, or the brain psychologist in Bakersville, where he had to take a six-hundred-question test that took over eight hours and two days to complete. It was obvious they were doing everything they could to make Kenny give up so they wouldn't have to pay the settlement.

At this point I gave up trying to help Kenny because I was exhausted after two years and had to get on with my life. Plus Kenny was loving the Brookdale retirement center with all of his meals provided and his own apartment. His former teammate, Lance Alworth, bought him a beautiful Rialto motor home. It was Kenny's lifelong dream to own one.

The Kerr Foundation also provided Kenny with a nurse and social worker to attend to his needs, take him to doctors' appointments, and help him with his favorite thing, going to the post office to get his mail to see if he won the sweepstakes so he could build on his land that his father left him.

Every now and again, I see Kenny either at Brookdale or with Howdy and Lois at Sandrini's restaurant, where we pick up where we left off about Kenny's situation. Kenny's situation brought us all together.

In closing, I must also mention the San Diego Chargers beat writer, the photographer who showed a great deal of interest in Kenny, and especially Bryce Miller, who writes for the *San Diego Union-Tribune*. They were instrumental in getting his story out, as well as the *Bakersfield Californian* newspaper, which printed around ten full-page articles, some of which were on the front page and written by the amazing Lois Henry.

A couple of things I want to add to round out Kenny's story. The motor home that Lance bought for him now sits under a tree on the Brookdale property outside of Kenny's window. When he was first given the vehicle, he didn't want anyone to see inside it. He covered all the windows in curtains, including the back windows. When he backed out of his parking area, he didn't see the tree behind him and rammed into it. Not knowing what was in his way he continued to hit the tree. Lacking sound judgment, spatial awareness, and a driver's license, it wasn't long before the van was permanently parked at Brookdale. To this day, Kenny yearns to return to his fig tree. It was his land willed from his father, the family homestead in reality. He fed five dogs that kept him company and trekked daily to the post office. He had a life that suited him.

* * *

Mark, Lois, and Howdy, through diligence and hard work and a passion to do right by Kenny Graham, have saved his life. They care for him as a family would. They respect him and often quote his philosophy. I've picked up a few of Kenny's sayings that I find particularly appropriate.

"If it's free, I always take two."

"I'm trying to solve my problems, but I want to solve them in the
order I want to solve them."

"Slow down; you're going to miss the stop signs."

"I've been around the block and in the alley too."

"Take me to the bank. I need some walking-around money."

The problem that his friends face is, are they cutting Kenny's wings for
him or for them? Yes, he likes the free food and the amenities, but he
misses driving his van to the beach and escaping to his fig tree for the
feel of his land. He wants to be the untethered man who makes the
decisions. His friends want him healthy and safe and well fed and cared
for. Do they feel guilty or rest easy? Hard to decide.

CTE AND THE LAW

Sports fans and doctors know of chronic traumatic encephalopathy as a
degenerative brain disease. But it has also entered the legal world, not
just as part of the NFL's concussion settlement but also as an argument
mounted by lawyers to defend their clients.

One example involves Kellen Winslow II, who followed his famous
father into the NFL after a successful college football career in Miami.
The Cleveland Browns drafted the tight end in the first round in 2004.
For his first season, he had to sit out with injuries sustained in the
second game of the season when he broke his fibula. He lost his incentives, which were built into his rookie contract.

He bought a motorcycle after signing his contract and obtaining his
signing bonus. In a parking lot with several friends in 2005, he decided
to ride the bike. He'd had no experience with large motorcycles and
taken no driving lessons. He jumped on the machine, revved it up, and
took off right over the street curb surrounding the parking lot. He fell
off the cycle, and it landed on his knee. He wasn't wearing a helmet
because he was only going on a short ride to test his new plaything.
Besides sustaining a serious knee injury, he sustained a head injury as
well. A prosecutor in the area charged him with disregarding safety. He
pleaded to failing to control his bike.

Kellen's rookie season was spent on the bench or in the locker room
rehabbing his broken leg, which required multiple surgeries. The following year he was on the Unable to Perform (Non-Football Injury) list.

This was not an auspicious start for a man chosen sixth overall in the NFL draft.

Kellen played in Cleveland through the 2008 season and then moved to the Tampa Bay Buccaneers through 2011. He spent 2012 with the New England Patriots and the following season with the New York Jets. While with the Jets, Coach Rex Ryan was complimentary of Winslow's play. However, he was suspended for four games for using performance-enhancing substances.

For three years, Winslow waited to be called by an NFL team. He kept in shape on the chance a team would need him. After waiting in vain, he scheduled a workout with the Green Bay Packers on August 8, 2016. After no one offered him a contract, Winslow participated in the Spring League in 2017.

His father tried to intervene several times to explain that every player must leave the league at some point. He knew his son was not physically fit enough to play in the NFL the last several years he played. He tried to get his son to psychologically accept his career was on the wane and that it would be better for him to stand aside. This caused a great divide between them.

Out of the league, Winslow's life spiraled downward. He was convicted of raping a homeless woman, exposing himself to a woman in the street, making sexual gestures with his exposed genitals to a seventy-seven-year-old woman at the gym. He pleaded guilty to sexually battering a hitchhiker in 2018 and raping an unconscious teen in 2003. In 2018, he was charged with felony first-degree burglary. Two weeks later (June 14, 2018) he was arrested on charges of kidnapping and rape.

Winslow II has been sentenced to fourteen years in prison as part of the plea agreement he made in November 2019. Because the courts were closed due to the COVID-19 virus, his hearing has been postponed. His family and attorneys are trying their hardest to have him serve only twelve years because they say he needs therapy more than imprisonment.

Winslow's legal history is hard to understand. His attorneys are defending his erratic behavior by saying he has CTE, a defense that has become popular recently even though the disease still cannot be diagnosed in the living. Any football player is assumed to have had many undiagnosed head injuries. According to this defense, these head injuries have caused brain dysfunction, and therefore, the perpetrator of the crime cannot be held guilty because he is suffering from brain injury. In other words, while he committed the crime, he was not in his right mind and therefore he should receive a lesser sentence. Winslow's attorneys said their client's brain damage began with the motorcycle accident and mounted with the hits he took on the field.

Kellen's attorneys are faced with defending his consistently bad behavior. His dad believes it stems from Kellen's disappointment and severe depression that resulted from not becoming an NFL icon. He wanted to challenge his dad, I'm sure, to be "the greatest Kellen Winslow in the NFL." The attorneys attribute his behavior to brain injuries on the football field and the motorcycle accident. You need to decide.

Then there is the notorious case of Aaron Hernandez, a star athlete on his high school football team who was so highly coveted that Urban Meyer, then the coach at the University of Florida, talked to Hernandez's high school in Bristol, Connecticut (home to ESPN's headquarters), and convinced them to let Aaron graduate a semester early. Meyer wanted to give Hernandez time to learn the offensive plays so that he'd be ready when the season began in August. Because Hernandez was a weak student, Meyer enrolled him at the Santa Fe Junior College in Gainesville, where a few other Florida football players were studying. Hernandez took courses such as personal gardening and bowling. When he took an academic course such as statistics, he couldn't finish it. The material was too difficult. Never mind. Hernandez was never valued as a student. He was a football player.

Unfortunately, his appetite for marijuana followed him to Gainesville. He made it known that every time he took the field, he was high. Occasionally, he'd be drug tested and then suspended for a few games. Tim Tebow, his straight-laced quarterback, tried to mentor him, but it was really no use. After three years of playing for the Gators, Aaron was told by Coach Meyer that he'd better declare for the NFL draft because he wasn't wanted back on the Gator team.

At age twenty, he was the youngest player to be drafted in 2010. He would have been picked in a higher round, but his marijuana use was well known and he was considered immature. Finally, the New England Patriots—Hernandez's "hometown" team—took a chance on him but structured his contract with a low signing bonus and lots of incentives. They thought they could control his behavior by having him strive to behave and do well on the field. Tebow called his friend, Patriots quarterback Tom Brady, and asked him to look out for Aaron. He needed a good mentor. Fairly quickly, Hernandez distinguished himself as a tight end alongside Rob Gronkowski, the team's other young, talented tight end. They were a powerful duo that hoovered up Brady's passes. Hernandez started in Super Bowl XLVI and caught eight passes for sixty-seven yards, including a twelve-yard touchdown.

In August 2012, the Patriots offered Hernandez a five-year, $40 million contract extension. Even with the generous salary that showed that the team appreciated his hard work, Hernandez was an immature force in the locker room. He worked harder than most team members but was a distraction. He wasn't liked and he seemed a bit crazy. He was actually running a secret second life, one filled with weapons, criminals from his hometown in Connecticut, and drug dealing. He was using drugs recreationally as well. That is what contributed to his behavioral issues that the team members couldn't understand. He brought two childhood friends to Boston to be his assistants. One was to procure drugs; the other, weapons. He rented a second, secret home to store his cache.

Aaron lived with his fiancée and daughter in an upscale neighborhood. His high school sweetheart had been through the ups and downs with Aaron and had come to accept what piece of his life she could occupy. She knew about his other female companions and drug dealing and drug usage to some extent. She chose to accept him as he was.

But this antisocial behavior was consistent throughout Aaron's tumultuous life. His parents were always disruptive and fighting in the home. His father would leave and then return. He was known to be violent and hit Aaron and his brother for no reason. The boys were afraid of him but also respected him as a tough-man role model. His dad didn't care about school grades but cared about athletic ability. So his sons were multisport athletes. Like most children from violent homes, Aaron re-created that violence in whatever environment he lived.

In the summer of 2013, a year after signing his contract extension, Hernandez became increasingly paranoid and was convinced someone was trying to kill him. He even went so far as to ask to be traded from the New England Patriots to a West Coast team. The Patriots said they would not release him under such circumstances. Fearing for his family's safety, he installed an elaborate security system in his home. Additionally, he purchased a retrofitted armored car with compartments for weapons. According to teammates, his mood would swing wildly from child to tough guy. He only traveled in vehicles with tinted windows so no one could recognize him when he drove by. He was immersed in a world of constant marijuana usage and cocaine.

His behavior was building to a crash. It was the only way it could go at this point. Aaron wouldn't let anyone help him. Then it happened: he was charged with first-degree murder. The Patriots immediately released him from the team. Two months later, a grand jury indicted him for the murder of Odin Lloyd. He pleaded not guilty in September 2013. On April 15, 2015, he was found guilty of first-degree murder.

Not surprisingly, the National Football League, which is quick to celebrate athletes on the field, erased Aaron Hernandez immediately. All merchandise bearing his name was confiscated; all photos and mentions of him at the Patriots and NFL offices were eliminated. The University of Florida did the same. *Madden NFL 25* and *NCAA Football 14* video games erased all signs of Hernandez. Even Pop Warner removed all references to Aaron's records. One would never know Aaron Hernandez existed as a football player. Never mind that football is a violent sport and players before and in the years to come will be accused of violence and crimes. The league believes it's imperative to keep the sport's image clean.

Facing life in prison, Aaron Hernandez hung himself with a bed sheet in his cell on April 2017. During the four years he was imprisoned, he was belligerent and obnoxious. He was put in a special section for men who acted out and needed extra supervision. In other words, even though he was in a different environment, his behavioral patterns remained the same. He suffered from migraines and a poor memory that were inconsistent with a young man of twenty-seven.

After his death, his family donated his brain to scientists at Boston University, who have the largest brain bank in the country and are the leading researchers into CTE. In September 2017, the scientists, led by neuropathologist Dr. Ann McKee, came back with their shocking verdict: Hernandez had such a severe form of the brain disease that the damage was similar to that found in players in their sixties.

In a diagnosis that linked one of football's most notorious figures with the sport's most significant health risk, doctors found Hernandez had Stage 3 CTE, which researchers had never seen in a brain younger than 46 years old, McKee said. The extent of that damage represents another signpost in football's ongoing concussion crisis, which has professional players weigh early retirements and parents grapple with whether or not to allow their young sons to take up the sport.[1]

Although the brain had been clearly destroyed by injuries, we have to wonder if we can blame Hernandez's behavior on CTE, or whether perhaps the events of his childhood were partly to blame. He was reared in a violent environment lacking the security children need to gain confidence and succeed. He began to smoke weed at a young age, which is known to stunt maturity. He was pushed through high school to college before he was socially mature enough to enter a university and complete courses successfully. No coach took responsibility for his education. He was used throughout high school and college as a great addition to the football team but not as a young boy needing guidance and role models.

I believe during the years he played football in college and the pros, he took many hits to the head. I doubt he reported any of them to his trainers. He kept playing because that's what he was supposed to do. That's when the tau protein, which is the signature of CTE, began to weave tangles in his brain and his brain began to shrink. By this point, he really could not tell right from wrong. He had huge memory losses, migraines, and paranoia. He thought people were out to kill him. Paranoid delusions are one of the many signs of CTE. By this point, Hernandez had no functioning ability to assess situations and make decisions. He was reacting rather than acting with thoughtfulness. At some point, the drug-induced paranoia was taken over by the CTE-induced paranoia to make a mush of Aaron's brain. He would never have gotten better. He was going to deteriorate more month by month. There is no drug to reverse this brain damage.

CTE SUICIDES

As of June 2018, there were forty-four documented instances of players in the NFL who had committed suicide. I'm sure there are more by now, but that is the latest official number. It's not a census the NFL wishes to be made public. The men reached the point where they could no longer stand to be less than the men that they once were, and they rarely remember who they were in the worst of cases.

On December 1, 2012, a linebacker on the Kansas City Chiefs, Jovan Belcher, created a media blitz by killing his fiancée, with whom he had an infant, and then driving to the Chiefs training facility, where he shot himself in the head. Although he was an undrafted free agent, he saw a lot of action playing for the Chiefs and was re-signed by Kansas City before the 2012 season. The sensationalism of this story was that the suicide took place not in private but in the parking lot adjacent to the training facility in front of team officials. When Jovan arrived, he ran into the general manager of the team and confessed that he'd just murdered his girlfriend. The head coach and linebackers coach then arrived and tried to talk Jovan into giving up his weapon. When he heard the police sirens and realized they were soon to be there, he made the sign of the cross while kneeling and shot himself in the head in front of the staff.

An autopsy later revealed that Belcher, twenty-five, had a blood-alcohol level more than twice the legal limit when he shot his girlfriend nine times. The police had found Belcher sleeping in his car with the motor running several hours before the murder-suicide but let him go.

One year later, in December 2013, Belcher's mother insisted on exhuming his body. She wanted his brain tested for chronic traumatic encephalopathy. While awaiting the results, she filed a wrongful death lawsuit in Missouri state court against the Kansas City Chiefs. In the suit, she said the Chiefs should have been aware of the changes in Jovan: his speed, his cognition, and all the other symptoms associated with CTE. Continuing to play made his physical and mental situation worse, she claimed.

By the end of September 2014, the medical examiner who did an autopsy of Jovan Belcher's brain determined that he in fact suffered from CTE. His illogical and out-of-control behavior was a result of brain injuries suffered on the field of play, it was presumed.

Perhaps the most notorious and saddest case of a player with CTE was Junior Seau, who was one of the league's most dominant players from his rookie season in 1990 with the San Diego Chargers until his retirement from the New England Patriots in 2009. He was a Pro-Bowler twelve years running and the NFL Man of the Year in 1994. He easily made the One Hundredth Anniversary All-Time Team. Junior was a linebacker who set the standard for what a linebacker should be in the NFL. The Chargers retired his number and inducted him into the team's Hall of Fame. Hailing from Oceanside, California, just up Interstate 5 from San Diego, Seau was a hometown hero who was friendly, visible, and giving, even after he left the Chargers in 2003 to finish his Hall of Fame career in Miami and then New England.

Following his football career, he started a successful clothing line and ran a popular restaurant. Junior was active in the Samoan community in Southern California and created a foundation to help abused and neglected children. On the surface, Seau was the perfectly adjusted retired NFL player, with money in his pocket, a pillar in the community, and three young kids. He set the example everyone pointed to as the man who knew how to make the adjustment to life after football.

But beneath the surface, his mind was slipping away. He was too generous with customers at his restaurant, and the business began to falter. His memory was erratic. He would call his ex-wife and ask for directions. He would miss appointments or turn moody, which was surprising given his upbeat attitude. In 2010, Seau drove his SUV off a cliff in Carlsbad, California. He said he had fallen asleep. He had also been arrested on suspicion of domestic violence involving his girlfriend. His depression deepened.

"He said, 'I had no idea how many hours are in a day, the days are so long,'" Gina Seau, Junior's ex-wife, told the *New York Times*. "That was a completely obvious statement of a man who was scared. He had so many opportunities, and he couldn't get there. He was stuck in a bubble."[2]

And then that bubble burst. On May 2, 2012, Junior Seau was found by his girlfriend in their home with a bullet in his chest. There was no note, but he presumably chose to shoot himself in the chest and not the head so that his brain could be preserved for science. There was a frenzy of doctors trying to reach the Seau family to win the right to do the autopsy. His family ultimately chose doctors at the National Institutes of Health to examine his brain. Seven months later, in January 2013, the family made the results of the autopsy known. Seau's brain looked just like those brains that have experienced repetitive head injuries. In other words, he tested positive for chronic traumatic encephalopathy. His family filed a wrongful-death suit against the NFL because of Junior's injuries. After years in limbo, the family ultimately settled the case with the NFL in 2018.

Seau was not the first player to plan to leave his brain to science. In early 2011, Alice Duerson, the ex-wife of Dave Duerson, received a startling text from her former husband. The former star defensive back on the Chicago Bears wanted her to donate his brain for research. Panicked, she called her children to alert them to call their dad. She continued to text and call. The man who was selected to four Pro Bowls, played on two Super Bowl championship teams, and received the Man of the Year Award in 1987 was dead.

As he requested, his family sent his brain to Boston University School of Medicine, where scientists have diagnosed the most cases of CTE. Duerson had carefully fired the weapon into his chest so as not to disturb his brain. He wanted people to know what he suspected: that he had chronic traumatic encephalopathy. Duerson was looking for a reason his life had fallen apart in every domain. Once a successful franchise owner of three McDonald's restaurants, he had purchased the controlling interest in a sausage company. He sold it a few years later and formed Duerson Foods, which before long was forced into bankruptcy. All of his businesses ultimately ended up in an auction. He couldn't seem to make a wise financial decision. Everything was falling apart around him. But he had more than an inkling why. Duerson had once sat on the benefits committee that approved or declined disability payments to ex-players with physical and cognitive problems. He read hundreds of reports. At some point, he must have turned inward and seen himself in these reports.

Boston University neurologists confirmed what Duerson believed to be true: he had CTE. He wasn't there to hear the diagnosis, but he knew before he pulled the trigger what the results would show. Now his family and friends also knew why he acted so strangely and lost his financial acuity.

CTE PATHOLOGY

For all the research done on CTE, scientists continue to work in their laboratories trying to understand the exact physical mechanisms that cause the brain to malfunction because of the disease. Millions of dollars are now distributed annually to institutions such as the National Institutes of Health, Harvard, and the University of North Carolina at Chapel Hill. The NFL has pledged millions along with government entities to help crack the code on this devastating situation occurring in the brains of our top athletes and increasingly in soldiers.

CTE itself is not new. The original diagnosis was called "dementia pugilistica" and found in boxers in the 1920s. The name stuck and was widely referred to as "punch drunk syndrome." As a child, my father, who boxed on his college's team, would have me listen to the weekly fights on the radio with him. Then he'd explain to me what was happening. We followed boxing together for years, and during that time many of the athletes began showing the symptoms associated with dementia pugilistica. Even as a teenager, it was easy for me to see the deterioration evident in these men. When Muhammad Ali started showing signs of verbal slurring and a shuffling gait, I wasn't surprised. I was sad, but this man had faced many opponents and never backed down from a tough fight. In 1984, he was diagnosed with Parkinson's disease, which, not coincidentally, many NFL football players get as well. It is believed to be related to repeated brain injuries in violent sports such as football, rugby, and boxing.

It is only recently that I quit following boxing. It seems that ultimate fighting has overtaken boxing in terms of popularity. I liked the rules and regulations of boxing. I liked the quickness and athleticism of the boxers. I used to travel to Las Vegas and New York specifically to watch certain matches. It was a sport, not a free-for-all. During my many years of following boxing, I could see the decline in some of the boxers. Like football players, some remained mentally intact while others did not. That's the medical conundrum to this day. What separates the two groups?

The symptoms of CTE begin with headaches and memory loss. They progress to migraine headaches and difficulty planning and completing tasks. Impulsive behavior and depression, or just not caring about anything, often follow. The next steps may be substance abuse, suicidal thoughts, and emotional instability. The worst of it is that there is no treatment. The symptoms creep into daily life stealthily. Years pass before stage 4, the most full-blown version of CTE, is reached.

At the time athletes injure their brains, their bodies don't recognize any significant change. A number of years later—and the time varies for everyone—small changes begin to take place. In the brain, big changes are taking place; tau protein tangles are building, the brain is shrinking in size, and it is aging rapidly. By that I mean, if you slice a mushroom and leave it overnight on a paper towel, the next morning it is wrinkled on the outside and has turned brown. It is shriveling from lack of moisture. That is what a brain with CTE looks like under the microscope. The small, natural empty spaces are larger and tinged brown. With all of this going on simultaneously, the victim has no control over his disease. He knows it will only get worse every day. Walking and thinking and speaking will become more difficult. Out-of-control emotional outbursts will terrify his family and friends. Fairly soon he'll be socially isolated. Maybe he'll find solace in alcohol, drugs, or both. He can only guess he has CTE because no doctor can diagnose him definitively until he dies. And that brings up suicide and why so many former players have turned in that direction for peace.

BENNET OMALU

Bennet Omalu, the man who connected CTE and the NFL, was a changed man. He was initially disappointed that the league did not recognize his accomplishments in discovering CTE in football players. He thought his research would help change the game and make it safer. He thought the NFL would be happy to have his findings and hear his ideas. Not only was his research ignored, but also the NFL brain committee attacked his writings and substituted their own that claimed that football players suffered no damage to the brain. One report even claimed that players were actually immune to concussions because they had absorbed so many hits throughout their lives.

Realizing his findings were not reaching the audience he had hoped, Omalu left the autopsy room and began giving paid speeches worldwide. He wanted everyone to know what he had found.

"Omalu portrays CTE as an epidemic and himself as a crusader, fighting against not just the NFL but also the medical science community, which he claims is too corrupted to acknowledge clear-cut evidence that contact sports destroy lives," Will Hobson of the *Washington Post* wrote in 2020.

As time has passed and Omalu has traveled the world, his message has mutated. Instead of being a voice of reason, he's become a frightening profit of doom. There is no scientific evidence to back up his current claims of the percentages of athletes who will be affected by CTE. Researchers are trying to answer these questions, but as of yet, there are no definite answers. Omalu believes children who play football and other contact sports will develop hyperactivity and attention deficit disorder as well as delinquency, though there is no research that even hints at that fact.

"Billing himself as the man who discovered CTE, Omalu has built a lucrative business as an expert witness for hire in lawsuits, charging a minimum of $10,000 per case. He also maintains a busy schedule of speaking engagements charging $27,500 per appearance," Hobson wrote.

Although Omalu bills himself as the man who discovered CTE, in the 1920s it was discussed in boxing circles openly. Twenty years later, the term chronic traumatic encephalopathy was in wide use, coined by Dr. Critchley of Britain. Omalu did not autopsy Mike Webster, the NFL player, until 2005. The term *chronic traumatic encephalopathy* preceded him by decades. Periodically, Omalu will admit he was not the first to name this brain disease, but he usually sticks with the fallacy that he was the first to identify it. "Some people who give me credit of discovering CTE, that is not true, really," he said. Later, Omalu said he had only "been successful in rebranding this disease concept." Omalu was an expert witness in a lawsuit in federal court against Pop Warner, the youth football league. He stated that playing this contact sport would lead to increased risk of mental problems, drug abuse, and death before age forty-two. This was filed officially in February 2018. After a year of consideration, the judge decided Omalu's testimony was "unreliable." Acting as an expert witness in another case against Ford Motor Company (an area in which he had no expertise), he claimed that "100 percent of NFL players have CTE and suggested parents who let their children play football or soccer are committing child abuse."

Omalu's grandstanding has muddied the waters in an already-contentious debate. Naysayers have started to deny CTE is a distinct diagnosis, and called into question any and all links with repeated head trauma. Omalu's strident advocacy has been matched by a growing list of "CTE deniers," some of whom are, not surprisingly, team doctors, advisors to sports leagues, and paid consultants to contact sports organizations.

Meanwhile, the scientific community continues its work in labs across the country, trying to find the hard data that will turn back the tau protein from creating havoc in the brains of athletes who play contact sports. Parents need reliable data to make the difficult choices of when and at what levels to allow their children to participate in sports. We trust our medical people to help us make the correct decisions.

Hugh Culverhouse. The founding owner of the Tampa Bay Buccaneers, Culverhouse convinced his daughter, Gay, to work at the club, where she eventually became president and one of the highest-ranking women executives in the NFL.

Coach John McKay. The original coach of the Buccaneers, McKay's intelligence and humor diffused the many years of losing and endeared him to fans during the team's three surprising playoff runs.

Jerry Eckwood. Beset by health problems in retirement, Eckwood disappeared from view until Culverhouse tracked him down and helped him apply for benefits. He was approved for the NFL's 88 Plan, which includes money for assisted living.

Gary Anderson. Culverhouse pulled Anderson out of a preseason game after his infant baby died while he was on the field. Culverhouse and "Mama Buc," who helped players and their families, met Anderson's wife at the hospital until Gary could get there. "Twenty minutes previously, he'd been running down a football field. Now he was saying goodbye to his daughter at the hospital."

Randy Grimes. A stalwart on the Buccaneers in the 1980s, he endured brutal practices and a lot of losing. To cope, he gobbled fistfuls of painkillers. When he was cut, Grimes was left with a raging addiction and struggled to find work. It would be more than a decade before he became sober. Now he helps other athletes battle addiction. "Instead of bright lights and adoring fans, I'm getting white lung and being bossed around by idiots who barely have a GED," Grimes wrote about his frustration keeping jobs. "I had one comfort during this dark time: My pills."

Tom McHale. A longtime linemen with the Buccaneers and friend of Randy Grimes, McHale seemed to have it all in retirement: A loving family, his health, and a string of Irish pubs, where he was a jovial presence. But over time, the thousands of hits to his head playing football seemed to alter his behavior. He became angry, irrational, and irritable. After he died of an accidental overdose in 2008 at forty-five, neuropathologists found that he had an advanced form of chronic traumatic encephalopathy, the degenerative brain disease linked to repeated head trauma.

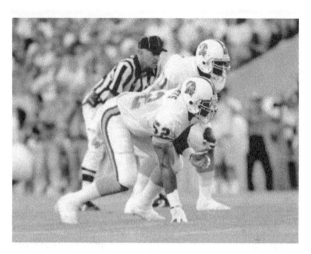

Keith McCants. A first-round pick from Alabama in 1990, McCants arrived in Tampa with injuries that would hamper his performance on the field and lead him to seek out drugs to overcome the pain. When he left the league after six seasons, he turned to harder drugs, lived on the streets, was arrested many times, and went in and out of rehab centers. The millions of dollars he made long gone, McCants has become a cautionary tale about players unprepared for the bright lights of the NFL.

David Lewis. A fan favorite during his five years in Tampa, the California-born linebacker battled a raft of health problems in retirement, including obesity and dementia. He died in 2020 at sixty-five.

Derrick Brooks. If there was ever a player to do it the "right" way, it's Brooks. He spent his entire fourteen-year career with the Buccaneers, a gifted leader on and off the field. He helped Tampa win its first Super Bowl title and was inducted in the Pro Football Hall of Fame in 2014. Since leaving the NFL, he has become a businessman and civic leader in Tampa.

Warren Sapp. Drafted in the first round in 1995 along with Derrick Brooks, Sapp was both brilliant and reckless on the field, winning accolades for his defensive prowess and infuriating opponents with his taunts. He could be charming, vexing, and confusing. He made and lost millions of dollars, getting in and out of trouble. He has since worked with the Concussion Legacy Foundation to help encourage players to consider donating their brains to further scientific research.

Warrick Dunn. A first round pick in 1997, Dunn spent the first five years and the last year of his twelve-year career in Tampa. He was as well known for his philanthropy as for his ability to run the ball. His rookie year, he started a charity, Home for the Holidays, and worked to help single-parent families pay their mortgages and furnish their homes. He dedicated his work to his mother, who yearned for a home for her six children. When she was murdered in a robbery, Dunn became the head of the household at eighteen. His philanthropy continues to this day.

8

DRUG ADDICTIONS

Josh Gordon was the quintessential child from the poor side of town who did drugs to escape from reality. Growing up in Texas, he also did drugs to survive in his neighborhood in Houston and fit in with social groups. Because he was physically talented, the supervisors in his life—teachers and coaches—covered for his foibles and failed to hold him accountable. In fact, they went so far as to enable him by allowing him to evade the consequences of his actions. I believe the adults in his environment wanted him to become a star athlete so he could escape the neighborhood. Given as much help as possible, given more chances than he deserved, he became a professional player and a Pro Bowl caliber star, earning millions of dollars. Yet he continued to do drugs and went to rehab repeatedly. Nothing changed. He was essentially still a seventh grader who was afraid. In his mind and heart, Josh never left the neighborhood.

"I've been enabled most of my life, honestly," Gordon told Uninterrupted in 2017. "I've been enabled by coaches, teachers, professors—everybody pretty much gave me second chances just because of my ability."

Gordon said he started abusing drugs in middle school. Here's what he told GQ magazine:

> Initially it started for me [because of] a lot of childhood and adolescent trauma-based fear. I was using in my childhood. That environment brought me into that a lot sooner than a normal—whatever normal is—kid should be brought into that, to be able to make a

decision on their own of what to do. I didn't want to feel anxiety, I didn't want to feel fear. I didn't plan on living to 18. Day-to-day life, what's gonna happen next? So you self-medicate with Xanax, with marijuana, codeine—to help those nerves so you can just function every day. That became the norm from middle school to high school. So by the time I got into my 20's, I was on an accelerated pace.

This pattern continued after he left Houston to attend Baylor University in Waco, Texas.

Not too long after I got arrested for possession of marijuana at Baylor, one of my coaches came by saying "you are going to get drug tested by the compliance office. This is how it's going to work, this is what they are going to do. If they call you in, here goes the bottles of detox." He showed me how to drink them, showed me how to take them. That was my first real experience with getting over the system and that authority not really being taken seriously because it was kind of being guided by someone that's employed by the same university.[1]

Despite the lessons in how to evade drug tests, Gordon was suspended from the team in 2010 because he and a teammate were passed out in the drive-through lane of a Taco Bell. However, he was reinstated before the end of the season. He failed a drug test for marijuana in the summer of 2011 and was suspended indefinitely by head coach Art Briles. A month later, he transferred to the University of Utah. However, once again he failed drug tests and did not play football in Utah.

The following year, in 2012, he was drafted by the Cleveland Browns in the second round of the supplemental draft. After a solid rookie season, Gordon was suspended for the first two games of the 2013 season for violating the league's substance abuse policy. Still, he ended up having his best season as a pro, with 1,646 receiving yards, good enough to be voted to the Pro Bowl and first team All-Pro.

In 2014, in a cruel twist, Gordon's roommate at the Browns was Johnny Manziel, the troubled quarterback out of Texas A&M who ended up bouncing out of the NFL because of his own substance abuse problems.

Gordon was then arrested for impaired driving. He was again suspended by the league but entered the NFL's substance abuse program. However, he violated the substance abuse policy and was suspended for the 2015 season. In 2016, he made another attempt at dealing with his drug problems by entering a rehabilitation center. He missed the 2016 season. In 2017, he played a few games for the Browns and in 2018 he signed with the Patriots. He injured his knee in the sixth game of the 2019 season and was placed on waivers, where he was claimed by the Seattle Seahawks. In December 2019, he was suspended again by the NFL, his eighth suspension, for failing a test for performance-enhancing drugs as well as abusing recreational drugs. According to NFL Network, Gordon relapsed in November 2019 after his brother passed away.

Some players never do drugs before they enter the NFL but pick up the habit while they are in the league. That's what happened to another Baylor football player, Randy Grimes, whose route to addiction started not with recreational drugs but with the painkillers that the trainers and team doctor readily prescribed to keep him on the field.

Grimes was drafted in the second round out of Baylor by the Tampa Bay Buccaneers in 1983. He remained with the team his entire career, which ended after ten years when he was unceremoniously released by his coach, Sam Wyche, with a simple but stinging sentence: "We won't need your services next year." Stunned, Randy cleaned out his locker and headed for his truck. Addicted to prescription drugs and alcohol to cope with his pain and anxiety, and having not finished his college degree, Randy was at a loss how to support his wife Lydia and two children. Like many other former players in similar straits, his life descended into a hellish pit of addiction that transformed a Christian boy raised in a small town in the heart of Texas.

Grimes played center, which means he was large. He had a baby face, however, that endeared him to everyone. He was uber polite like many Texas cowpokes and had a twang to his voice that melted hearts. When he arrived as a rookie fresh from a drive from Baylor, he brought his yellow rose of Texas, Lydia. Tall with blond hair curling down her back and a smile that stretched across her face, she and Randy were the rookie class king and queen. Lydia was the daughter of a Baptist preacher and the sweetest, most caring woman you'd ever meet. I and others at the Buccaneers knew in an instant this couple had everything they needed for a successful career.

Still, Randy, like a lot of rookies, was insecure initially, wondering if he could make it in the NFL. He had bouts of anxiety before he took the field. Slowly, he realized he could play in the league and not embarrass himself. For ten years Randy threw his body into the game. He practiced nearly every day during the week and competed on Sundays sixteen weeks a year. The other months he conditioned his body with weight training. He was a warrior. He needed to stay fit. However, he'd played football since childhood and his body was beginning to prove he wasn't invincible. Aches, bruises, and muscle tears built up. His pain was affecting him. He was anxious. He was scared.

"Ironically, prescription drugs were never mentioned as a problem," Grimes wrote in an unpublished manuscript. "But they were offered as a solution. After home games, trainers would stand at the locker room door with a cart and hand us a bag with two beers and two pills for pain as we walked out. I never took the beers. Lydia was always outside waiting for me, so I just took the pills. We never had a beer in the house, and I wasn't about to disappoint her."

> But after away games, I didn't have to worry about carrying beer out to the car or having Lydia smell it on my breath. There would be plenty of time to drink and medicate on the plane. After away games, the bus would drive to the airport and head straight onto the runway where we would board. We didn't have designated seats, but we learned where we could play dominos together, where the quarterback sat, where the linemen grouped. The coaches always sat up-front, so we left those seats open.
>
> As soon as we plopped our big, beat up bodies in those plane seats, prescription meds and beer flowed. The crew pushed a cart down the aisle loaded with beers. Following the crew, our trainer walked the aisle with a little bottle of pills, pouring them freely into our eager, beat-up hands.[2]

Though he did not know it, this was the start to Grimes's drug addiction, and it started at the hands of the football trainer himself. The trainer is supposed to watch for addictions or aberrant behavior in the locker room. In order to score more drugs, Randy asked his seatmates for their pills. Then he asked more and more players for their pills. He stored them up and began taking them at home. He had to find more as his body was adjusting to the first batches and he required more pills to achieve the same effects. It was known in the locker room that the combination to the safe where the drugs were stored was the jersey numbers of three players. Everyone knew the combination and used the drugs in the safe as their personal medicine cabinet. Randy didn't want to be known as someone who took drugs from the safe, so he asked more teammates for the prescription meds passed out on the team charters. But then his career came to a halt, and Grimes had to find new work.

> While I didn't have a firm plan of what to do after leaving football, for years I'd talked to my agent about joining him after I left the game. Even though we never really ironed out the details, I knew that he lived in a nice place in Chicago and was still connected to sports. Becoming an agent became my new dream. However, when my football career ended, I quit hearing from my agent. That hurt a lot. First, I thought we were pretty close. He'd spent so much time with me and he was someone I could call at any time. Second, I'd been building a backup plan based on working with him. Now I'd have no one showing me the ropes. [3]

Randy tried to build his own a stable of clients. He visited Baylor and a few other colleges. He met many athletes but didn't understand how to turn them into clients. Without a mentor, he was lost. It quickly became apparent to him that he no longer had the income he previously did for ten years. There was no money coming in; there was a new home in Houston and a family that had basic needs. Randy needed to find a job. However, after the glamour of an NFL career, after being Tampa Bay Buccaneers Man of the Year, and after being featured in commercials and eating for free at restaurants, how was he going to settle for selling cement in Texas?

But Randy had no other options. Lydia's brother worked at a concrete business and put in a good word with the owner. Soon Randy was selling the product for $38,000 a year and feeling humiliated that his life had come to this point.

> For three years, I sold concrete. To say that my heart wasn't in it would be a profound understatement. Bitterness ate at me. I'd be on a job and tell myself, "You've got to be kidding me. This is what the rest of my life looks like? Instead of bright lights and adoring fans, I'm getting white lung and being bossed around by idiots who barely have a GED." I had one comfort during this dark time: My pills. I took opiates whenever I could get them, but benzos were still my

staple. . . . Before Christmas I snorted cocaine and stayed up all night decorating.

Randy found a drug dealer in his affluent Houston neighborhood and took full of advantage of his take-it-now, pay-later approach to dealing. Within a few years, Randy was out of work and had lost his truck and his house due to nonpayment. His wife was working as a teacher, holding the children together and living with her parents. She had witnessed Randy's near death from an overdose. She'd suffered through failed drug treatments and had lost her jewelry and valuables, which Randy sold at pawn shops. Randy stole from her to feed his addiction. He even took his son's hunting rifle to the pawn shop in order to get another handful of pills. He missed the major events in his children's lives lying in a stupor in either his truck or a motel.

Lydia's prayers for Randy's turnaround were answered in a strange and somber way. Tom McHale, who played on the Bucs offensive line with Randy, was found dead of an overdose in 2008. Tom was a graduate of Cornell and had opened several pubs and restaurants after his career. He was a popular Buc with a ready smile and twinkling Irish eyes. Tom was married to Lisa, and they had three young boys. He looked to have made the transition to regular life successfully after playing football. However, looks can be deceiving. Behind the smile, Tom was suffering increasingly from headaches, depression, anxiety, and anger. He could no longer live at home because he was afraid he might harm his wife or children. He got an apartment with a roommate and descended into a hell of drug addiction and delusions.

Tom's brain was donated to doctors at Boston University's neuropathology laboratory, and his autopsy showed startling results. His brain was riddled with the tau protein that signaled he had the degenerative brain disease chronic traumatic encephalopathy. Tom could not help his behavior. It was linked to the violence he suffered on the football field during games and practices. This is the dark cloud that hovers above all players. Will I succumb to CTE?

Randy was shocked that his friend and pill-sharing buddy was dead. He realized that if Tom overdosed, he could easily be next. This time, he got serious about treatment. It was what he wanted, so now it would work. A group of doctors in a rehab group in New Jersey got him the addiction treatment he needed. It was a long and gruesome road to recovery.

Randy now works in recovery for several organizations and started Athletes in Recovery. Lydia is a certified family addiction coach.

Josh Gordon and Randy Grimes played football at Baylor University, where the mission of the educational program is to inculcate Christian commitment into leadership and service within the academic environment and beyond. I'm sure their parents and coaches thought this university would be a good environment for them as student-athletes. However, it begs the question that regardless of the philosophy of the institution, students are not protected from the allure of drugs. And neither Gordon nor Grimes graduated.

The path to opioids often begins in the locker room. The football culture, like the culture across our country, is to find quick, easy solutions. The pharmaceutical industry spends tens of billions of dollars a year trying to deliver pills that offer quick, easy solutions, and allow Americans to defer tackling the hard work needed to address the underlying conditions that ail them. So when players are in pain—just like factory workers injured on the job—they become dependent on swallowing a pill to make their pain disappear and allow them to get on with their lives. In the NFL, where players live week to week and in perpetual fear of getting cut, it takes too much energy and time to massage and stretch out the body of a player in pain. It's easier to hand him a pill. The pain will disappear, but the reason for the pain will remain. There's a game just days away. No time to waste.

Back in the day, in the Buccaneers locker room, there was a bowl filled with Tylenol and Aleve. If that didn't solve your problem, the drug locker combination was known by all players. There was no shame in raiding the locked box. Drugs were the answer. No one wanted to have surgery or miss games due to rehabilitation, so it was patch and play. If a player missed a game, the backup player may have a great day at his position, and suddenly that injured player would become a second stringer in the following game. Players have to cover their pain at all times, just like in the animal kingdom, where animals know that the weakest in the herd will get picked off and die. Men aren't thinking about the wear and tear on their body, and what would be the best thing physically to do. No. They are worried about keeping their position and getting a paycheck. If opioids get them through, who cares about the ultimate addiction or dependence on drugs? They can worry about that in retirement, assuming they recognize it as a problem at the time.

Studies conducted on retired players' opioid use are faulty because players disappear after playing in the NFL, making it hard to get a representative sample size. The most famous players who had careers in excess of ten years are an exception. They are featured in advertising campaigns and can be found in broadcast booths. The vast majority of players who were in the NFL, though, played for an average of four years and are basically unknown once they leave the league. Perhaps he was a lineman and continued to gain weight after his playing days. That additional weight compromised his already-injured hips and knees. He's in constant pain but doesn't have access to the team's drug locker anymore. So, as Grimes did, he starts to visit doctors who, no surprise, prescribe normal doses of painkillers. It isn't hard for former players to convince these doctors to write prescriptions. All they need to do is show the doctor x-rays and medical records from their days in the NFL to illustrate how much damage has been done to their bodies.

But the player usually isn't forthcoming about the amounts of opioids he's used to taking, which are more than a normal, healthy person would need. So after he gets his prescription of drugs, he takes a handful instead of one every twelve hours. He then has to visit another doctor and another doctor to get enough pills to keep up with his addiction. Finally, having exhausted all legal means of obtaining the opioids he needs, he turns to the street dealers. And like most addicts, the pain is beside the point. They need to keep taking pills so they don't have withdrawal symptoms, which are horrific and debilitating, sometimes more than the pain from the injuries.

No player wants anyone to know he's addicted and roaming the streets trying to buy his drugs for pain. Researchers don't know where to look for these players, and no one is going to admit to this behavior even if they are identified. When I read statistics that 26 percent of retired players are addicted to opioids, I wonder where the researchers found those men and what questions they asked. Once a player is in recovery, I can understand him admitting that he was addicted. But rarely will someone—especially an NFL player—say they are currently addicted. Retired players still have immense amounts of pride that they are supermen capable of enduring pain and never showing weakness.

How does a team release a player who is dependent on drugs to get through the pain he experiences? Easy, if you're the NFL. The business is cutthroat, and the minute a player cannot perform up to a coach's standard, the team releases the player. Teams will and do insist that they carefully prescribe painkillers in accordance with federal laws. Anything that happens after the player leaves the team is the player's problem.

This is a recipe for addiction, and that's the reality. There needs to be some way to help move players to a rehabilitation center so they can deal with their pain issues before they are sent home, where there is little professional support. Of course, it is an expensive step for the team or league, and it requires the league to admit that players in fact get hooked on painkillers during their NFL careers, but it would lead to a more viable retired player with a better quality of life. This would need to be pushed by the NFL Players Association and negotiated in the next collective bargaining agreement, which comes up for renewal in 2031.

Assuming the union makes it a priority and the owners are willing to contribute financially, such a program could be established. The league has relationships with treatment centers for players who are on team rosters to help them get drug counseling. Retired players who have insurance can get twenty-eight days of inpatient care at a drug treatment facility. But what is needed is a plan that negates that need for treatment. Drug abuse begins in the locker room, and that's where it needs to end. I suggest more treatment of injuries, more rest, and less drug dependence.

While vested players get access to several years of insurance when they leave the league, players with only a year or two of service get none and have to buy their own. Even the players who get five years of coverage from the league could confront their biggest problems after the insurance runs out. Jackie Wallace is one of those players without insurance. He has been missing since 2018. A six-year veteran of the NFL, playing with the Minnesota Vikings, Baltimore Colts, and Los Angeles Rams, and making it to two Super Bowls, Wallace was taken in the second round out of the University of Arizona. Although he spent his first year on the practice squad, he went on to lead the league in punt returns in 1978.

Following his NFL career, Wallace worked on an oil rig. He began a descent into addiction that included almost all the substances available at that time, alcohol and crack cocaine being his drugs of choice. There is some question as to when he began to be dependent on drugs. Some people in his circle believe his mother's death after he left the league was a catalyst. Others believe he used drugs during his playing days in the NFL. Regardless, they were his crutch. He turned to them in times of flux. Leaving the league under a shadow because he supposedly disrespected his Super Bowl coach, and losing his mother at the same time, was too much stress for Jackie to handle.

Wallace began seesawing in and out of recovery. At one point, he married and had a child. When he and his wife argued, he left and went back to drugs and began living on the streets in New Orleans, his hometown. He was imprisoned for check fraud and served about four years of a seven-year sentence. He was sober and living at a homeless shelter when, in 2014, he joined a concussion-related lawsuit against the NFL

Jackie had a pattern to his relapses. Whenever he had a loss, such as his career or his mother or his wife, he turned to drugs to ease his emotional pain. He numbed himself. This behavior completely destroyed his ability to transition from football to a career on the outside.

When he realized there was no quick payday waiting for him in the concussion settlement, Wallace was disappointed, and in 2017, he took off. The emotional pain was too much for him to handle without his drugs. True to the long pattern of behavior, Wallace lost himself in the streets, homeless.

PLAYERS AS DEALERS

"He's not being prosecuted because he's an NFL player," Assistant U.S. Attorney John Kull said. "He's being prosecuted because he's a drug dealer."[4]

Sam Hurd, a wide receiver for six years with the Cowboys and Bears, from 2006 to 2011, pleaded guilty in federal court in Dallas to one count of trying to buy and distribute large amounts of cocaine and marijuana. Authorities say that while teammates and friends knew him as a hardworking wide receiver and married father, Hurd was fashioning a separate identity as a wannabe drug kingpin with a focus on high-end deals and a need for large amounts of drugs. In many ways, Hurd was preparing for his life after the NFL playing days were over, trying to establish himself as a dealer to high-end clients. Unlike many players a few years from leaving the league, Hurd had a plan. Just the wrong plan.

Hurd was arrested in a sting operation outside a Chicago steak house. He talked to the investigator like a big shot wanting a thousand pounds of marijuana a week to distribute in the area. Likewise, he wanted to be supplied with large amounts of cocaine. He was on his first step to becoming the drug kingpin he wished to be. Unfortunately, in his eagerness to impress people, he failed to check with whom he was doing business. Due diligence was not his strong point.

At the time, he was in the first year of a three-year contract that would have paid him a total of $15 million. But NFL football wasn't enough of an ego boost for Hurd. He had to be a big player in the drug world of Chicago. "Sam Hurd Receives 15-Year Sentence for Drug-Distribution Role" was the headline in a story by the Associated Press on November 13, 2013.

Hurd, of course, was not the first player to get sucked into the world of drug dealing. In 1982, Mercury Morris was out of the NFL for six years when he began serving three years of a twenty-year term for trafficking cocaine. In 1986, Morris, one of the most decorated players in the history of the Miami Dolphins, had his conviction overturned. Morris convinced the Florida Supreme Court that evidence used against him had been hearsay. A new trial was ordered. However, Morris and prosecutors reached a plea bargain and he was released in a few months.

Having had a taste of the legal system, Morris began a legal career of sorts advising retired NFL players and helping them apply for benefits. This raised eyebrows with the league, which made a special provision to exclude Morris from advising players. They determined that no felon could act as a retired player's representative in seeking benefits from the NFL.

Still, Morris has become a popular motivational speaker. His stories span his three Super Bowl appearances and two championships with the Dolphins. In 1972, he and Larry Csonka both rushed for at least a thousand yards, the first tandem of running backs to do so in the history of the league. Morris was a popular player with Dolphin fans. He simply couldn't translate his success on the field to employment off the field.

Jeff Hatch graduated in 2002 with a degree in political science and economics from the University of Pennsylvania. He was a bright young man and a powerful offensive tackle on the Penn team. He was drafted by the New York Giants in the second round with the camera crew from ESPN recording the event for a TV special: *Hey Rookie, Welcome to the NFL*. Life was exciting for Hatch. Everything was opening for him. He reported to the Giants for rookie mini-camp and insisted on not signing the injury waiver. He sat out that first day of practice. With the financial protection in place, the next day he signed a standard three-year rookie contract worth $1.4 million, complete with a $500,000 signing bonus. His agent had insisted on the injury waiver, although Jeff was afraid it would affect how the team viewed him. More rookies should follow his lead but, like Hatch, they are afraid to upset their new employer.

When the full team was assembled for training camp, it only took a few practices to determine the injury waiver was the best part of the contract. Hatch had herniated a disc in his back and had to have surgery. His first year as a Giant would be spent in rehabilitation.

At three hundred pounds, Hatch had a lot of weight to support as he regained his strength and coordination. The drugs he was given to cope with the pain didn't seem to be enough to get through the daily physical and emotional grind. He began to see a series of doctors beyond his surgeon and team doctor to get his opioids. He found a dealer in New Jersey and bought from him regularly.

Prior to the surgery, Hatch had been a social drinker in college and a recreational drug user. He was certainly not an addict. But when he returned to the Giants, he was an addict. He was relegated to the inactive list or sat on the bench. Then came the day when the team suffered so many injuries that by the end of the season the Giants had no choice but to play Jeff at right tackle for the remaining four games. At the time, he was considered the Giants' biggest bust of a draft pick.

Jeff tried out for several other teams but never made it past the practice squad in training camps. An NFL doctor suggested he undergo spinal fusion surgery to alleviate his constant pain. That surgery in 2005 led to another round of muscle relaxers, antianxiety medication, and opioids. He went into a downward spiral until his parents arrived and took control. They placed him in a treatment center. He turned out to be such a successful client that after three months, the center offered him a position on the staff. He became their marketing representative.

However, Hatch had wanderlust and headed for California to make a name for himself in the movies. He did a few commercials and stunt work. The stunt work was hard on his repaired back and his joints that were injured from years of high school and college football. His agent dropped him because he was not getting acting jobs reliably. With nothing left, no money, and no job prospects, Hatch headed home to his parents in Maryland. While there, he got much-needed surgery to replace a knee. As he recovered, he began taking painkillers even more. Everyone thought he was in remission from his addiction, but he was using because he couldn't stop. He hid it well this time.

A longtime friend and head of a treatment center in New Hampshire offered him a job as their marketing representative. He moved from his parents' home into a cheap apartment, accepting a $35,000 salary. Hatch was still addicted and getting stronger drugs to deal with his increased appetite. He was dealing with more street dealers and fewer doctors. The dealers introduced him to different and stronger drugs, including heroin and fentanyl. His coworkers never suspected his addiction. They didn't see him evenings and weekends.

On July 2, 2019, Vice President Mike Pence abruptly cancelled a trip to visit the Granite Recovery Centers, where Hatch was working. The center had worked for weeks preparing for his visit with the staff at the White House. This was a momentous event, a way to highlight the addiction crisis in New Hampshire. The national news networks had no follow-up data, other than that the trip had been cancelled suddenly. Speculation ran high. A few days later, news broke that one of the administrators at the addiction center had pleaded guilty to a federal crime of drug trafficking. The vice president's office didn't want a photograph of Pence shaking hands with a criminal wrapped up in a drug sting. Air Force Two never left the runway that day.

The worker that scared off the vice president was Jeff Hatch.

> Court documents, which, along with the events they described, had been secret because Hatch was a cooperating witness, detailed the alleged chronology: How, on July 25, 2017, local, state, and federal agencies investigating a fentanyl supplier in Manchester, N.H., had learned that Hatch had made a call to arrange a drug pickup in Lawrence, Mass., and Hatch, by driving the drugs the 20-plus miles

back to his house, had crossed state lines and committed a federal crime, and how, after two years of silence, Hatch had then pleaded guilty the previous Friday in federal court to one count of using a communication device to facilitate distribution of a controlled substance (fentanyl) and now faced up to four years in federal prison and a $250,000 fine.[5]

Jeff Hatch is one more player who couldn't kick the painkiller addiction he developed while playing football. Once a player becomes addicted to opioids, pain relief after surgery can trigger a relapse. That is exactly the trap that caught Jeff. He had two spinal surgeries and a knee replacement. He couldn't handle the aftereffects without strong painkillers. He struggled, went to rehab, struggled, and moved in with his parents. He never got clean until he was forced to. His body craved the drugs. He was an ex-football player who was now an addict.

NFL SUBSTANCES OF ABUSE PROGRAM

This section was written by Dr. Camille Fildaro-Kraft, EdS (college student-athlete, Westmont College; MS in athletic counseling, Springfield College; MA and EdD in leadership and administration in higher education, USC), a former administrator of the NFL Substances of Abuse Program and longtime college administrator and consultant.

Nothing grabs the headlines more firmly than a story of a player who is caught with an illegal substance. Why is it, year after year, we are drawn to such salacious headlines blurting out athlete's bad behavior? Megastar athletes Josh Gordon and Randy Gregory have recently joined the long and infamous list of such fallen athletes. Both players have been trapped in the hands of illegal substance usage while playing in the NFL and were suspended multiple times. Josh Gordon "has been suspended eight times by either his team or the NFL," according to the Associated Press (Barry Wilner, June 19, 2020). Gregory has been suspended at least four times for his "marijuana addiction based on self-medicating his bipolar disorder" (K. D. Drummond, June 9, 2020).

These young men experienced humiliation and isolation as a result of being removed from their jobs, their income, and their teammates. It makes you wonder just how many athletes have fallen from grace and made it back for the win. America's long love affair with the *Rocky* movies speaks to our desire for great come-from-behind stories of the defeated athlete that wins against all odds. We have paid homage to movies such as *Any Given Sunday*, *Bull Durham*, *The Natural*, *Hoosiers*, *Raging Bull*, *Rudy*, and *Hoop Dreams* to name a few. The list is long. It seems as though only the really great stories make it to the big screens. The fairytales. But can there be that much of a difference between reality and make believe? If so, why?

As the former administrator of the NFL Substances of Abuse Program, I was responsible for coordinating the care for all those involved with substance abuse. During this time, I observed young men tangled in the residue of substance abuse consequences. I always wondered how many ever achieved their "Rocky" moment. How many of these young men had their comeback?

I have a theory based on fifty-three years of experience. I began competing in sports at the age of five. I graduated high school as the captain of two teams with eight varsity letters and an MVP award. I was a collegiate student-athlete. I hold a bachelor's degree in psychology, a master's degree in counseling student-athletes, and a doctorate in higher educational leadership. I conducted postgraduate research for ten years and wrote both a thesis and a dissertation while serving as a graduate assistant and postgraduate intern. I have served as an athletic counselor, an athletic administrator, a professor, a dean, and the administrator of the NFL Substances of Abuse Program.

During these experiences, I have had the good fortune of working with athletes from all backgrounds and all levels. Each one was different, yet the same. For the most part, athletes love to win. They are pleasers. They are gregarious, and they relish their brotherhood. They have leadership skills and listening skills. They know when to be patient, they know how to lead, and they know how to follow. They know grit. They know determination. They know what it is to give all they have until the very last second of the game; they are not quitters. They understand giving 110 percent effort and leaving it all on the field. They are loyal and team oriented. They inspire. They know success and they know failure. Through their experiences they have developed all the transferable skills one needs to succeed throughout their lifetime. So then, why is it that we don't often hear of an athlete overcoming struggles? More specifically, why don't we hear of athletes overcoming substance abuse?

My theory is simple: they aren't prepared for it.

They are not prepared for the recovery methods used for those who make poor decisions, particularly counseling. And so it is our responsibility to recognize this need and commit to designing programs specifically for athletes. Acknowledging the need for adjustments, designing programs that fit their audience, and implementing programs in a way that is effective. These modifications can be easily made by adapting three simple ideas based on the nature of sport.

First, sport encourages the repression of emotions. Second, athletes are overly prepared. And last, but most important, athletes are not well versed in the counseling experience.

Let's start with the idea that athletics encourages the repression of emotions.

This portion of my theory can be boiled down with the use of a valid argument form: hypothetical syllogism. This argument form illustrates my theory.

If A, then B. If B, then C. Therefore, if A, then C. Let's start with A. Follow me here. Most athletes are taught at a very young age to hide their emotions. Emotions in the athletic world are perceived as a sign of weakness. If you are seen as weak, then you can become vulnerable. And if you are vulnerable, then you create an advantage for your opponent. Therefore, sport teaches you the importance of repressing your emotions. This self-denial of emotional expressions is continually reinforced throughout athletic careers. For example, coaches reinforce this idea through mantras such as "suck it up." This ideology is compounded by a culture that says, for men, crying is a sign of weakness. As a result, an athlete can spend their entire career inhibited to express their emotions. So, for argument's sake, let's say that A equals conformity to repress emotions.

Next, let's explore B, which represents the acknowledgment that athletes don't possess the skills necessary to emote. If a person has repressed their emotions, then they don't possess the skills necessary to practice their expressions. For practical purposes we will refer to this as if A, then B, meaning, an athlete who represses their emotions is often without well-practiced emotional skills.

Last, C. This is the ability to develop emotional coping skills. Should a person have limited skills in which to express themselves fully, due to learned behaviors, they can pursue developing skills.

Hence, if an inhibited athlete (A), then the athlete is void of skills (B) but can then develop skills (C). If A (repressed), then B (no skills). If B (no skills), then C (develop skills). Therefore, if A (repressed), then C (develop skills).

The second portion of my theory centers on preparation. Not only are athletes trained to repress their emotions, but also they are intentionally overprepared. Award-winning author Malcolm Gladwell of *The Outliers* promotes the idea that only a small percentage of people will commit to 10,0000 hours of practice in order to master a skill. Athletes spend tens of thousands of hours, if not more, year after year, perfecting their craft. They prepare in a variety of ways.

They study playbooks and film, attend meetings, go to practice, lift weights, exercise, and monitor their eating and sleeping. In addition to their overwhelming physical commitment to their sport, they also undergo rigorous mental programming. This programing starts with conformity through the wearing of uniforms. They are conditioned to follow the team's rules, almost Pavlovian in practice. They know if they follow the rules, they will be rewarded with playing time.

They are an elite part of a special, chosen, talented brotherhood. Their job far exceeds employment regularities and operates more like a family. They are equipped with armor to go into battle and are expected to die for one another. They are taught team, as well as position-specific, philosophies. When it comes to preparation for performance, an athlete can tell you the color of the opponent's parking lot, the shape of the stadium and its smells, the color of the seats, the type of grass and its markings, and details down to the shadows caused by the sun's shifting and the wind's velocity throughout the contest. Mental conditioning includes believing refrains such as no pain, no gain; fight to the end; sweat and sacrifice equal success; whatever it takes; eleven players, one heartbeat; and trust no one. Their environment is rote repetition. Hours are spent memorizing plays and studying opponents as well as their own performance. The depth of analysis allows an athlete to prematurely recognize an action and possibly be able to preemptively strike. Anything to gain an edge over an opponent. Athletes are coached to be prepared for every possible outcome. Their job is their entire life, resulting in their existence being athletically highjacked. As a result, they conform to repressing their emotions (A) and demonstrating repetitive inoculated expectations (B). Both experiences eliminate the freedom to express their emotions.

The last portion of my theory focuses on the missing link, counseling. The intent of counseling is excellent, the execution can be horrific, and the reason is simple: counseling is counterintuitive for athletes. Therefore, athletes need to develop counseling knowledge in order to excel at the process.

Occasionally, when an athlete decides to explore unsanctioned behaviors, such as substance abuse, they will most likely experience consequences. These consequences come in different forms. The most common forms are fines, suspensions, and counseling. The NFL, for example, offers its athletes extensive access to some of the best and brightest counselors and psychologists throughout the nation as part of their Substances of Abuse Program. These professionals provide counseling sessions to help process personal journeys that led to substance abuse.

Kudos to the NFL for offering counseling as its process for deterring poor behavior for its Substances of Abuse Program. The program is thorough, well structured, and comprehensive. However, it is limited in its ability to help the athlete because it is designed without the understanding of the athlete. Rather, it is designed from a psychological model and not from the user's understanding. Just as an architect may design a building to look beautiful, its function may be minimal. The concept is good; however, the practicality is dismal. I believe a few minor adjustments could massively alter the program's current effect. For example, an enormous miss for me is the assumption that athletes have experience with counseling. I cannot emphasize this point enough. The supposition is that athletes know how to function within the counseling arena—that they are comfortable with counseling and that they have an understanding for the counseling process. It is as though they are being thrown into a swimming pool with the expectation that they can swim.

In its most basic form, counseling sessions are confessions of deeply private personal information. It is the process of exploring and sharing beliefs and experiences with strangers, expectations that are completely unrelatable to an athlete's ingrained value system. For example, therapy sessions—even more, substance abuse treatment centers—believe in group therapy. Group therapy is an experience in which it is expected that everyone will share. For an athlete, these experiences are very unfamiliar, not to mention there isn't anonymity for an athlete, so their level of participation is more likely contrived. It isn't that the athlete is weak or lacks the ability to engage in counseling; it is that the athlete has not been prepared to strengthen their counseling muscle in the same way they have been taught to hone their craft. Therefore, requiring an athlete to perform unfamiliar, untrained skills that run counter to years of programming can make them uncomfortable. For the most part, athletes are taught the importance of controlling their environment by mastering their experiences through repetition to the level of perfection. Additionally, their exposure to counseling is limited. Their expectations are biased by dramatized exaggerations. Their experiences are mostly formed from what they have seen in movies or on television, such as *Psycho* and *One Flew over the Cuckoo's Nest*. These misunderstandings add to the anxiety and fear predicated on false beliefs. Thus, it would benefit the athlete to be taught counseling etiquette and exercises, with the intent of availing them to the possibility of being more fully engaged in the counseling process.

Mostly, counseling is an unscripted, exposed setting in which the client is asked to profess vulnerability. Dr. Brene Brown professes that through vulnerability we can find our strengths. Brown has given well-acclaimed Ted Talks, teaches sociology at the University of Houston, and has written best-selling books. Brown is charming and convincing, especially when coupled with her southern charm, authentic personality, and overall relatable nature. She has cornered the market on cutting into reality and self-awareness with ease. She is a joy to listen to and a life changer for many people with her rich, deep discussions about shame, vulnerability, and strength. The ease in which she communicates allows an audience to disrobe their insecurities with one quick pull of the tie. And her down-to-earth humor just adds to the entertainment that provides the safety net of saving face. She is a whiz at decoding relatable self- deprecating thoughts that we all share. Her success has led her to numerous awards, including recently being selected as the University of Texas at Austin's 2020 commencement speaker and Women Leaders in College Sports keynote speaker for their annual convention in October 2020.

I would love to apply Dr. Brown's theories to athletes, and I am sure she has and does, but for me, again, there is a missing process—and a critical one—the teaching of the skills necessary to become vulnerable. This is especially a different request of an athlete. Athletes are not taught "the how" of being vulnerable. Every aspect of being vulnerable goes against their innate teachings, and they have not spent time to fully developed the skills necessary to be vulnerable.

So, I say, let's help athletes create their own playbook so that when they are in situations that require them to be vulnerable, they are equipped. In other words, if an athlete finds himself or herself facing counseling, for whatever reason, it would be spectacular to give athletes skills by providing them the ability to survive that experience and per-haps gain personal health. It seems to me as though young men who have been through a substance abuse program have chosen the tactic of survival through grit.

I'm not quite sure these young men have questioned or asked for help to better navigate the system in which they've been placed. Let's witness an athlete's comeback. We can watch them become role models for others. To right the wrong. We can demystify the experience and prepare an athlete for the situation they're going into just as they are prepared to play a game. They need to be able to evaluate what is happening, assess their surroundings, and make their own route or play. They need a counseling playbook just as they need a playbook for their craft. They need to have a reference guide and develop skills and an understanding for the experience and knowledge of the expected out-come. This skill set should make an athlete feel empowered so they can enter into counseling with the tools needed to successfully engage. To have control of their situation. Just imagine the success rate that is possible for these young men had they been provided the skill set and developed the skill set to excel in this environment. I believe there would be more *Rocky* comeback stories. I believe there would be a greater chance for success. They can master complicated skills and apply them, and they must also master counseling jargon, role-play counseling situations, and discuss the counseling process, what it looks like, what is smells like, what it is like for them to enter the situation with confidence and courage. With confidence and courage, they can then become vulnerable and unleash the shame that comes with experi-ences such as substance abuse and gain their inner strength to come out stronger. So back to my theory—when you put a highly prepared person into a situation they're unprepared for, they are most likely going to fail.

CONCLUSION

I firmly believe that the nature of sport is counterintuitive to counseling. If you were to place an athlete into counseling, they would most likely not perform at the same optimal level they are conditioned to perform. It seems almost too simple of an idea; however, I am passionate about my theory and am steadfast in my belief that most athletes will struggle when placed into a counseling setting for the simple fact that they lack the skills necessary. Athletes must be taught practices that will enable them to overcome ingrained habits.

Most people who struggle with developing self-discovery skills are provided a form of counseling to develop those skills. Although the NFL Substances of Abuse Program has recently undergone revisions to become more player friendly, it still lacks a comprehensive safety net for substance misusers. It does not allow for the athlete to prepare for the experience. In other words, for a player to fully use the Substances of Abuse Program to its maximum potential, they would have to demonstrate proficient self-awareness. For this specific population, I find this expectation to be highly unlikely and almost culturally impossible because counseling is diametrically opposed to athletic teachings. These teachings often include mantras. Such catchphrases have been ingrained into athletes their entire life, so unpacking these lifelong lessons takes substantial work. An elite athlete has little room within their craft for self- assessment and reflection. Most likely, they have been conditioned with repetition and choreographed plays, making the therapy process foreign.

So, just as good lawyers prepare their clients for court, I strongly believe there is a need to prepare people, especially athletes, for counseling. By constructing a comprehensive toolbox filled with a therapeutic repertoire, athletes can strengthen their counseling muscle, so to speak, and shorten the bridge between treatment and returning to their lives.

The goal for me is to prepare athletes for the counseling experience. As their counseling coach, I would have athletes rehearse counseling skills so they don't just survive treatment but also embrace it—to have their *Rocky* moment on top of the steps in Philadelphia with their arms raised and the song "Gonna Fly Now" pounding with trumpets and drums. They would have their comeback moment because they learned the other plays. They dedicated their attention to developing the skills necessary to excel in counseling.

9

DOMESTIC VIOLENCE

On May 23 (2018), I resigned from the NFL Players Association's commission on domestic violence. Susan Else, former president of the National Network to End Domestic Violence, resigned with me. I simply cannot continue to be a part of a body that exists in name only.

My resignation brought to an end a nearly four-year association with the NFLPA that was, by turns, promising, inspiring and deeply frustrating. The commission was formed as part of the sport's belated effort to confront the plague of domestic violence in the National Football League. The precipitating event was, of course, the viral release of a security video from an Atlantic City casino showing then-Baltimore Ravens running back Ray Rice knocking his then-fiancee unconscious in an elevator and then dragging her through the doors.[1]

As Deborah Epstein's resignation suggests, the NFL has yet to take the problem of domestic violence seriously. Clearly, penalizing players for a few games is not stopping the behavior. Drafting players who have abused women in college is tantamount to accepting violence in the league. From beating children to assaulting wives, girlfriends, and other women, the league has had more than its share of unseemly scandals that have shown how players at times act off the field.

Domestic violence, of course, is not confined to the NFL. It is a national problem, one that is often hidden from view. But as scandals involving Harvey Weinstein, Bill Cosby, and Jeffrey Epstein make clear, issues on the abuse of women cross all social groups, wealthy and poor, young and old, Black and White. As the country's most prominent sports league, though, the NFL gets outsized attention, good and, unfortunately, bad. That's why the video released in 2014 that showed Ray Rice knocking out his fiancée in an Atlantic City hotel was so shocking. It was graphic and powerful, of course, but it also involved a player who was at the time viewed as a "good guy" inside the NFL. The unemotional way in which he dragged his fiancée out of the elevator showed another, more startling view of the player and by extension the league.

The video shined a very uncomfortable light on the league, which is filled with men paid handsomely to express their rage in controlled, athletic ways on Sundays. The league at that time rarely suspended a player accused of domestic violence for more than two games, even though players caught taking banned substances were often suspended for far longer. After Commissioner Roger Goodell suspended Rice for two games, pressure built on the league to overhaul its policies. And so, in late August 2014, about a month later, Goodell issued a rare mea culpa and said the league's standards needed to be strengthened. Players involved in domestic violence would now get a six-game suspension.

Two weeks later, just as the season was getting started, the scandal website TMZ published another even more graphic video of Rice and his fiancée, this time taken by cameras from inside the elevator. It made national news and sparked a full-throated debate about the league, the issue, and the sad tolerance by male-dominated institutions. Rice was suspended indefinitely, and other players, including Adrian Peterson, were sidelined by the league. Two months later, Rice would win a legal battle over the league when a former judge agreed that the league couldn't suspend him twice for the same infraction, or double jeopardy. Although he was then eligible to sign a contract, he was too toxic for any team to handle.

Chastened again, the league said it would no longer rely solely on law enforcement to determine if a player committed domestic violence. Goodell also abandoned his prior practice of interviewing the player with his spouse or partner in his office to decide how sincere they were. Experts said that women who have been abused are far less likely to admit this in front of the men who abused them. The league hired a former prosecutor and other people familiar with sex crimes to work on an internal investigative unit. Public service announcements were created that included players denouncing domestic violence, and these were shown during games.

And yet, cases of domestic violence continue in the NFL, vexing the league. In 2016, the league suspended New York Giants kicker Josh Brown for one game for an incident of domestic abuse with his wife. Then police documents were unearthed that showed Brown had been "physically, verbally and emotionally" abusive to his wife.[2] Brown then confessed and was suspended indefinitely with pay. After his contract expired, Brown did not return to the league.

Missteps continue. Sometimes, the league cannot get local law enforcement to share what they know about the cases. Other times, video footage of an incident might indict a player, but the league is unable to get its hands on all of the available video to determine who is at fault. The league has said it is unwilling to pay for video, some of which might be stolen from internal security cameras and sold to websites such as TMZ, because it would create a slippery slope whereby profiteers might videotape players with the intention of selling it.

Then there are cases like the one involving Tyreek Hill, a star wide receiver on the Kansas City Chiefs. Hill played junior college football for two years before being recruited by Oklahoma State University. He was there a year, setting records for the football program but at the end of the year was dismissed from the team because he had choked and beaten his girlfriend. As part of his plea arrangement, he had to work or attend school. He impressed the University of West Alabama and signed on to play for their football team.

He was drafted in the fifth round of the 2016 NFL draft by the Chiefs. Although the fans complained that an abuser who had beaten up his pregnant girlfriend would be on the roster of their beloved team, he quickly made an impact and the complaints died down. (Such is the Faustian bargain that fans make.) Not only was Hill fast, but also he could catch the ball. His first three seasons on his rookie contract were outstanding. He was then offered a three-year $54 million extension. But the extension was in jeopardy after Hill was suspended from the team over child abuse allegations. His three-year-old son had a broken arm and was temporarily placed in custodial care, while the Kansas Department of Children and Families conducted an investigation of the incident. Audio also surfaced of Hill talking in a threatening way to his girlfriend. Yet the local prosecutor ultimately decided that while a crime had most probably been committed, he was unable to assign blame directly to either Hill or the mother of their child. By July, the league ruled Hill would not be disciplined because he did not violate the NFL personal conduct policy.

The decision by the league to let Hill off the hook did not surprise experts in domestic violence. Dr. Epstein was hired as a consultant to the players union to change the image of a league filled with abusers. She saw her role as more. She wanted to stop domestic abuse. She worked for four years doing studies of violence at the league and offering suggestions of how to mitigate this behavior by the players. The league had her sign a nondisclosure agreement, something it requires of all employees. Never were her ideas given credence or put into action. The NFL Players Association (NFLPA) hired her as window dressing to throw over the problem. Unfortunately, because of her signing the employment document, her study is not available to the public. Her ideas to change the violent behavior by players toward their family members and girlfriends are locked away in an NFLPA closet gathering dust.

It's difficult to understand the reason Ray Rice, one of the best players in the league, would hit his girlfriend so hard that she'd pass out in an elevator. He literally pulled her by the arms out into the lobby. She was in a tight-fitting cocktail dress that rode up high on her legs as Rice was dragging her. There was a crowd that gathered. She did not deserve to be humiliated and beaten up by this man. No one should be treated this way. The security camera didn't lie. The league, however, fumbled his punishment, initially giving a very light tap on the wrist until the second, more revealing video made the public scream for justice. Roger Goodell then readjusted his stance yet again.

Dr. Epstein was hired to add gravitas to the situation. The same thing happened when they hired a director for drug education. Lots of great curricula were produced with ideas for implementation created by a leader in the field of drug prevention. It's buried now in a closet with Dr. Epstein's work.

Although we can agree this problem of domestic violence is bigger than something the league can entirely control, the major problem is the violence that you do not see on hotel video or read in the newspaper. In one stretch between 2012 and 2014, thirty-three NFL players were arrested for domestic violence, battery, assault, and murder, according to *Sports Illustrated*. They include players who were accused of beating their children, assaulting police, and beating girlfriends.

One case that illustrates the dilemma faced by the NFL involved Greg Hardy, a star defensive lineman on the Carolina Panthers who was convicted of assaulting his then girlfriend. Hardy beat her and threatened to shoot her. He was convicted on two counts and was sentenced to eighteen months' probation. He appealed, and the charges were dropped because the woman declined to testify. The NFL put Hardy on the commissioner's exempt list, which allowed him to collect his salary while sitting out as the case played out. Then the league suspended Hardy for ten games in the 2015 season. He appealed, and a league-appointed arbitrator cut the suspension to four games. Dallas Cowboys owner Jerry Jones didn't wait for the suspension to end. He signed Hardy, who played twelve games for the Cowboys in 2015. He hasn't played since. But by signing Hardy, Jones in effect normalized his behavior.

Many of these cases, though, involve retired players who are no longer in the spotlight and thus rarely warrant a mention in the sports media.

The retired player is likely to get a divorce after he leaves the NFL. There are no hard data because these families rarely take part in studies or fill out questionnaires. But it is commonly believed the divorce rate is in excess of 60 percent. These families face an inordinate amount of stress from the moment the player is told the coach wants to see him, which often means the coach wants to cut the player. Without a steady paycheck, how will the mortgage, the car payment, and the credit card bills be paid? Rarely is a player ready for the last day of his career. When rookies are initially asked how long they think they'll play in the NFL, they often answer ten years. The reality is between three and four years. With rare exceptions, players and their families are not ready to transition to a new career.

No player wants to start another career being paid the basic salary of a new recruit. They feel it's demeaning to their sense of self and masculinity. It's difficult to be older and more experienced yet working alongside guys who are just starting their careers. It's difficult to hold their heads up and be proud of what they are doing. They are no longer NFL players. Their wives are no longer NFL wives participating in fashion shows and attending luncheons with other wives. They've lost their status as well.

One family whose husband played for the Buccaneers faced many of these problems. During his stellar and popular career, J fathered a son with a local woman, who gave the child his father's name. He, too, became an outstanding football player at a local high school and then at Florida State University. He now plays professional football and is considered a success.

However, J's wife is constantly reminded of his illegitimate son's presence in their community. The wife's daughter was also hurt because she had a half brother constantly in the news and the sports media often referred to her father. It was a stress-filled situation. The father made some poor investment decisions after he retired from the league and never managed to save his money. Soon, the family was depending on the mother's and daughter's incomes to hold the household together. Mom and Dad started abusing alcohol. Dad would borrow money and leave for days of drinking. Mom had to hide her money so she'd have money for rent and a car.

Every one of his NFL pension checks was spent on alcohol. The daughter's job took her to another Florida city. She was upset that she could no longer take care of her father. Without the daughter to witness his behavior, the former NFL star began beating his wife whenever he was home. He threw her out of the house in her sleepwear one night. He did everything to get her to leave. He wanted to drink and have a pity party for himself. She tried to cook and keep up the house, but it was a losing battle. Before long, she left to live with her daughter.

Tom McHale, a Buccaneer offensive lineman who played from 1987 to 1995, seemed to make a smoother transition. He had a degree in hospitality from an esteemed program at Cornell University. He opened an Irish-style pub. It was so popular that soon he had a few around town. He was the perfect barkeep: He knew your name, he knew your drink, and he made you laugh. His wife Lisa was a mom with three active sons, one with a disability. She and Tom had been college sweethearts, and the love radiated from their faces.

Then Tom changed. He became angry and irrational. He was no longer the teddy bear daddy. He was brusque and noncommittal. Lisa thought it was her fault in some way. Tom moved out of the house, saying it was better for her and the boys. His bars were losing money as he was no longer on top of the accounts or present.

One night, Tom accidently overdosed in his apartment and died. He was just forty-five years old. His wife insisted that his brain be sent for an autopsy. She knew there was something wrong with the man she'd loved forever. Boston University neuropathologist Dr. Ann McKee found that he had an advanced form of chronic traumatic encephalopathy (CTE), the degenerative brain disease. Lisa was relieved to know there was a physical answer to Tom's problems. But she was left with the emotional abuse of their breakup. She didn't understand what was happening to the man she loved, and Tom couldn't explain it either. Domestic abuse can be physical or emotional; the latter can be more difficult.

While we can blame Tom McHale's behavior and ultimate death on CTE, there are other players whose behavior may be caused by other factors. Antonio Brown, a star wide receiver, is a serial abuser of women. In 2019, there were two cases in the Florida courts filed by women who said he abused them sexually. In September 2019, Britney Taylor, Brown's former trainer, alleged that he sexually assaulted her three times, ending with rape. A week later, a second woman who was working for Brown, creating a mural for a wall in his home, accused him of sexual misconduct.

Brown should have been in team meetings during the week and playing football on the weekends. However, four days after the second accusation was filed, the New England Patriots released Brown. He had played just one game for them before they became aware of the sexual accusations against him and the intimidating text messages that he had been sending to one of his alleged victims. Prior to his one game with the Patriots, Brown had been with the Oakland Raiders, who released him because of a different spat with team officials.

On the opening day of training camp in California, Brown arrived at the practice field in a hot air balloon. It was a grand entrance meant to dazzle his new teammates. However, Brown could not practice. While vacationing in France, he did a new spa therapy called cryotherapy, or cold therapy, designed to treat tissue lesions. During the therapy, his feet froze because he did not wear the protective footwear that was recommended. Brown missed ten of eleven training practices. After his feet healed, he filed a grievance with the NFL because he wanted to continue to wear his longtime helmet that the league had since banned because it did not meet its minimum safety standards. Brown lost his battle in arbitration and told everyone that he would retire unless he could wear his old helmet. He found another helmet, but it too did not meet the league safety standards. He did not practice with the team because he refused to wear an approved helmet. He filed a second grievance and again lost in arbitration. Finally, Brown chose a helmet to wear that was approved by the league. By this time his helmet had garnered much publicity. The helmet company paid him handsomely to wear their helmet for the season.

But Brown continued to cause problems for the team's management that ultimately led to a physical altercation with the general manager, Mike Mayock. Players rushed to hold Brown back. The following day he apologized to staff and players in the locker room. Twenty-four hours later he demanded to be traded. He was released that afternoon just in time for the Patriots to pick him up before closing time. He agreed to a one-year contract worth a potential $15 million with a $9 million signing bonus.

You may ask why the Steelers, the Raiders, and the Patriots put up with Brown's antics and outbursts. The answer is simple. No matter what chaos he caused off the field, he was one of the best receivers to ever play the game. He is highly talented physically and is pathologically charming. He constantly scores as the best at his position. He runs, he receives, and he occasionally throws touchdowns. He knows no equal. Teams try to overlook his game-day mischief such as climbing the goalpost after a touchdown, twerking in celebration of a play, and hurdling over a player but hitting his face mask with his foot. He gets fined but continues his antics. After one playoff game with the Steelers, he took a video of the locker room celebration for Facebook Live. He was paid almost $250,000 by Facebook, even though videotaping in the locker room is against club rules. At least one of his teammates was unwittingly videotaped entirely naked.

Brown was a two-sport athlete in high school, playing football and running track. He played quarterback and was impressive. He tried to go to Florida State University, but they rejected him because his grades were insufficient for their program. The same was true for Alcorn State. He finally enrolled at North Carolina Tech Prep. He played quarterback his lone year there and was offered a scholarship to Florida International University based on his outstanding play. Unfortunately, Brown was expelled before the season began when he got into a fight with university security. He finally found a spot at Central Michigan and played there for three seasons; he then entered the draft.

Brown keeps his name in the news because of his outlandish behavior, particularly now that he isn't tethered to a football schedule. He recorded a music video of a song he wrote. The lyrics are a repeat of the words "I've got money." The video includes a large contingent of barely dressed females gyrating around him in his home.

He also called the police to report a theft of $500,000 in jewelry. When the police arrived, he told them he'd invited two women to his house. They fell asleep. He awoke and went to the gym. When he returned, they had disappeared with his jewelry. Unfortunately, he did not know their names or where they lived.

Renting a luxury condo on the fourteenth floor of a building in South Florida, Antonio became upset when he thought the furniture was not up to the standard of what he was paying in rent. He began tearing the furniture apart and throwing it over the outside railing. A child below was almost hit by flying debris, and the parents sued Brown. Brown pleaded no contest and settled the case.

Antonio has four children. He regularly gets upset because the mothers of his children say they don't have the money they need to raise the kids. There was an altercation in January 2020 when he called the police and told them to remove two of his children and their mother because they were trying to steal his car. He videotaped the incident and played it on social media. He cursed the police using horrible language. The upshot was that the police in Hollywood, Florida, returned a donation he had made to the Police Athletic League and told him to never step foot on their property again. They were finished with him.

Retired players often resent their wives because they don't see their lives being affected by no longer being employed by the NFL. The wives still have to go to the grocery store, cook meals, take care of the children, and possibly hold a job. The man is lost, while the wife's role is the same as when the husband was a professional player. He feels guilty for not working but is reluctant to take a job he feels is below him. He thinks his wife and friends will no longer respect him. It's psychologically more acceptable to be unemployed as a football player than work at an entry-level position.

There are few coping strategies in this transitional time of their lives. They are young and basically healthy with some college education. Yet it's difficult to apply for a job. If the player has an agent or NFL influencer who guides him to save his money, perhaps he can make the transition. But whom do you trust with your money when you're setting up a business? The player has been so involved in football for the majority of his life that he relies on what others tell him. He really doesn't know much about investment opportunities, and he's unable to fully discern what's reputable when people flock to him with a nest egg trying to get him to invest in a new project. Ultimately, the player doesn't know how to read the fine print in a contract and signs away his future profit.

And when the money is gone, the feeling of going from a big business tycoon to broke is difficult. It happens regularly because the players aren't prepared for life after football. They then take out their frustration on their wives. It begins with cursing and escalates to blows. The wife often feels in some way she is responsible, so she keeps her mouth shut and doesn't report her abusive husband. She worries about what would happen to her and her children if he was jailed. She'd have no home. She hangs on, hoping her relationship with her husband will change. She does everything she can to placate him. She still gets beaten because his life outside the home has not changed. He turns to alcohol and drugs to soothe his pain. Ultimately, divorce is the only way out of this unhappy home.

10

SUCCESS VERSUS BANKRUPTCY

As we've seen, life after the NFL can be a mixed bag. Despite all the hard work and success the players put in and receive by making it to the NFL, the toll of remaining in the league can be high, and many players are unprepared for life after football. Regardless of their injuries, struggles at home, and other hurdles, plenty of NFL players move on with their lives, leaning on the skills they accumulated in college, making the most of their networking opportunities while in the league, or just following their long-held desires.

Because NFL players rarely announce their retirement formally, and because many of them simply drift away from the league, finding precise figures on what players are doing in retirement is difficult. But LinkedIn analyzed the pages of three thousand former NFL players (or those who identified themselves as former players) and determined that 48 percent of these men started their own small business, worked in sales, or helped manage clients. This makes sense. Employers love to hire former athletes because they tend to be disciplined and confident and are used to shaking hands and meeting strangers. A former NFL player who cold-calls a company or potential customer might have a better chance of getting his foot in the door than someone who doesn't have the cache of a professional athlete.

Another 17 percent worked in athletic professions, typically coaching or fitness training. This, too, makes sense. If professional athletes know anything, it's how to stay in shape. And again, their background as former professional athletes is a great calling card. What red-blooded American male wouldn't want to work out with a former NFL player?

Perhaps the most misunderstood group is the 3 percent who work in media and sports broadcasting. They are highly visible and appear to have it all—a big salary, a huge national platform, fancy suits, and the appearance of being smart since, after all, they are talking about the sport they played for years. But for every Tony Romo, who received rave reviews as a broadcaster for CBS Sports, there is a Jason Witten, a tight end and former teammate of Romo's who lasted just one year as an analyst on Monday Night Football, and decided to return to the NFL as a player, where he felt more comfortable. Where Romo was glib, Witten was shallow. Romo took chances; Witten leaned on clichés. Both made a lot of money, but Witten discovered how hard it was to learn a new craft.

Tiki Barber, the celebrated running back with the New York Giants, hung up his cleats in 2006. He quickly went to work for *The Today Show*, the most popular morning show on television, as well as a correspondent on Sunday Night Football. It seemed like a natural move. Barber was handsome, likeable, and well known. But Barber quickly realized how hard it was to be in television. Years after the experiment failed, he told a reporter how disarming it was to start a new career. He realized that he was thirty-five and his new coworkers who were his age had been working in television for ten or more years and were much more accomplished. He realized he had to start over.

But what to do? The *New York Post* ran a story in 2010 that said Barber wanted to return to the NFL because he had financial problems. Sure enough, in 2011, Barber filed paperwork to come out of retirement, though he insisted the move was not about making money. By the start of the season, the dream of a return was over. Barber's agent admitted that no team was interested in offering his client a contract.

Barber has cycled through several jobs since then.

Then there is the story of two Buccaneers, Warren Sapp and Derrick Brooks, who were both drafted in the first round in 1995 and both ended up in the Pro Football Hall of Fame. Both came from Florida high schools where they were stars on their respective teams and garnered many awards and accolades. In 2007, both were named to the Florida High School Association All-Century Team, comprising the top thirty-three players in the last hundred years of Florida high school football. Each went to a Florida university, one to the University of Miami and one to Florida State University. Both had successful professional careers in football. One went bankrupt, one did not. One is a cautionary tale about how easily the hard-earned gains made in the NFL can be squandered, while the other is the success story every fan—and especially the league—hopes players can be.

In 2013, the first year he was eligible, Warren Sapp, a star defensive lineman, was voted into the Pro Football Hall of Fame. That same year, the Buccaneers retired his number 99 and made him a member of their prestigious Ring of Honor. Sapp, the twelfth pick in the 1995 draft, played for the Bucs from 1995 to 2003 and then moved to the Oakland Raiders for the remainder of his career, retiring in 2007.

Sapp was an outstanding two-sport athlete in high school, playing three positions on his football team as well as third base on the baseball team. At one time he held the records for home runs, the longest field goal, and the most sacks. He, of course, was recruited by many college football programs. He chose the University of Miami, and they converted him to his sweet spot: defensive lineman. Accolades accrued, including a Consensus First-Team All-American (1994), the Lombardi Award (1994), the Bronko Nagurski Trophy (1994), the Bill Willis Award (1994), and Defensive Player of the Year by the Football Writers Association (1994).

As a Buccaneer, Sapp was given the starting job of right defensive tackle almost immediately and stayed in that position his entire nine years with the team. After the expiration of his rookie contract in 1998, Sapp was given a six-year extension of $36 million. In 1999, he rewarded the Buccaneers by winning the NFL Defensive Player of the Year Award. Three years later, in early 2003, Sapp was instrumental in helping Tampa win Super Bowl XXXVII over the Oakland Raiders, the Buccaneers' first championship. Despite being double- and triple-teamed, Sapp was a powerful defender in that pivotal game.

In 2004, Sapp found himself playing for the Oakland Raiders. He lost weight and became quicker, and he was once again a powerhouse. The 2005 season started the same. However, with six games remaining, Sapp injured his shoulder and was out of the lineup. For the following two seasons, he continued to lose weight and dominate on the defensive line.

By the time he called Al Davis, the Raiders owner, and said, "I'm done," he'd been selected to the Pro Bowl seven times, named a First-Team All-Pro four times, and voted to the All-Decade Teams twice. It was 2008, and Warren Sapp had reached the point of retirement on his own terms.

Although earning many awards during his football career, Sapp was also a disrupter on the field. During a game in Tampa against Green Bay, Sapp blindsided Packers offensive tackle Chad Clifton away from the play action. Clifton was paralyzed on the field and spent five weeks in rehab learning to walk. The Packer's coach Mike Sherman let Sapp have a piece of his mind, saying "That was a chicken-shit play."

Sapp's reply, "You talk tough? Put a jersey on!" followed by "[You are] a lying, shit-eating hound." Unfortunately, this exchange was picked up by television cameras. Players don't disrespect coaches on any team publicly.

Several games later in the 2002 season, Sapp skipped between the Pittsburgh Steelers players during their pregame warmups on the Tampa field. The poor sportsmanship escalated into a shoving match between the teams. Sapp was essentially baiting the opponents, an action he would repeat the following year against the Indianapolis Colts on Monday Night Football. Again, on October 6, 2003, he skipped through the opponents and disrupted their warmups. The following week while running onto the field for the game against the Washington Redskins, he bumped an NFL referee. He was fined $50,000. Sapp's response: "It's a slave system. Make no mistake about it. Slavemaster say you can't do it, don't do it. They'll make an example out of you."

On January 3, 2008, Warren Sapp declared to Al Davis that he was quitting football. He still had a few years remaining on his contract. However, it could be that the altercation that occurred on December 23, 2007, was the reason he was no longer interested in remaining in football. Nearing halftime, a misunderstanding developed. A linesman assumed the Raiders would decline a ten-yard penalty against their opponents, the Jacksonville Jaguars. However, Sapp was the defensive captain and wanted the penalty to stand. Things got out of control with heated language causing the linesman to flag him for unsportsmanlike conduct. Sapp and the Raiders wouldn't stop their barrage of insults at the officials and drew a second unsportsmanlike penalty. At this point, the coaches took the field to try and restore order. During the melee, the referee said Sapp bumped him. That necessitated a third penalty, and he was ejected from the game. Later, Sapp was fined $75,000.

During his thirteen years in the NFL, Sapp earned $59 million. Shortly before he retired, he invested in Urban Solutions Group. The goal was to build low-income housing in South Florida. His group was loaned money by PNC bank, which probably thought Sapp could personally guarantee the loan. Unfortunately, their timing was terrible because the housing market collapsed during the recession in 2008, and their project failed. This would haunt him.

Yet Sapp still had good things going for him. From 2008 to 2011, he worked as an analyst on *Inside the NFL* on Showtime. Although professionals in the field complained that he was not much of an analyst, his personality carried him. The videos of his appearances on *NFL Total Access* are still fresh and entertaining today if not professional. The same was true of his sense of rhythm. He was not much of a dancer, but in 2008, he made it to the finals on *Dancing with the Stars*.

Sapp seemed to make guest roles a staple on television for several years until he was arrested for solicitation on the Monday after the Super Bowl in 2015 in Arizona. His contract with the NFL Network was terminated. Luckily for him, the charges were dropped three months later.

In 1998, Sapp's third year with the Bucs, he signed a six-year multi-million-dollar contract. During the Pro Bowl in Hawaii, he married Jamiko Vaughn. They had two children: Mercedes born in 1998 and Warren Junior born in 2000. Sapp is also the father to two other children: Jaelon Austin Sapp born in 1997 and Autumn Adkins, daughter of Chantel Adkins.

According to Chantel, she and Sapp began dating the year he married Jamiko. She was a basketball player at Temple, and they would fly back and forth to Tampa and New Jersey to see each other. When their daughter was born, he claimed paternity on the birth certificate, bought them a large SUV, and paid for a nanny. With money tight, Sapp quit paying, and a paternity test was ordered. The day of the test Sapp had someone else stand in for him. An appeal was filed; Chantel flew to Tampa to make certain it was Warren Sapp who was tested for paternity. The test showed he was the father. He denied the result. A third test was scheduled when Sapp finally admitted he was the father to Chantel's daughter.

In 2009, Sapp's yearly paternity support for four children was $408,893.

PNC was awarded $988,691.99 in a judgment against Sapp in the failed real estate venture in South Florida. This was in 2010. By 2011, his NFL Network salary was being garnished monthly in the amount of $33,333. This left him approximately $12,000 per month. He also owed the IRS $942,778 in taxes on his income from 2006 and 2010. Additionally, he owed property taxes of almost $70,000 and child support/alimony in the amount of $876,000. He had to file for bankruptcy. There was no way out of this financial morass.

Sapp left the limelight for several years and tried to regroup. For an article titled "Strip Clubs, CTE Talk and a CBD Sales Pitch: A Weekend Inside Warren Sapp's World," *Sports Illustrated* (January 29, 2018) writer Tim Rohan spent several days with the former Pro Bowler in South Florida. This was the first I'd heard of him since his financial flameout in 2012 and prostitution solicitation charges in 2015. He basically tunneled underground socially. Upon his reemergence in 2017, Sapp aligned himself with Chris Nowinski at the Concussion Legacy Foundation, stating he was suffering the effects of CTE. His memory was slipping, and he was scared. He began to address groups such as veterans and high school parents. His message was twofold: don't play tackle before high school, and consider donating your brain, as he did, to the foundation.

Simultaneously, Warren has gone into business with Be Tru Organics, a company that sells CBD pain relief products. He swears he uses the pain relief spray twice a day. As the company's main spokesman, he is personally excited about the research that is being done by the company to protect brain cells and keep them from dying. Sapp has been pushing the NFL to let players use the Tru products. He is serious about wanting to repair their brains. Likewise, he sees the connection to the Concussion Legacy Foundation in the same way. When the scientists in Boston identify the CTE marker in the living patient, he intends to get them treatment with cannabidiol. He's reassured by preliminary research that the patients' brains will heal from the effects of the concussions they suffered.

Interestingly, CBD manufacturers and distributors have targeted former NFL players. Many players test positive for marijuana each season and suffer the consequences. In the latest collective bargaining agreement, the NFL and players union agreed to eliminate suspensions for the use of marijuana. The union's goal was to decriminalize it within the teams. Players argue that it is not an opioid like the ones doctors dispense freely for pain. The men want the pain relief and mellowing effects of marijuana. The argument for CBD usage is that the THC (hallucinogenic) is removed, thereby making the sprays and oils safe to consume without the possibility of psychotic breakdowns.

These business and volunteer aspects are redeeming Warren's reputation. However, always the split personality, he continues to degrade and embarrass women in professional and social situations. He becomes rude to people lined up at autograph events and can be caught staring in space. He makes poor choices, such as spending too much money buying lap dances and other sex acts at strip clubs. It's difficult to meld the two men in this one body. While he is relaxed in the company of scientists and authors on the dais discussing concussions, he is equally at ease putting bills in a dancer's G-string. His NFL alumni group in Florida is wary of inviting him to special events as they don't know if he will embarrass the brotherhood that night. As they say, he can be charming if he's in the mood, but he can also behave inappropriately, destroying the ambience.

The question is, Which Warren Sapp will win the battle for his future?

Derrick Brooks and Warren Sapp differed very little in the beginning of their careers. They both came from Florida, played college ball in their home state, and were good enough to be drafted by the "home town team" in the first round. Sapp was on the defensive line, while Brooks was an outside linebacker. Brooks played his entire NFL career in Tampa, from 1995 to 2008. Sapp moved on after Tampa and played in Oakland before quitting the Raiders.

Brooks had an excellent career with the Bucs. He was selected to the Pro Bowl eleven times and was an All-Pro nine times. In 2014 he was elected to the Pro Football Hall of Fame in his first year of eligibility. Importantly, he was a member of the NFL One Hundredth Anniversary All-Time Team. The Buccaneers retired his jersey number, 55, as a salute to his greatness. Sapp also had his jersey number retired and was voted into the Hall of Fame as well. They both have Super Bowl rings from their time with the Tampa team playing under coach Jon Gruden.

This is basically where the similarities end.

Having been coached by Tony Dungy during his tenure at the Bucs, Brooks molded his philosophy on that of his former coach. Family is first. Religion is always central. Never break an appointment. Be a leader.

Brooks took over as the leader when a vacuum was created in the locker room after Hardy Nickerson was traded to the Jacksonville Jaguars in 2000. He stepped up and kept the order and focus that were necessary to move forward. Brooks will tell you he was not ready for retirement. The day it happened, he wasn't expecting it. He had planned to train Ronde Barber, a teammate, to take over as leader of the clubhouse when he retired. "That's one of the areas they struggled with for years," he told Rick Stroud of the *Tampa Bay Times*. "There was more value to what I was willing to sacrifice and do. But we never had any dialogue."[1]

The year he was drafted into the NFL, Derrick received his bachelor's degree in business communications from Florida State. He completed his master's degree in business communications, also from Florida State, in 1999. Education had been stressed in his childhood. His stepfather would arrive at school unannounced to see how he was doing in his classroom. If he caught him not paying attention to the teacher, there was immediate punishment. Brooks became an excellent student, attaining over a 3.5 average throughout school.

Brooks's grandmother set an example of service for him when he was a small child. She ran a volunteer soup kitchen out of her home for strangers. Brooks helped in this endeavor and was imbued with the Christian ethic of giving back to those who are less fortunate. He has continued that work today in Tampa with the Brooks Bunch charity and youth scholarship foundation. The Brooks Bunch works with inner-city children at the YMCA, emphasizing education and the wonders of the world. The children have traveled to Africa and other countries, learning about the cultures and history of the places they visit. In the United States, they visited the Grand Canyon, marveling at this wonder of the world. Brooks wants these children to have an idea of what lies beyond Tampa and that there's a world awaiting them.

Brooks and Edward DeBartolo Jr., the former owner of the San Francisco 49ers who lives in Tampa, teamed up to create the Brooks-DeBartolo Collegiate High School in Tampa. With stringent academic requirements, the school now has a waiting list of new applicants.

Brooks visits the school and is very hands-on in the operations and the encouragement of students to do their best always.

For the last couple of years Brooks has been an investor in the Pensacola Blue Wahoos, a minor league baseball team. This is not just any team but one of the most successful minor league franchises in professional baseball. He's so excited about his team that he now keeps a residence in Pensacola, where he was born, as well as in Tampa. Occasionally, he throws out the first pitch and has even been known to sub in an inning.

The most exciting thing Brooks has been tapped to do was be the face and leader of Super Bowl LV, which was held in Tampa in February 2021. "Some people might think of [Brooks's] name being involved as ceremonial in nature, but I can promise you that he has rolled up his sleeves," said Rob Higgins, executive director of the Tampa Bay Sports Commission and the president and CEO of the Tampa Bay Super Bowl LV Host Committee. "He is in the meetings. He is helping direct traffic, and he has been absolutely phenomenal. That work started more than a year ago and will continue over the next 17 months and beyond. We're fortunate to have his leadership, his work ethic, everything he brings to the table."[2]

It's evident that Brooks made a successful transition from the NFL. He's been married to the same woman and they've raised four children. His philosophy was grounded in Christianity and reinforced by Coach Dungy. His fellow alumni respect him greatly and seek his advice. By the same token, they know he is no playboy seeking a night out from the family. He's a star in the community both in business and in good deeds. Whereas others may get into quick money schemes, Brooks carefully plans his business deals and the people with whom he associates. He's earned the title of Favorite Son in the Tampa Bay area.

Then there's Warrick Dunn, who also went to Florida State and began and ended his twelve-year career with the Buccaneers, with a six-year stint with the Atlanta Falcons in between. Like Brooks, he won the prestigious Walter Payton Man of the Year Award for his philanthropy, though he was recognized for this award while playing for the Falcons. As a rookie for the Buccaneers, who drafted him in the first round in 1997, he established a much-needed charity: Home for the Holidays. He realized the worth of a home to single-parent families and pledged through a partnership with Habitat for Humanity to provide mortgage money and furnishings to make this a reality. Approximately 150 homes have been provided to families in areas in which Warrick played football.

He was motivated to create this charity by his mother, who for many years yearned for a home of her own for her six children. Tragically, she was murdered by robbers as she helped a woman make a night deposit. Although a policewoman, she was off-duty at the time. Warrick, her oldest son, was eighteen at the time. With the support of friends and relatives, he became head of the household. He immediately took the money from his mother's insurance policy and bought a home for his siblings. His grandmother helped him raise his siblings while he attended Florida State in Tallahassee. Proudly, he graduated in 1997 with a degree in information studies and was drafted by the Buccaneers.

In Tampa, he was named NFL Rookie of the Year by *Football News*, *Pro Football Weekly*, and *Sports Illustrated*. After leaving the Buccaneers, he played for the Falcons for six seasons and then returned to Tampa for his final season. Arthur Blank, the owner of the Falcons, thought so highly of Dunn that he offered him a part interest in the team.

In 2002, he founded the Warrick Dunn Charities. His outstanding community work was a high-paying benefit of his time in football and was noticed by former president Bill Clinton. He received the Giant Steps Award for his civic leadership. Originally from Louisiana, he raised more than $5 million in donations from his NFL brothers to help victims of Hurricane Katrina. He also received the Bart Starr Award in 2009 and the Jefferson Award for Outstanding Athlete in Service and Philanthropy in 2011.

Let's compare and contrast these situations. Dunn grew up in poverty with a single, working mom of six children. He had to take on the responsibility of raising his siblings when his mother died. Who would have thought this young man would have succeeded in life with the many obstacles blocking his way? His grandmother was influential because she insisted he follow his plans to attend college. He graduated on time. His mother's desire for a home for her family drove Dunn in his charity work.

Likewise, Brooks was raised by a single mom for his first six years. His family took an active interest in his education and he graduated college the same year he was drafted by the Bucs. His grandmother set the stage for his charity work as she fed the homeless strangers that appeared at her door. He speaks of his Christian faith and the importance in his life of his mentor Tony Dungy.

Are education and grandmothers the answer? Sapp didn't finish his education. It was never a priority for him. He was known on campus for smoking marijuana more than studying. He was there to play football and get drafted by an NFL team. He wasn't concerned with life after playing in the NFL. He figured things would work out one way or the other. Sapp was raised by a single mom too, just as Dunn and Brooks were. But Sapp never learned to respect women. Ultimately, that led to his biggest problems. With the rise of the MeToo Movement, irresponsible male behavior is not tolerated anymore. Sapp has yet to acknowledge that times have changed. Perhaps we will never be able to find that unknown factor that leads to the difference in these men and others.

CONCLUSION

Football coaches across all levels of the sport, from Pop Warner to high school on up, love to promote how the game teaches teamwork—one for all and all for one. If you do your job, stay in your lane, and execute your assignment, and your teammates do the same, you'll succeed and learn lifelong lessons in the process. Trust your teammates to your left and right. Don't grandstand. Submerge yourself for the sake of the team. They're messages drummed into players' heads from a young age.

By the time they make it to the NFL, players have spent ten, fifteen, and even twenty years listening to these mantras and living according to regimented schedules, taking orders from a range of coaches, and with few exceptions, expressing themselves through the dynamic of sacrificing for the team. By giving themselves to the sport, there is an assumption the sport will give back to them. Of course, long-lasting friendships develop and players remain in contact with influential coaches for decades.

But the NFL is unique because it is a business that produces an entertainment product called football, and the players are paid to perform every Sunday. Of course, the players love what they do and they're good at it. But at the end of the day, their ability to entertain is governed by a collective bargaining agreement and many other rules of the game and codes of conduct governed by the commissioner, the league office, and teams and coaches.

So when the day comes when their bodies are just too battered to go on, or are no longer valuable enough to continue being paid to play in the NFL, their contracts end and their connections to the NFL move into another phase: the retired player phase. Unlike the college draft and orientation program for rookies, there is no mandatory program for former players now out of a job.

On paper, there are many services and benefits available to these former players, but they are complex and sometimes hard to acquire. Initially, though, the biggest challenges at the outset are psychological. Few players retire on their own terms. Most of them are instantly thrust into the world when their coach cuts them or when no team will give them a new contract. Suddenly, there are few schedules and no one barking orders. To some, this is liberation. No early wakeup calls, no pressing need to work hours a day in the gym, and no need for painkillers to deaden the pain from injuries. Most of all, no coach yelling in your ear.

The honeymoon doesn't last long. Freed of schedules, many former players go home and do the opposite: they sit on the sofa, watch TV, and maybe play some golf. They catch up with friends and family. But eventually, their wife or girlfriend kicks the player off the sofa and tells him to get busy. But where should he go?

Most players have not saved enough that they can quit working, so finding a new job is a necessity. Coaching is always an option, but becoming a college or pro coach takes many years, and a lot of moving from city to city. Working in sales is a possibility, but many sales jobs are heavily weighted toward commissions, so the income is unsteady. Broadcasting jobs are few and far between, and at least at the outset don't pay much.

Then the residual effects of the injuries kick in—surgeries on knees, elbows, feet, back, and so on. Each is necessary, but they can also be debilitating. For linemen, there's also the need to lose the weight they gained to do their jobs. Losing thirty, forty, or even fifty pounds is a difficult undertaking, even more so if the athlete has so many injuries that he has difficulty doing aerobic exercise, such as walking for long periods on a treadmill.

The NFL is the wealthiest sports league in the United States, now bringing in about $15 billion a year. Owners have seen the value of their franchises skyrocket. In 2018, Jerry Richardson, the founding owner of the Carolina Panthers, sold the team to David A. Tepper, a billionaire hedge fund titan, for a record $2.2 billion. That was roughly ten times the $206 million he paid for the team in 1993. And the windfall came after an investigation in *Sports Illustrated* tied him to allegations of sexual harassment in the club's front office.

The money will keep pouring in. In 2021 and 2022, the NFL will renegotiate its multi-billion-dollar media and broadcast contracts that generate about half of the league's revenue. The value of those new contracts is unknown. But NFL games are by far the most-watched programs on television, and networks from CBS to Fox to NBC are expected to bid billions of dollars more for the rights to keep broadcasting games. As the NFL's money pot grows, its salary cap will keep rising, which means average player salaries will keep growing too.

And yet, when it comes to helping take care of retired players, the money flows a lot slower. Sure, the current generation of players receives substantially larger pensions to go with robust 401(k) accounts and an array of other services, as well as five years of health insurance if they are vested. But most of the worst health issues, like degenerative arthritis and the replacement of hips and knees, typically crop up after those five years of insurance have run out. Then there is the cognitive and neurological damage and symptoms like memory loss, depression, and short tempers that are associated with it.

The NFL Players Association has fought for benefit programs to help retired players cope with these issues. But the operative word is "fought." The owners rarely provide anything for free. The union and the current generation of players pay for benefits that their predecessors use, and that they, too, may need. The league contributes as well, of course. But many of the benefits—for instance, the disability plan— are jointly administered by representatives from the league and union, and the league has a knack of denying player applications to get the benefits they bargained for.

This book detailed many of the hurdles that the players face in obtaining these benefits. But hope is not lost. Groups like the Retired Player Assistance (RPA) can help former players and their families get the medical and psychological attention they need. The battle does not have to be fought alone. The process is unnecessarily expensive and complicated. But RPA can help players clear the administrative hurdles. The more former players use these services, the louder the message is to the NFL and the union that there are players in need and services that need to be funded. Retired players—the people who helped make the league the giant business it has become—need to get their share of the wealth they helped to create.

NOTES

2. TRANSITION

1. Mike Wells, www.espn.com, 8/24/2019.
2. "The Homeless Husky," Dan Raley, Husky Maven, 2/10/2020.
3. "Bankruptcy Rates among NFL Players with Short-Lived Income Spikes," NBER Working Paper, Kyle Carlson et al., April 2015. Collected data on teams from 1996 to 2003.
4. Christopher R. Deubert, Sarah McGraw, Holly Fernandez Lynch, Alixandra Nozzillo, and I. Glenn Cohen, "NFL or 'Not for Long'? Transitioning Out of the NFL," *Journal of Sports Behavior* 42 (4): 475.
5. Deubert et al., "NFL or 'Not for Long'?" 475.
6. Deubert et al., "NFL or 'Not for Long'?" 472.
7. Pat Evans, "Why Athlete Retirement Transitions Can Be So Devastating," *Front Office Sports*, 3/7/19.
8. https://www.pro-football-reference.com/players/H/HartBe00.htm.
9. Evans, "Why Athlete Retirement."
10. https://bleacherreport.com/articles/1314232-50-most-crooked-athletes.
11. https://www.espn.com/nfl/story/_/id/14628604/former-raiders-defensive-end-anthony-wayne-smith-sentenced-life-prison and https://www.cnn.com/2013/06/17/us/jose-canseco-fast-facts/index.html.
12. https://www.biography.com/crime-figure/oj-simpson.
13. https://gossipgist.com/rae-carruth.
14. https://www.charlotteobserver.com/sports/spt-columns-blogs/scott-fowler/article222710650.html.
15. https://www.history.com/this-day-in-history/boxing-legend-convicted-of-raping-beauty-queen.

16. https://sabr.org/bioproj/person/pete-rose.

17. https://www.investopedia.com/financial-edge/1012/pro-athletes-and-their-bad-money-habits.aspx.

18. https://drugandalcoholattorneys.com/drug-and-alcohol-attorney-interview-with-darryl-strawberry.

19. https://drugandalcoholattorneys.com/drug-and-alcohol-attorney-interview-with-vance-johnson.

20. https://drugandalcoholattorneys.com/the-journey-from-addiction-to-recovery-podcast-with-jayson-williams-stuart-m-goffman-alan-mednick-and-sean-nassif.

21. https://www.espn.com/nba/news/story?id=4938372.

22. https://www.palmbeachpost.com/sports/basketball/nba-star-jayson-williams-life-rebound-helps-others-with-addictions/
vESfKCGtN6THrqNwIBA
uxH.

23. https://futuresrecoveryhealthcare.com/rebound.

24. https://www.facebook.com/reboundforlife.

25. https://www.youtube.com/watch?v=9ZDQOlVSar4.

26. https://www.investopedia.com/financial-edge/1012/pro-athletes-and-their-bad-money-habits.aspx.

27. https://www.statista.com/statistics/240102/average-player-career-length-in-the-national-football-league.

28. https://www.si.com/nfl/2017/06/27/vince-young-cfl-saskatchewan-finances-bankruptcy-titans.

29. https://www.si.com/nfl/2017/06/27/vince-young-cfl-saskatchewan-finances-bankruptcy-titans.

30. http://www.nfl.com/news/story/09000d5d82906166/article/vince-young-agrees-to-oneyear-deal-with-buffalo-bills.

31. https://www.si.com/nfl/2017/06/27/vince-young-debt-chapter-11-bankruptcy.

32. https://bossip.com/649499/vince-youngs-crazy-purchases-that-drove-him-broke3920.

33. https://thesportsdrop.com/infqv/money-lessons-learned-from-nba-players-financial-fouls/37.

34. https://www.ncbi.nlm.nih.gov/pmc/articles/PMC4140700/#b16-sar-5–095.

35. https://www.ncbi.nlm.nih.gov/pmc/articles/PMC4140700/#b16-sar-5-095, citing D. H. Catlin and T. H. Murray, "Performance-Enhancing Drugs, Fair Competition, and Olympic Sport," *JAMA* 276 (1996): 231–37; and J. D. Metzl, E. Small, S. R. Levine, and J. C. Gershel, "Creatine Use among Young Athletes," *Pediatrics* 108 (2001): 421–25.

36. https://www.ncbi.nlm.nih.gov/pmc/articles/PMC4140700/#b4-sar-5-095, citing F. Botre and A. Pavan, "Enhancement Drugs and the Athlete," *Phys Med Rehabil Clin N Am* 20 (2009): 133–48.

37. https://www.ncbi.nlm.nih.gov/pmc/articles/PMC4140700/#b12-sar-5-095, citing D. A. Baron, C. L. Reardon, and S. H. Baron, "Doping in Sport," in *Clinical Sports Psychiatry: An International Perspective*, ed. D. A. Baron, C. L. Reardon, and S. H. Baron (Oxford, UK: Wiley, 2013).

38. https://www.ncbi.nlm.nih.gov/pmc/articles/PMC4140700/#b16-sar-5-095, citing D. A. Baron, D. M. Martin, and S. Abol Magd, "Doping in Sports and Its Spread to At-Risk Populations: An International Review," *World Psychiatry* 6 (2007): 118–23.

39. https://www.mirror.co.uk/news/uk-news/east-germanys-forgotten-olympic-doping-6949436.

40. https://www.theguardian.com/sport/that-1980s-sports-blog/2013/oct/21/ben-johnson-carl-lewis-dirtiest-race-history.

41. https://www.libertyhouseclinic.co.uk/cocaine-addiction-cause-tyson-furys-problems.

42. https://www.libertyhouseclinic.co.uk/cocaine-addiction-cause-tyson-furys-problems.

43. https://www.thefix.com/content/diego-maradona-admits-past-drug-use-has-caught-him.

44. http://www.ncaa.org/sport-science-institute/mind-body-and-sport-depression-and-anxiety-prevalence-student-athletes.

45. http://www.ncaa.org/sport-science-institute/mind-body-and-sport-depression-and-anxiety-prevalence-student-athletes.

46. https://www.healthcentral.com/slideshow/famous-athletes-that-struggle-with-depression.

47. https://www.clickondetroit.com/health/2017/05/31/former-nfl-player-randy-grimes-delivers-sobering-message-hope-on-prescription-pill-addiction.

48. https://faithonthefieldshow.com/randy-grimes-and-his-christian-faith.

49. https://faithonthefieldshow.com/randy-grimes-and-his-christian-faith.

50. https://faithonthefieldshow.com/randy-grimes-and-his-christian-faith.

51. https://www.youtube.com/watch?v=VbwTMJroTbI.

52. https://www.usatoday.com/story/sports/nfl/2018/07/31/how-kellen-winslow-ii-went-nfl-star-accused-serial-rapist-san-diego/862358002.

53. https://www.usatoday.com/story/sports/nfl/2018/07/31/how-kellen-winslow-ii-went-nfl-star-accused-serial-rapist-san-diego/862358002.

54. https://www.usatoday.com/story/sports/nfl/2018/07/31/how-kellen-winslow-ii-went-nfl-star-accused-serial-rapist-san-diego/862358002.

55. https://www.nytimes.com/2019/06/10/sports/kellen-winslow-jr-is-convicted-of-rape.html.

56. https://www.usatoday.com/story/sports/nfl/2019/11/05/nfl-kellen-win-slow-ii-has-cte-symptoms-his-attorneys-say/4162028002.

57. https://harvardjsel.com/2015/07/bethany-withers-without-consequence.

58. https://harvardjsel.com/2015/07/bethany-withers-without-consequence.

59. https://harvardjsel.com/2015/07/bethany-withers-without-consequence.

60. https://harvardjsel.com/2015/07/bethany-withers-without-consequence, citing "Jeff Taylor Suspended 24 Games," ESPN.com, November 20, 2014, http://espn.go.com/nba/story/_/id/11904798/jeff-taylor-charlotte-hornets-sus-pended-total-24-games-pleading-guilty-domestic-violence-case, archived at http://perma.cc/573T-ZFKN.

61. https://harvardjsel.com/2015/07/bethany-withers-without-consequence.

62. https://harvardjsel.com/2015/07/bethany-withers-without-consequence, relying on Joseph Person and Jonathan Jones, "Carolina Panthers' DE Greg Hardy's Court Date Pushed Back into 2015," *Charlotte Observer*, November 4, 2014, archived at http://perma.cc/P9BL-LZB3l; Joseph Person, "NFL Nears End of Greg Hardy Investigation," *Charlotte Observer*; and https://www.espn.com/nfl/story/_/id/11547511/police-report-says-jonathan-dwyer-ari-zona-cardinals-head-butted-punched-wife-struck-young-son-shoe.

63. https://harvardjsel.com/2015/07/bethany-withers-without-consequence.

64. https://www.theguardian.com/society/2010/sep/05/men-victims-domes-tic-violence.

65. https://harvardjsel.com/2015/07/bethany-withers-without-consequence.

66. https://harvardjsel.com/2015/07/bethany-withers-without-consequence.

67. https://harvardjsel.com/2015/07/bethany-withers-without-consequence, citing "Manny Ramirez Tells Reporters He 'Closed' His Domestic Violence Case, Report Says," CBSNews.com, September 14, 2011, http://www.cbsnews.com/news/manny-ramirez-tells-reporters-he-closed-his-domestic-violence-case-report-says.

68. https://www.youtube.com/watch?v=VbwTMJroTbI.

69. https://www.cnn.com/2013/10/31/us/balco-fast-facts/index.html.

70. https://harvardjsel.com/2015/07/bethany-withers-without-consequence.

3. HEALTH IN THE LOCKER ROOM

1. https://www.nfl.com/news/niners-acquire-redskins-tackle-trent-williams-in-trade-0ap3000001111403.

4. RACIAL DISPARITY

1. https://www.cnn.com/2020/06/05/sport/roger-goodell-responds-nfl-stronger-together-video/index.html.

2. Nancy Armour, "Cornerbacks Suffer Most Concussions, according to NFL Report," *USA Today Sports*, November 9, 2017, https://www.usatoday.com/story/sports/nfl/2017/11/09/cornerbacks-suffer-most-concussions-according-nfl-report/849749001.

3. https://concussionfoundation.org/CTE-resources/what-is-CTE.

5. NFL BENEFITS

1. Patrick Hruby, "Bad News for the NFL: John Riggins' Wife Is a Lawyer," *Washingtonian*, February 10, 2019, https://www.washingtonian.com/2019/02/10/bad-news-for-the-nfl-john-riggins-wife-lisa-marie-riggins-is-a-lawyer.

2. Cameron Miller, "Sports Law Development of the Week: Federal Judge Rules Former N.F.L. Player Wrongly Denied Disability Benefits," *SLA Blog*, March 5, 2019, https://blog.sportslaw.org/posts/sports-law-development-of-the-week-federal-judge-rules-former-nfl-player-wrongly-denied-disability-benefits.

3. https://www.zuckerman.com/news/press-release/court-finds-nfl-broke-law-refusing-benefits-brain-injuries.

4. "Federal Court Exposes NFL's Quiet Travesty: Denial of Retired Player Benefits," *Forbes*, July 3, 2017.

5. "Appeals Court Rules against N.F.L. Pension Plan, Finds Ex-Player 'Totally Disabled' from Concussion and CTE," Zuckerman Spaeder Press Release, June 23, 2017, https://www.zuckerman.com/news/press-release/appeals-court-rules-against-nfl-pension-plan-finds-ex-player-totally-disabled-concussion-and-cte.

6. Michael Rosenberg, "Permanently Disabled, Harrison Fighting for Benefits N.F.L. Took Away," *Sports Illustrated*, January 24, 2014, https://www.si.com/nfl/2014/01/29/dwight-harrison-nfl-pension.

7. Dr. Harlan Selesnick, 2/24/10.

8. Alan Schwarz, "Before Dementia Assistance, Help with NFL Application," *New York Times*, January 21, 2010, https://www.nytimes.com/2010/01/22/sports/football/22eckwood.html.

6. CONCUSSIONS AND
THE NFL SETTLEMENT

1. https://www.nj.com/jets/2014/11/former_jets_receiver_wayne_chrebet_says_the_damage_is_done_regarding_impact_of_concussions_on_his_li.html.

2. Steve Fainaru and Mark Fainaru-Wada, "NFL Board Paid $2M to Players while League Denied Football-Concussion Link," PBS, November 16, 2012, https://www.pbs.org/wgbh/frontline/article/nfl-board-paid-2m-to-players-while-league-denied-football-concussion-link.

7. CHRONIC TRAUMATIC ENCEPHALOPATHY

1. Adam Kilgore, *Washington Post*, 11/9/17.

2. https://www.nytimes.com/2015/07/25/sports/football/junior-seaus-family-will-not-be-allowed-to-speak-at-his-hall-of-fame-induction.html.

8. DRUG ADDICTIONS

1. Uninterrupted interview, 10/17.

2. Randy Grimes, "Off Center," unpublished.

3. Ibid.

4. https://www.si.com/nfl/2013/11/12/sam-hurd-cocaine-bust.

5. Chris Ballard, "Jeff Hatch Was Dealing Fentanyl. And Helping Addicts. Then a Planned Visit from the VP Blew It All Up," *Sports Illustrated*, October 2, 2019, https://www.si.com/nfl/2019/10/02/jeff-hatch-ex-nfl-player-drug-dealer-arrest-opioid-epidemic.

9. DOMESTIC VIOLENCE

1. Deborah Epstein, "I'm Done Helping the NFL Players Association Pay Lip Service to Domestic Violence Prevention," *Washington Post*, June 5, 2018.

2. https://www.nytimes.com/2016/10/22/sports/football/giants-josh-brown-abuse-nfl.html.

10. SUCCESS VERSUS BANKRUPTCY

1. Rick Stroud, *Tampa Bay Times*, 7/30/14.

2. "Tampa's Super Bowl Has a Face and It's Derrick Brooks," *Tampa Bay Times*, 9/4/19.

BIBLIOGRAPHY

PREFACE

Goldstein, Richard. "Gay Culverhouse, Who Helped Injured Football Players, Dies at 73." *New York Times*, July 2, 2020. https://www.nytimes.com/2020/07/02/sports/football/gay-culverhouse-dead.html.

CHAPTER I

Ackerman, McCarton. "Diego Maradona Admits Past Drug Use Has Caught Up to Him." Thefix.com, September 22, 2014. https://www.thefix.com/content/diego-maradona-admits-past-drug-use-has-caught-him.

Associated Press. "Rams, Colts Ownership Reportedly Will Change." *Gadsen Times*, June 23, 1972. https://news.google.com/newspapers?id=ZAMkAAAAIBAJ&sjid=z9cEAAAAIBAJ&pg=5564%2C3166070.

———. "Stalker of Culverhouse Family Sentenced to 27 Years." December 15, 1995. https://apnews.com/article/02b522d11c53394b604df61ed3382f7a.

Harmon Wages Statistics. https://www.pro-football-reference.com/players/W/Wage-Ha00.htm.

Litsky, Frank. "Hugh Culverhouse, 75, Owner of the Buccaneers." *New York Times*, August 26, 1994. https://www.nytimes.com/1994/08/26/obituaries/hugh-culverhouse-75-owner-of-the-buccaneers.html.

Mayo, Michael. "Bucs President Fights the Country-Club Set." *Florida Sun-Sentinel*, October 20, 1991. https://www.sun-sentinel.com/news/fl-xpm-1991-10-20-9102120156-story.html.

Smith, Scott. "Forever #1: The Lee Roy Selmon Pick." Buccaneers.com, April 8, 2016. https://www.buccaneers.com/news/forever-1-the-lee-roy-selmon-pick-17004317.

Tampa Bay Times. "Culverhouse and the Bucs: A Chronology." August 26, 1994. https://www.tampabay.com/archive/1994/08/26/culverhouse-and-the-bucs-a-chronology.

Chapter 2

Armstrong, Jeremy. "East Germany's Forgotten Olympic Doping Victims Tell of Illness, Infertility and Changing Sex." Mirror.co.uk, December 3, 2015. https://www.mirror.co.uk/news/uk-news/east-germanys-forgotten-olympic-doping-6949436.

Associated Press. "Kellen Winslow Jr. Is Convicted of Rape." *New York Times*, June 10, 2019. https://www.nytimes.com/2019/06/10/sports/kellen-winslow-jr-is-convicted-of-rape.html.

———. "Williams to Serve at Least 18 Months." *ESPN*, February 23, 2010. https://www.espn.com/nba/news/story?id=4938372.

Astor, Mark. "Drug and Alcohol Attorney Interview with Darryl Strawberry." Drugandalcoholattorneys.com. https://drugandalcoholattorneys.com/drug-and-alcohol-attorney-interview-with-darryl-strawberry.

———. "Drug and Alcohol Attorney Interview with Jayson Williams." Drugandalcoholattorneys.com. https://drugandalcoholattorneys.com/the-journey-from-addiction-to-recovery-podcast-with-jayson-williams-stuart-m-goffman-alan-mednick-and-sean-nassif.

———. "Drug and Alcohol Attorney Interview with Vance Johnson." Drugandalcoholattorneys.com. https://drugandalcoholattorneys.com/drug-and-alcohol-attorney-interview-with-vance-johnson.

Belson, Ken. "The Class of '90: Where Are They Now?" *New York Times*, April 29, 2015. https://www.nytimes.com/interactive/2015/04/28/sports/football/nfl-draft-class-1990.html.

Bishop, Greg. "Taking Vows in a League Hit Hard by Divorce." *New York Times*, August 9, 2009. https://www.nytimes.com/2009/08/09/sports/football/09marriage.html.

Bossip.com. "How Did Former QB Vince Young Blow $30 Million in Three Years? Look at All The Crazy Isht He Spent His Money On!" September 20, 2012. https://bossip.com/649499/vince-youngs-crazy-purchases-that-drove-him-broke3920.

Burlew, Jeff. "Local Attorney, Former Boosters Chair, Charged in Alleged NFL Investment Scam." *Tallahassee Democrat*, August 29, 2019. https://www.tallahassee.com/story/news/local/2019/08/29/local-attorney-former-boosters-chair-charged-alleged-nfl-investment-scam/2156671001.

Carlson, Kyle, et al. "Bankruptcy Rates among NFL Players with Short-Lived Income Spikes." NBER Working Paper, April 2015. https://www.nber.org/papers/w21085.

Chavez, Chris. "How Vince Young Racked Up Millions in Debt by 2014." SI.com, June 27, 2017. https://www.si.com/nfl/2017/06/27/vince-young-debt-chapter-11-bankruptcy.

Davoren, Ann Kearns, and Seunghyun Hwang. "Mind, Body, and Sport: Depression and Anxiety Prevalence in Student-Athletes." NCAA Sport Science Institute, October 8, 2014. http://www.ncaa.org/sport-science-institute/mind-body-and-sport-depression-and-anxiety-prevalence-student-athletes.

Deubert, Christopher R., Sarah Mc Graw, Holly Fernandez Lynch, Alixandra Nozzillo, and I. Glenn Cohen. "NFL or 'Not for Long'? Transitioning Out of the NFL." *Journal of Sports Behavior* 42 (4): 461–508. https://papers.ssrn.com/sol3/papers.cfm?abstract_id=3497163.

Evans, Pat. "Why Athlete Retirement Transitions Can Be So Devastating." *Front Office Sports*, March 7, 2019. https://frontofficesports.com/athlete-retirement-psychology.

Fowler, Scott. "I Rang Rae Carruth's Doorbell in Pennsylvania. Here's What Happened Next." *Charlotte Observer*, December 11, 2018. https://www.charlotteobserver.com/sports/spt-columns-blogs/scott-fowler/article222710650.html.

Gillespie, Claire. "10 Famous Athletes Who Struggle with Depression." Healthcentral.com, May 31, 2017. https://www.healthcentral.com/slideshow/famous-athletes-that-struggle-with-depression.

Gough, Christina. "Average Length of Player Careers in the NFL." Statista.com, September 10, 2019. https://www.statista.com/statistics/240102/average-player-career-length-in-the-national-football-league.

Grimes, Randy. "Randy Grimes Talks About His Christian Faith." Faithonthefieldshow.com. https://faithonthefieldshow.com/randy-grimes-and-his-christian-faith.

History.com. "Star Boxer Mike Tyson Convicted of Rape." History.com, February 10, 1992. https://www.history.com/this-day-in-history/boxing-legend-convicted-of-raping-beauty-queen.

Liberty House Clinic. "Is Cocaine Addiction the Cause of Tyson Fury's Problems?" https://www.libertyhouseclinic.co.uk/cocaine-addiction-cause-tyson-furys-problems.

Moore, Richard. "Ben Johnson, Carl Lewis, and the Drama of the Dirtiest Race in History." *Guardian*, October 21, 2013. https://www.theguardian.com/sport/that-1980s-sports-blog/2013/oct/21/ben-johnson-carl-lewis-dirtiest-race-history.

Nanavati, Raj. "Famous NBA and NFL Stars Who Blew Their Fame and Fortune." Thesportsdrop.com, May 25, 2019. https://thesportsdrop.com/infqv/money-lessons-learned-from-nba-players-financial-fouls/37.

Palmer, Barclay. "Pro Athletes and Their Bad Money Habits." Investopedia.com, November 3, 2019. https://www.investopedia.com/financial-edge/1012/pro-athletes-and-their-bad-money-habits.aspx.

Raley, Dan. "The Homeless Husky: Ex-UW, NFL Linebacker Tim Meamber." SI.com, February 10, 2020. https://www.si.com/college/washington/legends/former-nfl-linebacker-tim-meamber-talks-about-his-homelessness.

Reardon, Claudia L., and Shane Creado. "Drug Abuse in Athletes." *Substance Abuse and Rehabilitation* 5 (2014): 95–105. https://www.ncbi.nlm.nih.gov/pmc/articles/PMC4140700/#b16-sar-5-095.

Rogers, Lee. "There's Only One Way to Play." 106.3 Word, January 16, 2020. https://1063word.radio.com/articles/news/theres-only-one-way-to-play.

Schrotenboer, Brent. "Convicted Ex-NFL Tight End Kellen Winslow II Has CTE Symptoms, His Attorneys Say." *USA Today*, November 5, 2019. https://www.usatoday.com/story/sports/nfl/2019/11/05/nfl-kellen-winslow-ii-has-cte-symptoms-his-attorneys-say/4162028002.

Shapiro, Leonard. "The Hit That Changed a Career." *Washington Post*, November 18, 2005. https://www.washingtonpost.com/wp-dyn/content/article/2005/11/17/AR2005111701635.html.

30 for 30. "Broke." ESPN. https://www.youtube.com/watch?v=9ZDQOlVSar4.

TMZ. "Ray Rice Knocked Out Fiancee." Tmz.com, September 8, 2014. https://www.youtube.com/watch?v=VbwTMJroTbI.

Wangler, Sierra. "Former NFL Player Randy Grimes Delivers Sobering Message, Hope on Prescription Pill Addiction." Clickonitdetroit.com, May 31, 2017. https://www.clickondetroit.com/health/2017/05/31/former-nfl-player-randy-grimes-delivers-sobering-message-hope-on-prescription-pill-addiction.

Wells, Mike. "Luck Retires, Calls Decision 'Hardest of My Life.'" ESPN, August 24, 2019. https://www.espn.com/nfl/story/_/id/27456682/luck-retires-calls-decision-hardest-my-life.

Wikipedia. List of Professional Sportspeople Convicted of Crimes. https://en.wikipedia.org/wiki/List_of_professional_sportspeople_convicted_of_crimes.

Withers, Bethany. "Without Consequence: When Professional Athletes Are Violent off the Field." *Harvard Journal of Sports and Entertainment Law*, July 12, 2015. https://harvardjsel.com/2015/07/bethany-withers-without-consequence.

Wyche, Steve. "Vince Young Agrees to One-Year Deal with Buffalo Bills." NFL.com, May 11, 2012. http://www.nfl.com/news/story/09000d5d82906166/article/vince-young-agrees-to-oneyear-deal-with-buffalo-bills.

CHAPTER 3

Associated Press. "NFL Players, Harvard Team Up for $100 Million Health Study." *USA Today*, January 29, 2013. https://www.usatoday.com/story/sports/nfl/2013/01/29/nfl-retired-players-harvard-medical-study/1873661.

Brandt, Andrew. "The Delicate Issue of Medical Disagreements between NFL Player and Team." *Sports Illustrated*, November 13, 2019. https://www.si.com/nfl/2019/11/13/trent-williams-redskins-kelechi-osemele-jets-nfl-medical-issues.

"C.B.A. Agreement: What All Former Players Need to Know." https://www.nflalumni.org/news/what-the-2020-cba-means-for-retired-nfl-players.

Cohen, I. Glenn, Holly Fernandez, and Christopher Deubert. "A Proposal to Address NFL Club Doctors' Conflicts of Interest and to Promote Player Trust." Harvard University Hastings Center, November–December 2016. https://footballplayershealth.harvard.edu/wp-content/uploads/2016/09/1-Hastings-Center-Report-The-Role-of-Club-Doctors.pdf.

Fainaru, Steve, and Mark Fainaru-Wada. "League of Denial: The NFL, Concussions, and the Battle for the Truth." October 8, 2013. https://www.google.com/books/edition/League_of_Denial/4VITAAAAQBAJ?hl=en&gbpv=1&printsec=frontcover.

Finkel, Adam, and Chris Deubert. "The NFL as a Workplace: The Prospect of Applying Occupational Health and Safety Law to Protect NFL Workers." *Labor Law eJournal*, 2018.   https://pdfs.semanticscholar.org/bdff/bd6ccfe6c38766839ce33f58a8adb61bf084.pdf.

Knight, Joey. "Former Bucs Linebacker, Tampa Catholic Coach David Lewis Dies." *Tampa Bay Times*, July 15, 2020. https://www.tampabay.com/sports/bucs/2020/07/15/former-bucs-linebacker-tampa-catholic-coach-david-lewis-dies.

Roberts, Andrea. "Number of Years in NFL, Certain Positions Portend Greater Risk for Cognitive, Mental Health Problems in Former Players." *American Journal of Sports Medicine*, August 30, 2019. https://footballplayershealth.harvard.edu/about/news/number-of-years-in-nfl-certain-positions-portend-greater-risk-for-cognitive-mental-health-problems-in-former-players.

Schwarz, Alan. "Congress to Hold Hearing on N.F.L. Head Injuries." *New York Times*, October 2, 2009. https://www.nytimes.com/2009/10/03/sports/football/03dementia.html.

Sessler, Marc. "NFLPA: 78 Percent of Players Don't Trust Team Doctors." NFL.com, January 31, 2013. http://www.nfl.com/news/story/0ap1000000133534/article/nflpa-78-percent-of-players-dont-trust-team-doctors.

Shook, Nick. "Niners Acquire Redskins Tackle Trent Williams in Trade." NFL.com, April 25, 2020. https://www.nfl.com/news/niners-acquire-redskins-tackle-trent-williams-in-trade-0ap
3000001111403.

U.C. Health Media Room. "The Bell Tolls for Outdated Sports Phrases: Dings and Rings Mean Mild Brain Injury." April 30, 2010. https://www.uchealth.com/articles/the-bell-tolls-for-outdated-sports-phrases-dings-and-rings-mean-mild-brain-injury.

CHAPTER 4

Armour, Nancy. "Cornerbacks Suffer Most Concussions, according to NFL Report." *USA Today Sports*, November 9, 2017. https://www.usatoday.com/story/sports/nfl/2017/11/09/cornerbacks-suffer-most-concussions-according-nfl-report/849749001.

Boren, Cindy. "The NFL Studied Every Concussion over Two Seasons." *Washington Post*, November 9, 2017. https://www.washingtonpost.com/news/early-lead/wp/2017/11/09/the-nfl-studied-every-concussion-over-two-seasons-what-happens-next-may-be-up-to-manufacturers.

Boston University Research CTE Center. "Frequently Asked Questions about CTE." Accessed January 19, 2021. https://www.bu.edu/cte/about/frequently-asked-questions/

#:~:text=
Chron-
ic%20Traumatic%20Encephalopathy%20(CTE)%20is,that%20do%20not%20cause%20s
ymptoms.

Bouchette, Ed, and Ray Fittipaldo. "Bill Nunn Jr., Football Pioneer Who Scouted Steelers Legends, Dies at 89." *Pittsburgh Post-Gazette*, May 7, 2014. https://www.post-gazette.com/sports/steelers/2014/05/07/Bill-Nunn-Jr-long-time-Steelers-scout-dies-at-89/stories/201405 070182.

Gertz, Michael. "NFL Census 2016." ProFootballLogic.com, April 19, 2017. http://www.profootballlogic.com/articles/nfl-census-2016.

Melas, Chloe. "NFL Commissioner Roger Goodell Says League Was Wrong for Not Listening to Players Earlier about Racism." CNN.com, June 6, 2020. https://www.cnn.com/2020/06/05/sport/roger-goodell-responds-nfl-stronger-together-video/index.html.

Patra, Kevin. "NFL Instituting Changes to Rooney Rule." NFL.com, May 18, 2020. https://www.nfl.com/news/nfl-instituting-changes-to-rooney-rule.

Pro Football Hall of Fame. https://www.profootballhof.com/players/fritz-pollard.

Rhoden, William. "The N.F.L.'s Embrace of Black Players Has Always Been Conditional." *New York Times*, December 20, 2019. https://www.nytimes.com/2019/12/20/sports/football/nfl-black-players-fritz-pollard-colin-kaepernick.html.

CHAPTER 5

Associated Press. "N.F.L. Hall of Famers Demand Health Insurance and Share of Revenue." *New York Times*, September 18, 2018. https://www.nytimes.com/2018/09/18/sports/football/nfl-hall-of-fame-eric-dickerson.html.

Belson, Ken. "Fight for Cash Goes On for N.F.L.'s Longtime Retirees." *New York Times*, September 7, 2018. https://www.nytimes.com/2018/09/07/sports/nfl-retired-players.html.

Belson, Ken. "Help for Disabled N.F.L. Players Is Sacrificed for Pension Deal." *New York Times*, March 25, 2020. https://www.nytimes.com/2020/03/25/sports/football/nfl-retired-players-benefits.html.

Groves, Roger. "Federal Court Exposes N.F.L.'s Quiet Travesty: Denial of Retired Player Benefits." *Forbes*, July 3, 2017. https://www.forbes.com/sites/rogergroves/2017/07/03/federal-court-exposes-nfls-quiet-travesty-denial-of-retired-player-benefits/#44710ca34ad1.

Hruby, Patrick. "Bad News for the NFL: John Riggins' Wife Is a Lawyer." *Washingtonian*, February 10, 2019. https://www.washingtonian.com/2019/02/10/bad-news-for-the-nfl-john-riggins-wife-lisa-marie-riggins-is-a-lawyer.

Miller, Cameron. "Sports Law Development of the Week: Federal Judge Rules Former N.F.L. Player Wrongly Denied Disability Benefits." *SLA Blog*, March 5, 2019. https://blog.sportslaw.org/posts/sports-law-development-of-the-week-federal-judge-rules-for-mer-nfl-player-wrongly-denied-disability-benefits.

Rosenberg, Michael. "Permanently Disabled, Harrison Fighting for Benefits N.F.L. Took Away." *Sports Illustrated*, January 24, 2014. https://www.si.com/nfl/2014/01/29/dwight-harrison-nfl-pension.

Schwarz, Alan. "Before Dementia Assistance, Help with N.F.L. Application." *New York Times*, January 21, 2010. https://www.nytimes.com/2010/01/22/sports/football/22eckwood.html.

———. "Wives United by Husbands' Post-N.F.L. Trauma." *New York Times*, March 14, 2007. https://www.nytimes.com/2007/03/14/sports/football/14wives.html.

Zuckerman Spaeder. "Appeals Court Rules against N.F.L. Pension Plan, Finds Ex-Player 'Totally Disabled' from Concussion and CTE." Press Release, June 23, 2017. https://www.zuckerman.com/news/press-release/appeals-court-rules-against-nfl-pension-plan-finds-ex-player-totally-disabled-concussion-and-cte.

———. "Court Finds NFL Broke Law in Refusing Benefits for Brain Injuries." Press Release, March 8, 2016. https://www.zuckerman.com/news/press-release/court-finds-nfl-broke-law-refusing-benefits-brain-injuries.

CHAPTER 6

Associated Press. "Neurologist Denies Concussion-Disease Link." CBS, January 5, 2010. https://www.cbsnews.com/news/neurologist-denies-concussion-disease-link.
Belson, Ken. "For N.F.L., Concussion Suits May Be Test for Sport Itself." *New York Times*, December 29, 2011. https://www.nytimes.com/2011/12/30/sports/football/nfl-faces-retired-players-in-a-high-stakes-legal-battle.html.
———. "N.F.L. Agrees to Settle Concussion Suit for $765 Million." *New York Times*, August 29, 2013. https://www.nytimes.com/2013/08/30/sports/football/judge-announces-settlement-in-nfl-concussion-suit.html.
———. "N.F.L. Doctor Who Discounted Dangers of Head Trauma Retires." *New York Times*, July 20, 2016. https://www.nytimes.com/2016/07/21/sports/football/nfl-doctor-elliot-pellman-concussions-retires.html.
Belson, Ken, and Kevin Draper. "The N.F.L.'s Favorite Helmet Maker Is in Financial Trouble." *New York Times*, December 17, 2019. https://www.nytimes.com/2019/12/17/sports/football/football-helmet-vicis.html.
Belson, Ken, and Jon Hurdle. "Crowded Courtroom for N.F.L. Lawsuit." *New York Times*, April 9, 2013. https://www.nytimes.com/2013/04/10/sports/football/judge-hears-nfl-arguments-to-dismiss-head-trauma-cases.html.
Fainaru, Steve, and Mark Fainaru-Wada. "NFL Board Paid $2M to Players while League Denied Football-Concussion Link." PBS, November 16, 2012. https://www.pbs.org/wgbh/frontline/article/nfl-board-paid-2m-to-players-while-league-denied-football-concussion-link.
Keating, Peter. "Doctor Yes." ESPN, November 6, 2006 https://www.espn.com/espnmag/story?id=3644940.
Luckasevic, Jason. "Luckasevic Motion to Enforce Settlement." U.S. District Court for the Eastern District of Pennsylvania, March 31, 2020. https://www.documentcloud.org/documents/6821778-11038-0-Luckasevic-Motion-to-Enforce-Settlement.html.
Seeger Weiss. "$4.85 Billion Settlement: Vioxx." Press Release, July 17, 2008. https://www.seegerweiss.com/news/merck-vioxx-settlement.
Slater, Darryl. "Former Jets Receiver Wayne Chrebet on Concussions: 'The Damage Is Done.'" NJ Advance Media, November 27, 2014. https://www.nj.com/jets/2014/11/former_jets_receiver_wayne_chrebet_says_the_damage_is_done_regarding_impact_of_con cussions_on_his_li.html.
WCVB. "Long NFL Careers Spell Greater Risk for 'Serious Cognitive Problems,' Harvard Research Finds." WCVB.com, August 30, 2019. https://www.wcvb.com/article/long-nfl-careers-spell-greater-risk-for-serious-cognitive-problems-harvard-research-finds/28869855.

CHAPTER 7

Breslow, Jason. "Junior Seau Suffered Chronic Brain Damage, NIH Study Finds." *Frontline*, PBS, January 10, 2013. https://www.pbs.org/wgbh/frontline/article/junior-seau-suffered-chronic-brain-damage-nih-study-finds.
Carey, Benedict. "Yes, Aaron Hernandez Suffered Brain Injury, But That May Not Explain His Violence." *New York Times*, September 22, 2017. https://www.nytimes.com/2017/09/22/health/aaron-hernandez-brain.html.

Gonzales, Richard. "Researcher Says Aaron Hernandez's Brain Showed Signs of Severe CTE." NPR.com, November 9, 2017. https://www.npr.org/sections/thetwo-way/2017/11/09/563194252/researcher-says-aaron-hernandez-s-brain-showed-signs-of-severe-cte.

Ilgore, Adam. "Aaron Hernandez Suffered from Most Severe CTE Ever Found in a Person His Age." *Washington Post*, November 9, 2017. https://www.washingtonpost.com/sports/aaron-hernandez-suffered-from-most-severe-cte-ever-found-in-a-person-his-age/2017/11/09/fa7c d204-c57b-11e7-afe9-4f60b5a6c4a0_story.html.

Pilkington, Ed. "The NFL Star and the Brain Injuries that Destroyed Him." *Guardian*, July 19, 2011. https://www.theguardian.com/science/2011/jul/19/nfl-star-brain-injuries-destroyed.

Schrotenboer, Brent. "Crimes of Ex-NFL Star Kellen Winslow Said to Be Driven by Brain Injuries." *USA TODAY*, March 10, 2020. https://www.usatoday.com/story/sports/nfl/2020/03/10/ex-nfl-star-kellen-winslow-committed-crimes-driven-cte-lawyers-say/5008271002.

———. "Why Ex-NFL Star Kellen Winslow II Descended into Darkness, according to Family Letters." *USA TODAY*, March 17, 2020. https://www.usatoday.com/story/sports/nfl/2020/03/17/kellen-winslow-descended-into-darkness-according-family-letters/5065811002.

Schwarz, Alan. "A Suicide, a Last Request, a Family's Questions." *New York Times*, February 23, 2011. https://www.nytimes.com/2011/02/23/sports/football/23duerson.html.

Sheets, Megan, and Alex Raskin. "Ex-NFL Star Kellen Winslow Jr's Wife Files for Divorce after His Rape Conviction." *Daily Mail*, September 16, 2019. https://www.dailymail.co.uk/news/article-7469983/Ex-NFL-star-Kellen-Winslow-Jrs-wife-files-divorce-rape-conviction.html.

Slideshow. "NFL Players with CTE." *CBS News*. Accessed January 20, 2021. https://www.cbsnews.com/pictures/nfl-football-players-with-cte.

CHAPTER 8

Associated Press. "Sam Hurd Receives 15-Year Sentence for Drug-Distribution Role." NFL.com, November 13, 2013. http://www.nfl.com/news/story/0ap2000000281352/article/sam-hurd-receives-15year-sentence-for-drugdistribution-role.

Ballard, Chris. "Jeff Hatch Was Dealing Fentanyl. And Helping Addicts. Then a Planned Visit from the VP Blew It All Up." *Sports Illustrated*, October 2, 2019. https://www.si.com/nfl/2019/10/02/jeff-hatch-ex-nfl-player-drug-dealer-arrest-opioid-epidemic.

Belson, Ken. "For N.F.L. Retirees, Opioids Bring More Pain." *New York Times*, February 2, 2019. https://www.nytimes.com/2019/02/02/sports/nfl-opioids-.html.

Bruno, Bianca. "Ex-NFL Player Sentenced for Selling Opioids for International Drug Ring." Courthousenews.com, July 5, 2017. https://www.courthousenews.com/ex-nfl-player-sentenced-selling-opioids-international-drug-ring.

Dryden, Jim. "Retired NFL Players Using Painkillers." Washington University School of Medicine in St. Louis, January 28, 2011. https://medicine.wustl.edu/news/podcast/retired-nfl-players-using-painkillers.

Dunne, Eugene, Catherine Striley, Zachary Mannes, Breton Asken, Nicole Ennis, and Linda Cottler. "Reasons for Prescription Opioid Use while Playing in the National Football League as Risk Factors for Current Use and Misuse among Former Players." PubMed.gov, June 28, 2018. https://www.ncbi.nlm.nih.gov/pubmed/29933284.

Spaeth, Emma. "How Opioids Are Destroying the Lives of NFL Players." *Daily Emerald*, May 14, 2019. https://www.dailyemerald.com/opinion/spaeth-how-opioids-are-destroying-the-lives-of-nfl-players/article_23834d64-768c-11e9-8abb-470fa65a8f5a.html.

Spiner, Trent. "Behind Pence's Air Force Two Cancellation: A Drug Dealer." *Politico*, July 22, 2019. https://www.politico.com/story/2019/07/22/pence-air-force-two-heroin-bust-1425823.

Swenson, Kyle. "From USC Football Player to Drug Lord: The Journey of Owen 'O-Dog' Hanson." *Washington Post*, December 20, 2017. https://www.washingtonpost.com/news/morning-mix/wp/2017/12/20/from-usc-football-player-to-drug-lord-the-journey-of-owen-o-dog-hanson.

Walter, Ashleigh. "Retired NFL Player Randy Grimes Helping Others with Addiction in Delray Beach." WPTV.com, September 6, 2019. https://www.wptv.com/news/region-s-palm-beach-county/delray-beach/retired-nfl-player-helping-others-with-addiction.

CHAPTER 9

Allen, Karma. "Arrest Warrant Issued for Former NFL Wide Receiver Antonio Brown in Assault Case." *ABC News*, January 22, 2020. https://abcnews.go.com/Sports/arrest-warrant-issued-nfl-wide-receiver-antonio-brown/story?id=68467212.

Alper, Josh. "Ufomba Kamalu Arrested on Domestic Violence Charge." *NBC Sports*, April 10, 2020. https://apple.news/AQPuXdx6SRqybfPSa084NcA.

Clickitticket.com. "The NFL and Domestic Abuse: A List of Players Arrested for Domestic Violence." March 27, 2019. https://www.clickitticket.com/nfl-domestic-violence.

Crosset, Todd. "Male Athletes' Violence against Women: A Critical Assessment of the Athletic Affiliation, Violence against Women Debate." *Quest* 51, no. 3 (April 20, 2012). https://www.tandfonline.com/doi/abs/10.1080/00336297.1999.10491684.

Doerer, Kristen. "The NFL's Problem with Violence against Women: A Story of Profit and Apathy." *Guardian*, December 7, 2018. https://www.theguardian.com/sport/2018/dec/07/the-nfls-problem-with-violence-against-women-a-story-of-profit-and-apathy.

Granderson, L. Z. "The Language Used in the Antonio Brown Case Is Telling." *Los Angeles Times*, September 14, 2019. https://www.latimes.com/sports/story/2019-09-14/language-used-in-antonio-brown-case-is-telling.

Hill, Jemele. "The Self-Destruction of Antonio Brown." *Atlantic*, September 23, 2019. https://www.theatlantic.com/ideas/archive/2019/09/self-destruction-antonio-brown/598603.

Maaddi, Rob. "NFL At 100: The Shadow of Domestic Violence Over League." Associated Press, September 6, 2019. https://apnews.com/52967a391a7c4aebbeb9135c7e881a3d.

Maske, Mark, and Adam Kilgore. "How Two Cases of Player Violence against Women Turned NFL Season 'Upside Down.'" *Washington Post*, December 5, 2018. https://www.washingtonpost.com/sports/how-two-cases-of-player-violence-against-women-turned-nfl-season-upside-down/2018/12/05/8fd69ed8-f7ea-11e8-8d64-4e79db33382f_story.html.

McCallister, Doreen. "Patriots Release Antonio Brown after Another Sexual Misconduct Allegation." NPR, September 21, 2019. https://www.npr.org/2019/09/21/762977002/patriots-release-antonio-brown-after-another-sexual-misconduct-allegation.

Moore, Terence. "NFL Still Clueless When It Comes to Players' Abuse of Women." *Forbes*, December 1, 2018. https://www.forbes.com/sites/terencemoore/2018/12/01/nfl-still-clueless-involving-players-abusing-women.

Morris, Benjamin. "The Rate of Domestic Violence Arrests among NFL Players." FiveThirtyEight, July 31, 2014. https://fivethirtyeight.com/features/the-rate-of-domestic-violence-arrests-among-nfl-players.

O'Toole, Shannon. "Wedded to the Game: The Real Lives of NFL Women." NFLwomen.com. http://www.nflwomen.com/excerpts.htm.

Shpigel, Ben. "For Antonio Brown, a Rape Accusation Raises a Question of Privilege in the N.F.L." *New York Times*, September 11, 2019. https://www.nytimes.com/2019/09/11/sports/football/antonio-brown-rape.html.

SI Wire. "15 NFL Players Arrested for Violence against Women in Last Two Years." *Sports Illustrated*, September 11, 2014. https://www.si.com/nfl/2014/09/11/nfl-players-arrested-domestic-violence-assault.

Springer, Shira. "This Season, the NFL Faced Renewed Scrutiny for How It Handles Domestic Violence." WBUR.org, January 18, 2019. http://www.wbur.org/news/2019/01/18/nfl-chiefs-domestic-violence.

CHAPTER 10

Brinson, Will. "Robert Griffin III Reportedly Filing for Divorce from Wife of Three Years." CBS Sports, August 17, 2016. https://www.cbssports.com/nfl/news/robert-griffin-iii-reportedly-filing-for-divorc-from-wife-of-three-years.
Merrill, Elizabeth. "How NFL Players Are Thinking about Life after Football." ESPN, March 7, 2020. https://apple.news/ANOB98c68S96YJ3TObS7_vw.
Terrill, Rachel. "My NFL Love Story, Part 3: An Exploration of Love, Marriage, Football and Infidelity." *Sports Illustrated*, August 25, 2016. https://www.si.com/nfl/2016/08/25/womens-week-nfl-wives-rachel-terrill-infidelity.

INDEX

ABOUT THE AUTHOR

Gay Culverhouse was the highest-ranked woman in the National Football League for ten years. As a president of the Tampa Bay Buccaneers and a longtime football advocate, she provides readers with an insider's view of the locker room and the men who inhabit it, as well as their days after leaving the league.

In 2009, Culverhouse testified before the House Judiciary Committee on legal issues relating to football head injuries. She then formed Retired Player Assistance, whose mission is to help retired NFL players get the benefits they are entitled to. RPA also has a special program for the wives and mothers of players.

Culverhouse was an expert in the field of concussions and head injury prevention. She earned a doctorate from Columbia University and was on the faculty of the medical school at the University of South Florida.